Gatewood & Geronimo

Gatewood & Geronimo

Louis Kraft

The University of New Mexico Press : ALBUQUERQUE

Other Books by Louis Kraft:
The Final Showdown (1992)
Custer and the Cheyenne: George Armstrong Custer's
Winter Campaign on the Southern Plains (1995)

Library of Congress Cataloging-in-Publication Data

Louis J. Kraft, Jr. 1947–
Gatewood & Geronimo / Louis Kraft
p.   cm.
Includes bibliographical references and index.
ISBN 0-8263-2129-1 (cloth)
ISBN 0-8263-2130-5 (pbk.)
1. Apache Indians—Wars, 1883–1888. 2. Gatewood, Charles B. 1853–1896
3. Geronimo, 1829–1909. I. Title. II. Title: Gatewood & Geronimo
E83 .88 K73 2000
973.8—dc21   99-6780
CIP

For the three special people in my life—
Marissa Kraft,
Cindy Tengan,
and
Louis J. Kraft, Sr.
(August 15, 1918–February 14, 1999)

Contents

Acknowledgments

༄

There are many people who helped during the creation of this book.

The project began in May 1995, fittingly in Arizona, when a conversation with Aaron and Ruth Kantor Cohen, owners of Guidon Books in Scottsdale, turned to Gatewood and Geronimo. This talk initiated a search that continues to this day (and most likely will never end). During the course of the following years, Ruth (February 9, 1921–January 10, 1999) graciously offered research suggestions and names of people I should contact. I cannot state how much her and Aaron's interest and unselfish assistance aided me during the project.

Any research of Gatewood and Geronimo cannot be considered complete until the historian concludes at least one in-depth visit to the Arizona Historical Society in Tucson, Arizona. Gatewood's papers are there, as are Camillus Fly's marvelous 1886 photos of Geronimo, Naiche, and their band in the wilds of Mexico. And these items constitute just the beginning of their holdings. The Society's entire staff assisted me at one time or another during the life of this project. One person, however, must be singled out: former archivist Mario M. Einaudi. Mario went way beyond the call of duty, constantly offering suggestions for other directions in my research.

Jessica J. Hurley, Archives Assistant, Arizona Department of Library, Archives, and Public Records, Archives Division, Phoenix, Arizona, located the indictments against Gatewood for the false arrests. Bill Doty, Archivist, National Archives, Laguna Niguel, California, gave invaluable assistance in locating the transcript of the Zuck, Kay, and Jones trial. Because Gatewood's problem with Zuck and company seems to be the key to Gatewood's career, their help was a godsend.

Nan Card of the Rutherford B. Hayes Memorial Library, Fremont, Ohio, made the George Crook Collection available to me. Michael Pilgrim of the National Archives, Washington, D.C., helped me find hidden treasures. The Arizona Historical Foundation, Hayden Library, Arizona State University,

Tempe, Arizona, also aided my research, while the staff of the El Segundo Public Library, El Segundo, California, constantly filled my orders of inter-library-loan requests and kept me up and running on their microfilm machines.

Many have helped in the assembly of photos, artwork, and cartography. The list includes Susan Sheehan, Arizona Historical Society, Tucson, Arizona; Randy Heckenburg, U.S. Army Military History Institute, Carlisle, Pennsylvania; and Lori Flemming, *Wild West* magazine, Leesburg, Virginia. Special thanks are owed Kim G. Walters, Director of the Braun Library, Southwest Museum, Los Angeles, for her extraordinary guidance of my research directions. I cannot say enough about Kim's efforts in my behalf—if you are researching Native Americans, do yourself a favor and contact her and the Southwest Museum.

Neil Mangum, Superintendent, Little Bighorn Battlefield National Monument, Montana, was most helpful, giving directions to various historical sites that are not on any maps. He also suggested others who might be helpful in the research. Neil gives generously of his time and information. Others would benefit greatly by following his lead.

Apache historian Edwin R. Sweeney discussed his research in Mexico, which includes the Archivo Historico de Sonora, Hermosillo, Sonora. I cannot thank him enough for helping me to correctly identify the prefect of Arispe.

Eleven friends offered their support and encouragement: writer Eric Niderost, editor Tom O'Neil, writer Gary McCarthy, publisher Dick Upton, writer-director Tom Eubanks, director Craig Lew, writer-editor Jeanne Dodge-Allen, editor Gregory Lalire, video producer and lecturer extraordinaire Mike Koury, and writers Kathy and Mike Gear. I hope that when called upon, I am able to reciprocate in a like manner.

Good friend George Carmichael read the first draft chapter by chapter as it was created. His comments, questions, and editing were of immense value. I can never repay him for the enormous amount of time he has generously given.

Cindy Tengan is my lady and my love. She has been involved in the project since its inception. Always there for me, she assisted in every way imaginable. Her untiring, enthusiastic help played a big part in the creation of the manuscript. Best of all, I had a wonderful time working with her.

My greatest supporter has been my father, Louis J. Kraft, Sr. All I can say, Dad, is thanks from the bottom of my heart.

Marissa Kraft is my girl and my life. Once again she proved she is the best traveling companion in the world. Always eager to explore, she is forever ready to follow one more trail that seemingly leads nowhere. Her only hesitation came when we slid to a dusty halt in front of a one-hundred-yard mud hole. While I foolishly considered our chances of getting to the other side of the goop, she wisely advised: "Don't try it, Dad." I prevailed. She was right. We got stuck (but luckily were able to work our way out of the mire). Our tracking of Gatewood and Geronimo has given me more cherished memories than I could count. My only hope is that we have many more trails to share together.

And finally I am grateful to Durwood Ball, my editor at the University of New Mexico Press, for his immediate enthusiasm, continued support, and fine editing of the manuscript.

Gatewood & Geronimo

CHAPTER ONE

Bay-chen-daysen and the Bedonkohe Warrior

By 1882 the last remaining opposition to white settlement of the Southwest, the Chiricahua Apaches, had been forced onto the San Carlos Apache Reservation in eastern Arizona. At least most of them were there. A nomadic people perfectly suited to roaming the arid deserts and mountains of Arizona, New Mexico, and northern Mexico, they were miserable with their confinement. As with any people whose entire lifeway faced cultural genocide, they sullenly accepted their fate. And though few white men made any attempt to know them, one, *Bay-chen-daysen,*[1] as the Apaches called him, did. Yet he, like the Native Americans with whom he associated, did not willingly choose his station.

Tall, slender, and southern born, Second Lieutenant Charles Gatewood[2] graduated from West Point in 1877. A veteran Indian campaigner since reporting for duty at Fort Apache, Arizona Territory, in 1878, he found himself the most celebrated member of the Sixth U.S. Cavalry's mess. He did not seek this distinction. If anything, he had a jaded view of the "glorious life" an officer's commission offered. He had no dreams of glory. Four long years had destroyed his youthful illusions of advancement. Service in the Southwest offered hardship, deprivation, and little else. Gatewood had been given a duty to perform and he did it—as well as he could.

Fellow officers considered him "cool, quiet, courageous; firm when convinced of right but intolerant of wrong; with a thorough knowledge of Apache character."[3] Although he did not court colorful descriptions of his capabilities, some reached print. *The Mining Journal* portrayed Gatewood as a paragon of heroism:

> It means that for months at a time he lives with these savages, risking his life upon their faith. . . . The officer who commands these savages must possess some unusual and even remarkable qualities. He must have a thorough knowledge of the Indian character and tongue. He must be brave, or they would despise him, for if he flinched for a moment they would see it and his influence would vanish.[4]

Gatewood had made a name for himself as an Apache man. He had achieved an enviable success as commander of Apache scouts. Bay-chen-daysen had led a company of Apache scouts from March 31, 1879, to June 30, 1880, and again from November 12, 1881, to the present time.[5]

This success came about in spite of a major shortcoming. Taciturn, Gatewood did not like documenting his activities. His "personal reports of the most thrilling affairs were short, scanty and unsatisfactory; just a report of the ordinary day's work."[6] Gatewood's knack of minimizing his accomplishments did not go unnoticed. "[His] wonderful success in the field was approved, but [his] meager reports as to when, where, and the attendant circumstances left much to be desired."[7] This garnered for him a bad reputation within the Sixth. In spite of this, Gatewood found himself "very popular with the officers and men in military circles,"[8] as well as highly regarded: "he was one of the best Indian war soldiers, one of the truest friends and one of the tenderest [*sic*] souls that God ever let live on this earth."[9]

A major contributor to his success in the field was the equality with which he treated his Indian scouts. Gatewood was a rarity on the frontier. He did not view the Apaches as subhumans to be robbed and stamped out. "I am convinced," he once wrote, "that Indians are no different from other persons . . ."[10] His view allowed him to accept the natives as coworkers. This did not mean that he was not careful. He was extremely cautious when it came to recruiting scouts. His reasoning was simple: "The Apache respects nothing, believes in nothing, & bows to nothing, but Force."[11] This understanding allowed him to accept a constant reality: "It therefore happened that the scouts of one year would be turning the Territory topsy-turvy the next, & the officer commanding a company of scouts would be pursuing a party of ex-scouts with an assortment of ex-hostiles."[12] Bay-chen-daysen excelled in his risky business. Time and again, he was able to ride out on a scout with men whom he had hunted just a short time before. Perhaps the main reason Gatewood had achieved so much success by 1882 is that he willingly included the Indians he worked with in his decisions. When on patrol, Gatewood always discussed the next day's line of march with his Apache scouts. He invited their participation and considered their suggestions and concerns. He paid particular attention to anything that worried the scouts. He set great store by their opinions.[13] The Indians could see Gatewood's trust, respect, and lack of fear, and, in turn, they reciprocated.

The Apache people naturally resented the white invasion of their land. As mountain and desert people, they were well prepared to resist the encroachments of the *White Eyes*.

[The Apache's] mode of warfare was peculiarly his own. He saw no reason for fighting unless there was something tangible and immediate to be gained.. . . . His creed was "fight and run away, live to fight another day." Corner him, however, and you would find him as desperate and dangerous as a wounded wolf.

Only when cornered, or to delay pursuit of his women and children, would he engage a force anywhere near the strength of his own. To fight soldiers merely in defense of his country, he considered the height of folly; and he never committed that folly if he could avoid it.[14]

Years of contact with the Apaches gave Gatewood a thorough understanding of their mode of operations:

Contact with others meant war, for war was his business. . . . He assembled his warriors near an unsuspecting, or unprotected, settlement, or lay in ambush for a traveling party, and then, at the most propitious moment, a surprise, a rapid & furious attack, women & children carried into captivity, property destroyed or spirited away, & the dead left horribly mutilated & unburied. These wily guerrillas always took good care to have accurate information as to the numbers of their intended victims & their means for defending themselves, so that whenever they attacked, success was pretty well assured.[15]

The Apache nation consisted of four tribes: the Lipan, the Jicarilla, the Mescalero, and the Chiricahua. Each of the tribes was made up of a number of bands. The bands, in turn, were also broken into smaller groups or clans, which could be as small as two families.[16] These bloodlines and family ties, although strong, could not prevent the Apaches from returning again and again to their calling. "Even when they were on their reservations," Gatewood wrote, "they were not peaceable. The most bitter feuds existed between families, bands, tribes & clans, & were handed down from one generation to the other."[17]

The Chiricahuas, the fiercest of the tribes, consisted of three bands (or four bands, depending upon the source). The northern- and eastern-most band ranged westward from the Rio Grande in New Mexico Territory almost all the way to Arizona Territory. The Chiricahua called them *Chihenne* (*cíhéné, Chi-hen-ne, Chihinne*), meaning *Red Paint People*. This band included the Warm Springs (Ojo Caliente), Membreños, Coppermine, and Mogollones Apaches; war chieftains Mangas Coloradas, Victorio, Nana, and

Loco came from this band. The central band ranged from southwestern New Mexico through southeastern Arizona territories. Called the *Chokonen* (*cókánén, Cho-kon-en*) by the Chiricahuas, they were the first band to have the term *Chiricahua* applied to them. The band has also been called the *Cochise Apaches,* after their famous leader; Naiche belonged to this band. The southern band ranged mostly through the northern portions of the Mexican states of Sonora and Chihuahua and the southern tip of New Mexico Territory. They called themselves *Bedonkohe* (*Be-don-ko-he, Bedonkohes,* *ⁿdé'ïⁿdàˑí*), meaning *Enemy People*; Geronimo, who was also known as *Hieronymo* (the actual pronunciation of his name) and *Goyahkla, Goyankla,* or *Goyathlay* (all of which mean *One Who Yawns*), belonged to this band. The fourth band called themselves *Nednhi* (*Netdahe, Nednai*). They ranged through the Sierra Madre in Mexico; Juh belonged to this band.[18]

Although bathed in blood since the coming of the Spaniards, the tribe never came together to meet the continual onslaught by invaders. Struggling against very unfavorable odds, they usually prevailed because they could thrive in their rugged homeland, while other races could not. Finally subdued in the 1870s, the Chiricahuas (except for a portion of the tribe that remained free in Mexico) found themselves banished to a reservation in eastern Arizona. In 1875, all the Arizona reservation Apaches were removed to the White Mountains. Their new home—which mixed Apache tribes unfriendly with each other—would eventually be called San Carlos. The Chiricahuas did not understand why all this had come about.

> They kept asking what or whom it was that gave [white] men the
> right to act in such a way. Had their God told them to behave so?
> If that were the case, they certainly wanted nothing to do with Him!
> . . . The Whites plundered their land, stole their horses, killed their
> people, and destroyed their villages; why then did the Whites find
> it so strange when the destitute Apache raided in return? Finally,
> the Whites said they would give them reservations. Yet how could
> they give the Apache that which already belonged to them in the
> first place?[19]

By 1882 Cochise and Mangas Coloradas were dead; and so was Victorio, killed by Mexican treachery. Juh, the Nednhi chieftain, became the dominant war leader. Also known as *Ju, Ho, Whoa,* and sometimes *Who,* he stood over six feet and weighed 225 pounds.

Two others, Geronimo and Naiche, would play prominent roles in the last Apache wars. Geronimo,[20] an aging Bedonkohe warrior (approaching his sixtieth birthday) and sometime mystic, burned with a desire to be free. His heart also burned for vengeance. There were not many who dared to cross him. His ferocity in battle was well known, but there was much more to him than merely blood lust.

Some twelve years before, about 1870, he traveled at great risk to Juh's camp in southeastern Arizona, to be with his favorite sister, Ishton, as she gave birth to Juh's son, Daklugie. After Ishton suffered for four days without delivering her child, Geronimo, who officiated as medicine man, feared his sister would die. Distraught, he went off by himself into the Chiricahua Mountains to pray to *Ussen*—God, the Creator of Life. Daklugie, who as a boy saw much of the horror of the final years of his peoples' freedom, retold the story as he heard it:

> As Geronimo stood with arms and eyes upraised, as our people
> do, Ussen spoke. Geronimo heard His voice clearly, . . . Ussen told
> Geronimo that his sister [would] live, and he promised my uncle that
> he would never be killed but would live to a ripe old age and would
> die a natural death.[21]

Continuing, Daklugie offered an insight that may be very close to the mark:

> Ussen's promise is what gave Geronimo his wonderful courage. He
> was by nature already a brave person; but if one knows that he will
> never be killed, why be afraid?

During this time, Geronimo and a small group of Bedonkohes—mostly his relatives—who followed his lead although he never was elected chieftain, frequently found themselves living near Juh's Nednhis.

The other Chiricahua who would soon be pressed into the limelight was indeed a chieftain. As Cochise's son, the twenty-six-year-old Naiche (*Natchez, Nachite*) was both an elected and a hereditary Chokonen chieftain. Tall, slender, good-looking, he performed well on the warpath, but his hatred for the White Eyes did not begin to match Geronimo's. Even though they were different in temperament, Geronimo and Naiche would become partners in the final fight to save their culture and their lives.

Officers who drew Apache duty found it to be very demanding. Although still a young man, Gatewood had already begun to feel the consequences of his continued exposure. Patrol duty often lasted for months, and he found the harsh rigors of living in the field increasingly difficult. Shortly after recruiting a company of Apache scouts (in April 1880) to watch Juh and Geronimo, who had come in to San Carlos, Gatewood became ill with

inflammatory rheumatism and reported to Camp Thomas for medical treatment. His condition worsened and he was relieved of command.[22]

Even though he recovered, his rheumatism never left him. On May 1,
1881, Bay-chen-daysen furnished his superiors with a certificate, signed by
Dr. Basil Norris, that stated "he had rheumatism of knee, ankle, hip and
shoulder, the result of exposure in line of duty in Arizona."[23] Based on this
report, Gatewood drew leave from May 5 to July 5. Aches and pains aside,
he had a much more important reason for wanting time off. His health be
damned; he was in love. In June, he traveled east to Frostburg, Maryland,
where he married his sweetheart, Georgia McCulloh, on June 23. Whenever
he found himself in the field, he always came back to this memory—especially during the month of June. Although they would have many separations in the years to come, Georgia happily braved life on the various barren
military posts—sometimes living in garrisons other than those where Gatewood was stationed.

July 5, 1881, came and went. Gatewood did not report back to Fort
Apache or return to duty. Perhaps he needed more time to recover his health.
Maybe he did not want his honeymoon to end. Probably it was a mixture of
these two reasons, combined with government inefficiency that caused a
request for extended leave to be lost. For several months his idyll continued,
uninterrupted. Suddenly, on September 5, Gatewood found himself *absent
without leave*. He was informed that the General of the Army *desired an
explanation*. The AWOL lieutenant hastily returned to active duty that September.[24]

Duty as a soldier kept him in the field for long intervals, and during these
extended absences Gatewood's concern for Georgia deeply troubled him. His
letters to her often spoke of his worry over her well-being and of his love for
her and their children to be.

Five hundred Chiricahua recalcitrants remained in Mexico's Sierra Madre,
where Mexicans did not welcome their presence any more than the Americans. Blood was often spilled, only to be followed by a time of peace. This
usually happened when the Apaches needed supplies, rest, or wanted to go
on a drunk. Unlike the situation in the United States, they could make peace
with individual Mexican towns.

There was another need that drove the militant Chiricahuas: their dimin-
ishing numbers threatened their survival. In order to prosper in the wild, a
unique division of labor had to be observed. Women played an essential role
in Apache society, and when there were too few females, more had to be
recruited. By April 1882, Geronimo knew they needed more people to join

them in the Sierra Madre. Along with Juh, Naiche, and Chatto (a Chiricahua war leader), he led a group across the international boundary and headed north to the San Carlos Reservation.

The raiders chose Loco's Chihenne band to merge with them. It did not matter that most of Loco's people wanted to remain at peace on the reservation; Geronimo forced the old chieftain's people—it was said at rifle point—to leave their homes between the Gila and San Carlos rivers. None dared disobey; they saw their abductors kill chief of police Albert Sterling and one of his Indian scouts. When some of the reservation Apaches resisted, one of Geronimo's warriors shouted: "Take them all! No one is to be left in camp. Shoot down anyone who refuses to go with us!"[25]

During the flight for freedom, Geronimo led everyone southeast, doing everything he could to avoid contact with the white troops he knew hounded his trail. Traveling at night, he skirted the mountains that paralleled the San Simon River. By this time, his raiders had killed more than fifty people.

Geronimo's captives were exhausted when he reached a spring in the Stein's Peak Range, some forty miles due east of Fort Grant, Arizona. During the break, his warriors discovered Indian scouts from the soldiers closing in and killed four of them. Then the soldiers attacked, and one warrior died in the engagement.[26] Geronimo held his ground; his position was good and the soldiers left. Even so, the White Eyes were too close, and Geronimo had to move again. That night he moved out onto the wide San Simon Valley.

> When he was on the warpath, Geronimo fixed it so that morning
> wouldn't come too soon. He did it by singing. Once we were going
> to a certain place, and Geronimo didn't want it to become light
> before he reached it. He saw the enemy while they were in a level
> place, and he didn't want them to spy on us. He wanted morning
> to break after we had climbed over a mountain, so that the enemy
> couldn't see us. So Geronimo sang, and the night remained for two
> or three hours longer. I saw this myself.[27]

By morning Geronimo and his people reached an assembly point in the Chiricahua Mountains. The old warrior rested everyone during the day. Traveling again at night, he reached Mexican soil without further trouble. But outdistancing the threat of American bullets did not staunch the possibility of bloodshed, for the Mexicans also tried hard to kill Apaches. Yet Geronimo felt safe. Apaches usually handled the Mexicans easily, and he knew the white soldiers could not follow him across the Mexican border. He knew he was safe.

❖❖❖

Geronimo was wrong. Captains Tullius C. Tupper and William A. Rafferty, with two companies of Sixth U.S. Cavalry and two of Indian scouts, reached the international boundary. Although they had no authority to cross the line, Tupper, who outranked Rafferty because of his seniority, decided to risk his career and illegally continued the hunt.[28]

Further north, Gatewood's Apache scouts were dispersed in an irregular line, moving "at a rough, shambling walk . . . with no semblance of regularity; individual fancy alone governed [their advance]."[29] They typically wore a calico shirt, cotton trousers, and moccasins that were highly prized and never abandoned. Each scout also wore a scarlet headband.

Gatewood and his scouts accompanied Captain Charles G. Gordon's (Sixth U.S. Cavalry) pursuit of the Chiricahuas, pounding down the southbound trail. On the morning of April 24 they came upon Lieutenant Colonel George A. (Sandy) Forsyth's command of six companies of Fourth U.S. Cavalry, and outranked, Gatewood and Gordon joined Forsyth.

Under a blazing sun, men and livestock suffered from thirst as the combined command continued to track the fleeing Indians. Forsyth's command rested at Horse Shoe Canyon, where everyone drank a pint of water; then they pushed on to Stein's Pass. At noon the next day, scouts found Geronimo's trail six miles to the west. The signs remained easy to follow, until at 6:30 P.M. the trail abruptly ended. The Chiricahuas had scattered in all directions. But tired as they were, Forsyth's command pressed onward and did not make camp until 10:00 P.M. Half an hour later, Captain Adna Chaffee (Sixth U.S. Cavalry), with a troop, and Lieutenant Frank West (Sixth U.S. Cavalry), with Indian scouts, found the camp.

Next day the hunt continued without Chaffee. When scouts again found the Indians' trail, the tracks showed clearly that they were heading for the Mexican border. First their trail hugged the foothills of the Chiricahua Mountains, then ventured out onto the San Simon Valley. After another long day, the march ended at 9:30 P.M. They had covered forty miles and had not drunk any water since ten in the morning.

At daylight, everyone was back in the saddle. Suddenly the trail ended; the fleeing people had scattered once again. Gatewood and everyone else knew it was unlikely they would catch the Indians before they reached the border. But now there was something even more important—water. The chase halted until good water was found at Cloverdale Ciénagas, then it continued on to the border. As expected, the Chiricahuas had won the race to the international line. Forsyth had orders not to cross into Mexico, but after seeing evidence that Tupper and Rafferty had already done so, he decided to follow their lead.[30]

❖❖❖

Geronimo moved southeastward. Now in Chihuahua, but still far from his destination, he continued to travel at night. He camped at a spring at the base of the Sierra Enmedio, a small mountain range. Since freeing Loco's people, Geronimo had lost one in battle, along with a few of Loco's band who refused to go to Mexico and had slipped away under the cover of darkness.

Both Geronimo and Juh—who, Geronimo once said, "was like a brother to me"[31]—liked to party. They had pulled off a pretty big coup, and it was time to celebrate. The people cooked mescal, ate, and drank long into the night. Just before dawn, a man and three women left camp looking for more mescal and walked right into a company of Indian scouts, who opened fire; all four died. Although not ready to attack, soldiers fired into the camp from a hill on the opposite side of the valley. The camp sprang to life as soldiers' bullets slammed into it from above.

Apaches returned the soldiers' fire, with Geronimo, Juh, and their brothers holding their ground. However, most of their shots went high as they fired at the soldiers above them. The fight did not go well for the Chiricahuas. Too many people had fallen, including a woman who thought her son was fighting with the attacking Indian scouts. Loco was wounded in the leg. Then, as the sun neared its zenith, the soldiers unexpectedly pulled away.[32] Geronimo knew they had been hit by Americans. This was not a good sign. American soldiers had followed him into Mexico.

Some eight hours after the fight, Forsyth pounded into Tupper and Rafferty's camp; Gatewood, Gordon, and West rode with him. Everyone realized that had they gotten there sooner, they could have dealt the Apaches a crippling blow. Forsyth—whom the Apaches called *Always Too Late to Fight*—vented his fury at missing an opportunity to crush the recalcitrant Indians.

With the addition of Rafferty and Tupper's force, Forsyth now commanded 450 men. Sensing victory within his grasp, Forsyth wanted to move out, but Rafferty and Tupper's men needed rest. Instead of dividing his force, Forsyth remained in camp. The next morning, Forsyth found the battle site deserted, and decided to press deeper into Mexico.[33]

Geronimo and the people with him moved out onto the Janos Plains. Most were now afoot, many were wounded. When Geronimo called a halt, Naiche, Chatto, both of whom had horses, and about a dozen other warriors refused to stop. They continued on, oddly not remaining with the women and children.

After sleeping for a little over an hour, Geronimo and Juh had Loco's band once again on the move. They covered twenty-nine miles that night. East of

Aliso Creek, they found themselves surrounded by small hills. They could see their destination—the Sierra Madre—in the distance, but first they had to cross the Janos River.

As they moved, Geronimo and most of the warriors who did not desert the women hung to the back of the strung-out line, guarding against another American attack. A few warriors who were in the lead of the line of march stopped to rest and smoke. Not tired, or perhaps anxious to reach the safety of the Sierra Madre, the women and children passed them. Suddenly, after only traveling a few hundred yards, shots rang out. They had walked into an ambush. Mexican soldiers charged into the long spindly line of refugees, shooting women and children as they ran. "People were falling and bleeding, and dying on all sides of us. Whole families were slaughtered on the spot, wholly unable to defend themselves."[34]

Geronimo and the other warriors in the rear raced to their peoples' defense. Geronimo yelled for "the men to gather around him and make a stand to protect the women and children."[35] Thirty-two warriors responded to his cry. Women dug a rifle pit in an arroyo. By now the Mexicans had surrounded the Apaches. The fight lasted until dark.

Someone set the grass on fire. Geronimo claimed the Apaches did it to hide their escape. Batsinas, an eleven-year-old Chihenne Apache who would later be known as Jason Betzinez, said the Mexicans torched the vegetation to force the Indians into the open.

Geronimo yelled: "If we leave the women and children we can escape."[36]

Those within hearing of Geronimo could not believe what they heard. "What did you say?" Fun, Geronimo's half-brother, asked. "Repeat that."

"Come on!" Geronimo said. "Let's go."

Fun pointed his rifle at Geronimo. "Say that again and I'll shoot."

Geronimo did not bother to reply. He turned, climbed out of the rifle pit, and disappeared into the smoky darkness.

Knowing the infants' cries would alert the Mexicans, the warriors asked—and received permission—to kill them. A harsh reality, but one that Chiricahuas accepted. Then, miraculously, they slipped beyond the Mexican lines and escaped. Seventy-eight Apaches died, most of whom were women and children. Another thirty-three women and children were captured.

Forsyth came upon Colonel Lorenzo García and the Sixth Mexican Infantry the day after the battle. Told by García to vacate Mexican soil, Forsyth stated that he was in pursuit of the fleeing Indians. The Mexican commander curtly showed the Americans the battle site, then repeated his demand, making it clear that if the Americans did not leave he would attack them. With García's formal complaint in hand, Forsyth returned to the United States.

Pleased that the Mexican government had not made more out of the illegal entry onto their soil by American soldiers, the U.S. Army brass turned its back on the excursion into Mexico. Reports were returned to officers who had written them. As far as the army was concerned, the expedition into Mexico had not occurred. The less known about the disobedience of orders, the better.[37]

The pursuit most likely affected Gatewood's painful joints. Luckily, this time the malady did not require sick leave. Changes were about to take place in Arizona, and it was no time to be absent.

Although Geronimo had been at San Carlos in 1880, Gatewood had yet to meet him. Certainly he had no idea that the Bedonkohe Chiricahua's excursion that April of 1882 precipitated a multitude of events, . . . events that would place him in a pivotal role and thrust both of them on a collision course that would put their lives at stake.

CHAPTER TWO

Apache Duty

Controlling Apaches had never been easy. It seemed that as soon as the military forced one recalcitrant band back to the reservation, another group went out. As unrest on the frontier continued, settlers demanded protection, but nothing the army did satisfied them. In contrast to the frontier cry for extermination, city dwellers back east bemoaned the inhumane treatment of the poor natives. This trapped the military in a catch–22—damned if you did and damned if you did not—situation. Lieutenant General Philip Sheridan, who would become commander-in-chief of the army in less than a year and a half, put it best:

> If we allow the defenseless people on the frontier to be scalped and ravished, we are burnt in effigy and execrated as soulless monsters, insensible to the sufferings of humanity. If the Indian is punished to give security to these people, we are the same soulless monsters from the other side.[1]

In an attempt to ease tensions and bring a lasting peace to the territory, the army named General George Crook commander of the Department of Arizona in July 1882. Crook often wore a tan canvas suit and a cork helmet, cropped his hair close, and sported a forked beard. Labeled an eccentric, he was also methodical. Crook generally had a reason for everything he did. His manner of dress was well suited to the burning temperatures and hostile terrain of the Southwest.

Some called Crook a fool who did not know his business. He did suffer setbacks, such as a starvation march during the Sioux War of 1876. Still, he was considered one of the army's best Indian fighters. His success consisted of three ingredients: Indians, mules, and humanity. Knowing the value of an Indian's special knowledge, and his hatred at times, of his brethren, he used Indians to fight Indians. This demoralizing factor weighed heavily on the recalcitrants when they saw other Indians helping the whites hunt them down. Crook never underestimated the endurance, strength, and mobility of the mule. More importantly, they could go where wagons could not go, allowing the general to track warring Indians almost anywhere. Finally, he treated his adversaries like humans.[2]

Crook had commanded the Department of Arizona once before (1871–1875). Gatewood, along with every other officer in the department, had heard of Crook's unbending but common-sense approach to getting a job done, and knew he would shape the command to suit his style of operations.

The remnants of the refugees finally reached Juh's main Nednhi camp in the Sierra Madre, about thirty miles southwest of Casas Grandes. The addition of the Chihenne Apaches increased the size of the camp to several hundred.

The Sierra Madres are actually two mountain ranges that rise from the Chihuahuan Desert: the Sierra Madre Oriental (Eastern) and the Sierra Madre Occidental (Western). Mammoth in size, the Oriental is 810 miles long while the Occidental is 775 miles long. Both are over one hundred miles wide and have peaks that easily reach twelve thousand feet. "In the north they are desert regions, sandy and dry, dotted with creosote bush and mesquite, yucca and ocotillo and a host of other plants . . . Farther south, where the ranges increase in altitude, their peaks and high draws are home to trees and wild flowers of the temperate zones."[3] Born of volcanic upheaval, the Occidental "is more rugged, more austere." It has huge waterfalls, and "contains complex, steep-sided canyons called barrancas" that are sometimes deeper than the Grand Canyon. "The Oriental, composed largely of limestone laid down by an ancient sea that once covered the region, is lusher and slightly more gentle."

Although the escape had begun well, much tragedy had befallen the people. They needed a time of peace. Besides, the warriors had booty to trade that had been taken in raids. A thirsty Geronimo had another objective: mescal or aguardiente. The leaders decided to seek peace at Casas Grandes, a pueblo located on the northeastern rim of the Sierra Madre Occidental range. Geronimo, Juh, Chatto, and about one-third of the Apaches who were then at Juh's camp traveled to Casas Grandes. They met the *alcalde* of the pueblo, who forgot past outrages and invited them to visit his town and trade.

Even though some of the Apaches remained wary, most of the Indians ventured within the pueblo's adobe walls. Mexicans gave them mescal, which they downed eagerly, and soon a festive atmosphere replaced any fear of treachery. The day ended with both sides enjoying each other's company. The second day mimicked the first: Mexicans and Apaches drank and traded, and by nightfall many Apaches were drunk. Instead of moving a safe distance from Casas Grandes, they camped just outside the city walls, where they drank, howled, and danced deep into the night.

Next morning, Mexicans fell upon the Indians as they slept off their drunken stupor. At least twelve warriors died, though the death count may have been much higher, as supposedly very few Apaches who accepted the Mexicans' hospitality escaped. Geronimo's wife, Chee-hash-kish, along with twenty-nine other women were taken. Geronimo's luck held. He avoided the slaughter, but at the cost of a loved one, for he never saw Chee-hash-kish again. The incident increased his hatred for Mexicans. Juh and Chatto also escaped, but Chatto's entire family was captured.[4] Instead of peace, war erupted in northern Mexico.

North of the border, an uneasy peace continued. American authorities realized that this was just the lull before the storm. Recent months had seen two severe American engagements with Apaches and the deaths of at least fifty whites. Some 600 Chiricahuas—150 of whom were warriors—roamed free in Mexico. It was inevitable that they would cross the international boundary and raid the United States again. Rumors claimed Juh planned a strike into Texas.

Crook, who had definite ideas on how to drive the Chiricahuas from the warpath forever, found the situation a shambles when he returned to Arizona Territory on September 4, 1882.[5] He began by selecting his aides with care, wanting only officers who knew and understood the Apache. Captain Emmet Crawford and Second Lieutenant Britton Davis (Third U.S. Cavalry), along with Gatewood, fit the bill.

The general arrived at Fort Apache, located on the White River in eastern Arizona, by the middle of September. The fort served as headquarters for the White Mountain Indian Reservation. Here he found about sixteen hundred Indians incarcerated. Another four thousand lived south of the Black River on the San Carlos Indian Reservation. Both reservations, created in 1872, were now considered as one reservation encompassing somewhere between eighty and ninety square miles. The Indian population on the two reservations consisted of Tonto, White Mountain, Cibicue, San Carlos, and Chiricahua Apaches, along with Yavapai. This was not a happy blend of people. Originally there had been four reservations grouping the tribesmen by clan, but now these people were herded together at San Carlos and Apache. Some of the groups avoided each other. They looked upon foreign subtribal groups with distrust and suspicion.

The Apaches lived in wickiups that the women built. Constructed of poles and limbs that were tied together, the circular, dome-shaped dwellings were covered with yucca leaves, rushes, brush, or bear grass—whatever the women could find. Living conditions at Apache were better than at San

Carlos. The higher altitude of pine-covered mountains and upland meadows produced more natural materials for the Indians to use, while the desert at San Carlos did not provide much useful material.

At Apache, Crook and his new assistants called a council. They found the Apaches sullen, distrustful of the whites who controlled them. "[O]ne officer of the gov[ernment] would tell [the Indians] one thing and another, something else, until [the Indians] lost confidence in everybody."[6] Interpreters were incompetent or prejudiced, or both. When the reservation had been set up, the Indians had received more supplies than they could use. Then the supplies began to dwindle. The so-called Indian Ring of agents and their contractors enriched themselves by defrauding the Indians.

This ring struck an angry chord in Gatewood every time he discussed the matter:

> Uncle Sam was exceedingly liberal in his donations to [the Apaches], but his servants had an awful capacity for absorption. In [time], he had to satisfy the rapacity of the celebrated Indian Ring, besides individual officials, before the beneficiary was allowed to receive anything. . . . All this was done openly, so that the latter knew it well.[7]

These were not idle words; nor were they a one-time occurrence. Gatewood had been aware of the situation for some time, and it bothered him. With his appointment as military commandant of the reservation at Fort Apache, he found himself in a position where he could do something. Putting a halt to some of the blatant stealing would become a priority for him.

For Gatewood, corruption was an issue of morality. Once he decided to take a stand, there would be no turning back. It did not matter who the enemy was. Or how dire the consequences might be. He would fight for what he knew was right.

A review of the current situation on the reservation showed that the flour distributed weekly to a family probably did not last one day. What passed for beef on the hoof amounted to little more than walking skeletons.[8]

The White Mountain Apaches, who had recently abandoned the warpath, listened to Crook's proposal with an open mind. Gatewood summarized their decision after hearing the general out: "[They] agreed, that if allowed to occupy their old country, the northern end of the reservation in which Fort Apache is situated, & given aid in farming implements, seed, & food enough to carry them thr[ough] until they could gather their crops, they would ask nothing more of the Gov[ernmen]t."[9]

On October 5, Crook issued General Orders No. 43: "Officers and soldiers serving this department are reminded that one of the fundamental prin-

ciples of the military character is, justice to all—Indians as well as white men
. . . In all their dealings with the Indians, officers must be careful not only
to observe the strictest fidelity, but to make no promises not in their power
to carry out . . ."[10]

Later that month, Crook, Gatewood, and Davis traveled to San Carlos,
at the confluence of the Gila and San Carlos rivers. Naked, dirty, hungry, and
frightened children hid from the white men. Infrequent rains, constant
winds, summer temperatures that reached 110 degrees in the shade, and
swarms of insects would later prompt Britton Davis to call the agency *Hell's
Forty Acres*.[11] Here they found the situation worse. The Apaches "had been
driven into th[e] barren waste at San Carlos with no provision for their self-
support. A nomad[ic] people who had lived off the country, subsisting on
game, wild fruits, nuts, and certain herbs, they had not the faintest idea how
to subsist by agriculture and no means to that end had they known how."[12]

That first night Gatewood and the others slept on the ground without
tents. One officer pulled a centipede from his bedding, while another found
a tarantula, and yet another a young rattlesnake.

Crook called a second council on October 15. Eight hundred Indians
attended. "They presented a picturesque sight,"[13] Gatewood remembered,
"clad as they were in all the colors of the rainbow & in all imaginable cos-
tumes from a breech clout to a stove pipe hat." Crook gave the Apaches the
freedom to live anywhere on the reservation. At the same time, he insisted
upon keeping track of all males old enough to bear arms—fourteen years
of age and older. In all, there were fourteen hundred males in this classifica-
tion. Each warrior was issued a brass tag that identified him, and it was
mandatory that the Indians wear their tags at all times. Failure to appear at
a roll call or to wear the tag meant a visit to the calaboose.

The general knew he could improve the situation only by total military
control; nothing less would satisfy him. He got his way. Rationing—subject
to military supervision—remained the San Carlos Indian agent's lone duty.
Indian agent P. P. Wilcox, who had assumed his position as civilian agent at
San Carlos near the time that Crook returned to the Southwest, promised his
cooperation, but his words would prove to be empty rhetoric. A political
appointee with a religious background, he spent very little time at San Carlos. He hated the job, had nothing but contempt for his wards, and only took
the position because of the salary and the fact that he could not find anything
better. Nevertheless, the usurpation of power bothered him.[14]

The next few days of roll call passed without incident. Then, one morning, a dust cloud billowed ominously in the distance. About sixty White
Mountains appeared on the mesa one mile from the agency. Heavily armed

with cartridge belts, rifles, and revolvers, they formed ranks like the cavalry, and rode forward in perfect mimicry of soldiers marching in column. The Indians at the roll call looked about anxiously. Gatewood enjoyed the scene, knowing they (there were no Chiricahuas present) would have run had the soldiers not been present. Next to the Chiricahuas, the White Mountains were the most feared warriors.

Alchesay, head of the largest band of White Mountain Apaches, halted before Gatewood. At twenty-nine, the chieftain, who had served Bay-chen-daysen as first sergeant in the late seventies and early eighties, was slender and yet muscular. His piercing black eyes and high cheek bones stood out in the early light. Gatewood liked and respected him. "Anzhoo [Good]," Alchesay said in greeting. He shook Gatewood's hand, hopped off his horse, and asked to see Crook.

While Alchesay and a few of his headmen went to see the general, the rest got in line to have their names entered in a roll-call book. Gatewood knew each of them personally. All had served as scouts under his command at one time or another and insisted upon shaking the nantan's hand. This was accompanied by a barrage of jokes:

> "Hello, Bay-ch[e]n-days[e]n, your nose has grown since we saw you last," "Ah! the billy-goat has kept himself thin so that he can run fast & far when the wolves get after his sheep." (They regard them-selves as wolves, coyotes,—coyotero, man-wolf—& the Yumas & Mojaves, a company of whom they knew I commanded in [a recent] campaign against them, as sheep. . . .) "Say, old goat, did you wear a bell so that your sheep could follow you?" "Ba-a-a." "Hold your head up, now that you are among *men* once more," & so on. All this was received with bursts of laughter & great good humor, & return of these compliments in kind only added to the general good feeling.[15]

Yes, the White Mountain Apaches were Gatewood's friends. Of all the Indians who served under him as scouts, they were his favorite. And now he was in a position to be more than a commander and a friend to them. Now he was military agent of their reservation.

As Crook's military agents, Gatewood, Crawford, and Davis drew diffi-cult assignments. Crook realized this: "These officers constantly carried their lives in their hands; the service in which they were engaged was one of the greatest possible delicacy and danger, where the slightest indiscretion would have proved fatal to them."[16] Gatewood called his new position "more dan-gerous than following [Apaches] on the war path."[17] Placed on detached duty from their regiments, they reported directly to Crook. "Other officers in the Department, regardless of their rank, had been told it was 'hands off.'"[18] On paper, their assignment appeared ideal.

But appearance belied reality—especially for Gatewood. Soon he would be known as a *Crook man*. The title did little to advance his military standing. In fact, the opposite happened. In the near future, being a Crook man would basically render him an exile—not at first, but certainly in the coming years, Gatewood saw the irony of the situation. He served under Crook, becoming one of the general's key subalterns. However, he was not a Crook man, for he constantly locked horns with the general and their relationship forever remained a far cry from cordial. One of Gatewood's contemporaries wrote: "it is queer but Gen[eral] Crook did not have any use for any of our Regiment—Gatewood included."[19]

Although Indian tensions seemed to relax somewhat after Crook's return to the Southwest, peace did not come to the territory. To Gatewood's dismay, another war loomed. He did not crave another outbreak. War brought never-ending patrols, the inevitable breakdown of his health, and long separations from his wife and soon-to-be-born child. There would be little acknowledgment and no advancement.

His trepidation was not unfounded. While Crook set up the reservation system, Geronimo could never forget the massacre of his first family in Sonora. With the recent loss of Chee-hash-kish, he justified his hunger for vengeance with the need for supplies. Geronimo, who did not take scalps as it was not an Apache custom, raided first in Sonora, then the United States, before returning to Sonora for a second strike. The rugged life had kept him in shape. He could run almost as long and far as the young men—but not quite. On many days, he would be one of the last arrivals at a pre-arranged destination. Although two warriors died during the depredations, stealth, ferocity, and fear guaranteed success. His blood lust satiated, Geronimo retreated back to the safety of the Sierra Madre, where he once again merged with Juh's band.[20]

At San Carlos, Crook set about altering the Indians' situation on the reservation. He called a third and final meeting on November 3. The Apaches—no Chiricahuas were present—told the general and his subordinates that "many of their people were sick and . . . many had already died from disease."[21] They also said that no crops would grow on the ground where the agent made them live.

Agent Wilcox agreed. He then pushed the blame on the Interior Department, saying they insisted the Indians live near the agency buildings so they could be counted regularly. This kept them far from fertile land and stopped them from becoming successful farmers.

Crook repeated his decree that the Apaches could live anywhere they desired on the reservation. He also told them that they had to become self-supporting; and they were to manage themselves, which included enlisting their own police force and conducting their own trials. All in all, it was a good beginning. Many families packed their scanty belongings and moved to the pine forest of the Mogollon Rim, north of San Carlos. The general, however, never became a generous benefactor to his Indian wards. Although sympathetic toward the Apache, he constantly found himself in a no-win situation with them. And no wonder: some laws he insisted on infringed upon the Apache way—mainly, a ban on *tizwin* drinking and wife beating.

Crawford, with Davis assisting, took military charge of the Indians at San Carlos and Gatewood assumed control of the Indians at Fort Apache.[22] As military agent of the White Mountains, Gatewood spent a lot of time thinking about his new position and the power he now wielded. His assignment was simple: control the Indians. This made him "judge, jury, sheriff, & legislature," and gave him the power "to take all proper & legal steps necessary to preserve the peace, prevent the manufacture & consumption of . . . [tizwin], encourage & aid them in agricultural & other peaceful pursuits: in other words, to keep them quiet & make them self supporting."[23]

He agreed with Crook—wife beating had to end. This part of the Apache lifeway was wrong. He had seen women brutally attacked for no apparent reason, and made it a priority. Treating girls as if they were property to be traded, bought, or sold like horses also bothered him.

Gatewood knew the new order would bring about dissent, and might even cause his wards to bolt the reservation. If this happened, he knew he would be held accountable. His task would not be easy. At the same time, he was now in a position to do some real good, and this possibility far outweighed any negativity.

Back at Fort Apache, Gatewood called his own meeting and explained the situation to his Indians. He told them they would grow their own crops to eat and sell. Loafers would not be tolerated. Nor would wife beaters. As expected, the warriors did not like his words, for loafing and wife beating had always been their right and they saw no reason to stop. Farming was not men's work: it was women's work. They did not know how to grow crops and did not want to learn.

Gatewood tried a new approach. He explained that the old ways were going away, that raiding and fighting were things of the past, and that to continue riding the war trail meant death. It was time they learned to live in peace, in permanent homes like white men. Some of the chiefs had visited eastern cities, and they knew his words of the future were true. They agreed to try to walk the white man's road.[24]

Gatewood set about allotting plots of land to the heads of households. Within just a few weeks, the bands had selected their farm and grazing lands, and women and children and even a few men began to clear the land. This gave Bay-chen-daysen yet another priority—farming implements. Agent Wilcox had plenty of shovels, hoes, and rakes. But he was angry the Indians were not remaining near his son-in-law's trading post and refused to give the Indians the needed tools. Obtaining tools became a never-ending problem. Gatewood's Indians dug their ditches with sticks and butcher knives. Then they planted their crops.[25]

Crook also reorganized the Apache scout companies. Crawford, Davis, and Gatewood immediately set about recruiting Apaches to serve as scouts. Crawford enlisted his companies at San Carlos and Gatewood his company at Apache. After the enlistments were filled, Crawford took 150 scouts to patrol two hundred miles of the Mexican border. Gatewood, who personally commanded Company A, Apache Scouts, remained at Apache. His scouts were all White Mountains, while those enlisted at San Carlos were Chihenne or Chokonen. Scout duty would soon include police work as well. The new scouts, when not on active duty, were "scattered among the bands to which they belonged."[26] They watched their people, reporting what they saw to Gatewood and Crawford.

The women liked the new order and complained whenever their men roughed them up, causing the accused to spend time behind bars. This had the desired effect: wife beating and mutilation declined. The Indians on the entire reservation also produced less tizwin.

While the White Mountain Apaches made great strides forward in their new life, the Chiricahuas dragged their feet. Turning them into farmers did not really succeed. Their women tended fields, but for the most part, the warriors refused to perform such unmanly tasks.[27] The "feeling of restlessness, discontent, fear, and uncertainty"[28] continued, and this mood carried over to the white soldiers who served among them. As a precaution, Gatewood and Davis selected seven Apaches to remain with their bands and listen to the talk of their brothers. They would serve as the ears and eyes of the two lieutenants, who felt that the only way to prevent another break for freedom was to know of such a plan in advance. The informants also served another purpose. Ever since the Apache scouts mutinied at Cibicue (1881), when the medicine man Nokaydeklinne was shot and killed,[29] white officers watched their backs, always alert to the possibility of sudden Apache treachery. Two of the spies worked for Gatewood, the other five for Davis. Their identities were kept hidden, and they only reported in the dark of night.

Gatewood enjoyed the *all-knowing* power the Indians thought he possessed; "it puzzled them to guess how the *Nantan* could know so much of what was going on in & around their villages,"[30] he wrote. "This had a good effect, for it often caused an offender to give himself up, & turn state's evidence on his companions."

Ever vigilant lest they put themselves in jeopardy, Gatewood and Davis found their lives uniquely bound together. Living on the edge created a bond that lasted the rest of their lives. As Davis put it: "[We knew] each other in a way that is seldom given to men to know."[31] Gatewood often traveled to San Carlos to visit the clean-shaven Davis, who the Apaches called *Nantan Enchau*—Stout Chief.[32]

Access to Fort Apache was not easy. The trails cutting through the rocky mountain terrain that surrounded the post were narrow and difficult to traverse. The fort consisted of barracks, officers' quarters (log construction in 1873–1874), hospital (standing on an isolated promontory), post trader (also isolated), a sawmill and pump house, reservoir, and target range. Some of the buildings were made with stone, while others were adobe. During the 1880s, a number of wooden buildings were constructed, including several structures on officers' row. There was no stockade. The White River swept through a gorge that skirted officers' row at the northern side of the post. Rough wooded country, "gashed with arroyos," stood behind the barracks to the south and east.[33]

Gatewood, who had served four months in 1878 as Post Quartermaster and Commissary at Fort Apache, thrived in the managerial assignment, for he enjoyed taking charge of Indian affairs on the reservation. Bay-chen-day-sen had the patience and discretion that Crook felt were needed to properly oversee a *regeneration* of the Apaches.[34]

As isolated as Gatewood's domain was, he did not have total control of it. At times he found that his power to select which Indians could serve as scouts was overruled by Crook. This usurpation of what should have been his absolute right put him in unnecessary jeopardy. Crook had no qualms about stepping in and dictatorially insisting that he use a particular Apache as scout. At one time, Crook demanded that he take as first sergeant an Apache called Sanchez, who had been at Cibicue, although not as a scout. Bold and aggressive, Sanchez may have fired the initial shot at the troops at Cibicue. Crook's continual interference with his subordinates at this time appears insignificant when compared to later episodes. However, as time passed and the number of these incidents increased, Crook's intervention "hurt the feelings of some of the best men in the service."[35] By not trusting Gatewood and Davis to do their jobs, Crook ultimately undermined the working relationship between himself and his subordinates.

Gatewood's position as an Indian supervisor suited him well. Although friendly with his fellow officers, he was basically a loner, and working with Apache scouts filled his need for solitude. Gatewood's personal reserve, combined with his keen eye, allowed him to understand the Indians he worked with. He realized that Apaches respected force,[36] but at the same time he knew that "the best way to get along with an Indian," as interpreter George Wratten once said, "is to make him a pal."[37] To do this, he could not maintain a chasm of racial separation. This was especially true during the many long periods of time he spent in the field with scouts. Gatewood readily adapted their mode of fighting and surviving. At the same time, he never turned his back on white culture.[38]

The Apaches, after centuries of Hispanic influence, spoke a smattering of Spanish. They also knew a few English words. Over the years, the Apaches became adept at using an Apache-Spanish-English pidgin. To help matters, the army hired interpreters capable of Apache-Spanish and Spanish-English translations. For some reason, reliable English-Apache interpreters were almost nonexistent. Gatewood knew language was the key, and he refused to depend totally on interpreters—although he always had them present if possible. Speaking of himself, Gatewood once wrote: "The Nantan spoke & understood the Apache dialect somewhat but not to an extent that would always insure accuracy of interpretation, especially in important matters. As it was, even with great care, misunderstandings arose frequently, sometimes leading to serious complications, & again with ridiculous results."[39] As the years passed, his Apache proficiency increased, and so did his Apache-Spanish-English pidgin.

The year 1882 became 1883. Geronimo did not remain with the Nednhi for long. When Juh took over half the people and moved deeper into the Sierra Madre, he and Chihuahua moved near the headwaters of the Bavispe. After several months of peace, he raided Sonora again.

While Geronimo's band enjoyed this time of prosperity, Juh's people were attacked by Mexicans. They lost women, children, and much of their belongings. Arguments between Juh and the other leaders resulted in his band splitting and going in different directions. Juh and the people who remained with him joined Geronimo's camp, increasing the warrior strength to eighty.[40]

More supplies were necessary. Geronimo decided to return to Sonora to steal more stock. At the same time Chihuahua, Chatto, and Benito planned to slip north of the border to get bullets.[41] That March the Bedonkohe and Chokonen war parties moved out together, separating after the first night's camp. Geronimo and the Bedonkohes moved toward the Bavispe River while Chihuahua and the Chokonen turned northward toward the United States.

While Arizona experienced a lull in depredations, Gatewood and Davis found their Indian wards more than willing to remain peaceful. They kept the Apaches working their plots of land, which was not an easy task when there were so few farming tools to go around. Gatewood's wards constantly asked for hoes and rakes and more seed, but there was none to give. Then, at the end of January, Gatewood heard that Agent Wilcox intended to distribute some tools, along with barley and potatoes, to the White Mountain Apaches. This pleased him, and on February 8, he wrote to Wilcox, requesting hoes, rakes, a plow and harness, and a wagon.

> I take this occasion to ask you to let [my wards] have all you can possibly give them, which I fear cannot be much. Still, as they are so willing to work & help themselves, even a *few* things would be considerable encouragement. I have never seen them in such good humor & so ambitious to become possessed of property of some kind.

Gatewood said the Indians preferred pumpkin, melon, corn, and potatoes. He closed the letter with:

> Everything up here is quiet. The Indians are getting along well & all they want is something to plant & tools to plant with. Scarcely any trouble among them, nothing to amount to much.[42]

Satisfied with the progress being made on the reservation, Crook traveled to the southeast corner of Arizona. Wanting to open negotiations with the Chiricahuas in Mexico, he sent emissaries across the border. Although the effort failed, he did catch two Chiricahua women attempting to return to San Carlos. What they said almost sounded like a challenge: "the Chiricahuas ha[ve] sworn vengeance upon Mexicans and Americans alike; . . . their stronghold [i]s an impregnable position in the Sierra Madre, a 'great way' below the International Boundary."[43]

Left with only one option, Crook began planning his next move—to hit the Chiricahuas as soon as opportunity presented itself. Back in July of 1882, the United States had signed an agreement with the Mexican government that allowed troops from either country to pursue warring Indians across the border when in close pursuit.[44] He would not have long to wait.

Geronimo took his time during the trek to Sonora, making many stops to eat beef and rest. After being spotted near Baviacora, he picked up his pace, and avoided Mexican soldiers. After stealing some horses, he crossed the Sonora River, then dropped into a valley. Here, he attacked a ranch and killed some people. Turning southward, Geronimo attacked every village he came upon. He captured a lot of booty, but did not kill many people.[45]

The old warrior's war party made better time than the other war party. Chihuahua crossed the United States border, raiding first in Arizona and then in New Mexico. His raid began on March 21. With twenty-six warriors, including Chatto, he struck with cyclonic swiftness; first at Charleston, a charcoal camp ten miles south of Tombstone. Chihuahua drove north to the Gila, then headed east, crossing into New Mexico north of Stein's Peak and continuing northeastward. He passed through the Burro Mountains, skirted Silver City, then dropped southward. In six days he traveled 450 miles through hills and canyons, stealing horses and killing twenty-six whites while only one warrior was killed (another warrior, tired of war, returned to the San Carlos Reservation). "Chihuahua and his raiders moved so rapidly," Kaywaykla said, "that military officers thought two or more war parties were operating in New Mexico and Arizona."[46]

Chihuahua's raid sent shock waves of terror throughout Arizona. Crook mounted a massive pursuit, but not once did any of the pursuing troops set eyes on a Chiricahua. Gatewood and his scouts took part in the hunt. After reporting to the commanding officer at Fort Huachuca, he scoured the country between the Dragoon and Huachuca mountains.[47] He found nothing— not one sign. The raiders had vanished as quickly as they had appeared. But Crook had what he wanted: a reason to enter Mexico.

CHAPTER THREE

The Sierra Madre

A telegram sent to Crook on March 31, 1883, got right to the point. Departmental and national boundary limitations no longer applied. Pursue and destroy the Chiricahuas.

Leaving orders to prepare for an invasion of the Chiricahuas' stronghold in the Sierra Madre, Crook traveled to Mexico to discuss the impending expedition. Stopping at Guaymas and Hermosillo in the state of Sonora, he met with Mexican army generals José Guillermo Carbo and Bonifacio Topete, along with Sonoran governor Luis E. Torres. Next, Crook traveled to Chihuahua in the state of Chihuahua. Here he met Governor Mariano Samaniego, General Ramón Reguera, and Chihuahuan mayor Zubrian.[1]

The United States and Mexico had previously worked out an agreement that allowed a pursuing army to cross the border if in hot pursuit of Indians. However, there were several stipulations that impeded swift action. The invading force had to cross the international boundary in an unpopulated or desert area. The crossing could not be made any closer than two leagues (roughly three miles) of a town. The invading troops had to notify the host nation of its intent, preferably before making the crossing. And finally, and most importantly, the invaders had to retreat as soon as they engaged the quarry or lost the trail. Under no circumstances could the invasion last for an extended period of time.

This would not do. Crook pleaded for permission to hound the trail until he succeeded. The Mexicans agreed. Topete was especially supportive. The Americans could cross the border on May 1, but not before.[2]

Troops began to organize at Fort Willcox, about sixty miles north of the border in southeast Arizona. Located on the western side of the Dos Cabezas Mountains, the post also served as Crook's headquarters. Six companies of Third and Sixth regiments of Cavalry (under Major James Biddle and Captain William Dougherty) prepared for the campaign.[3]

Gatewood's orders were specific. Hurry to San Carlos and enlist an additional seventy Indian scouts; then join the main force at Willcox. Gatewood had no trouble finding enlistees. He explained the dangers of the campaign, stressing that the scouts would walk well over one thousand miles. As their salary—thirteen dollars per month—was not considered enough compensation, Gatewood told the enlistees they could keep whatever booty they captured from the Chiricahuas. As soon as he had recruited the allotted number of men, he led them to Willcox. Joining Crawford, he prepared the expedition for the invasion.[4]

The Southern Pacific Railroad passed through Willcox. During stopovers, passengers aboard the trains often rushed to get off. The attraction? They wanted to see the soldiers who would soon hunt Indians. One such passenger approached some of Crook's officers and said he and his wife wanted to see an Arizona bad man. Lieutenant G. J. Fiebeger, remembered the occasion: "Gatewood was as tough a looking specimen as we had, so he was pointed out."[5] Undoubtedly, Bay-chen-daysen, anticipating the march into the unknown of the Sierra Madre, had already donned the nonregulation clothing he wore while in the field. In appearance, the mustachioed nantan probably looked more like the scouts he commanded than the general population's perception of what an officer in the U.S. Army should look like.

Satisfied that Gatewood was just what he was looking for, the traveler walked up to him, introduced himself, and invited the *Arizona bad man* to meet his wife and pass the time with a glass of champagne. Gatewood gladly accepted the invitation.

By April 23 all preparations had been completed. Crook wanted to be at the border and ready to cross at the appointed time. He ordered his combined force of Indian scouts and companies from the Third and Sixth out from Willcox.

Howling winds swept the top layer of sand from the desert. The flying sand blasted everything that ventured from cover. Designated to lead the way, Gatewood shouted: "*Ugashé!*—Go!"[6] His Indian scouts—their faces painted with deer's blood, red ochre, or roasted mescal juice to protect them from the sun and wind—moved out on foot. Forming small groups of two and three, they scattered over the terrain. Moving quickly, the scouts covered a lot of ground. Soon, opaque clouds of swirling dust hid them from sight as Gatewood fought his way forward riding a mule.

Although mules easily outperformed horses in the Southwest, Gatewood preferred horses and he had a favorite, Bob. Gatewood thought the world of Bob, whom he lost during a heated engagement with Victorio's Chihennes at Lake Guzman in October 1879. During the fight, Apaches captured some of Gatewood's mounts, Bob included. It broke him up every time he thought about the captured animal. As Bob was his personal property, Gatewood requested a reimbursement of 125 dollars. The government refused payment, which remained a sore point with him.[7]

While Crook's army advanced, Geronimo and Juh's bands camped a few miles northeast of the Sierra Madre in a pine forest. Food had again become scarce. A war party raided Oputo on the west side of the Bavispe River, capturing one hundred head of cattle and driving them back to the waiting village, where everyone feasted and danced. Soon after the celebration, the bands moved up into the Sierra Madre, eventually camping west of Huachinera. Shortly after the move, on April 25, they ambushed a detachment of Mexican soldiers following their trail.[8]

Crook did not know of the latest depredation. But even if he had known, he would not have hurried because his army could not cross the border until May 1. The command slowly worked its way one hundred miles southeastward across the scorching sand, reaching San Bernardino Springs on April 28. Final preparations complete, Crook divided his command. Most of the white troops would patrol the border and prevent Chiricahuas from reentering the United States. The Indian scouts spent the dark hours between dusk and dawn dancing. Crook sent telegrams to the Mexican officials, informing them he would cross the line at the agreed-upon time.[9]

Strict orders reduced everyone's baggage to one blanket, forty rounds of ammunition, and the clothing on their back.[10] As planned, the invasion force crossed into Mexico on May 1. It consisted of 193 Indian scouts (Chiricahua, White Mountain, Yuma, Mojave, and Tonto), one company of Sixth Cavalry (Company I), and two pack trains, which were later divided into five trains (pack mules carried enough hard-bread, coffee, and bacon for sixty days, as well as 160 rounds of extra ammunition per man). Captain John G. Bourke (Third U.S. Cavalry) and Fiebeger (Engineer Corps) acted as aides-de-camp. Captain Adna Chaffee, Lieutenant Frank West, and Lieutenant W. W. Forsyth of the Sixth U.S. Cavalry commanded forty-two enlisted men. Crawford, along with Gatewood and Lieutenant James Mackay (Third U.S. Cavalry), commanded the scouts. A. A. Surgeon Andrews was medical officer. Al Sieber, a German who had served as both packer and scout since the 1870s, acted as chief of scouts. Archie MacIntosh, who was half-Chippewa and had been employed as scout and interpreter since 1855, assisted Sieber. Mickey Free, a red-haired Mexican blind in one eye; Severiano, a Mexican who became the Spanish-Apache translator at Fort Apache after living and raiding with the Apaches thirty years; and Sam Bowman, who was part-Choctaw, were interpreters. Tzoe (Peaches), along with To-klanni and Alchesay, acted as guide.[11] Peaches, a White Mountain married into the Chiricahua tribe, had left the Chihuahua/Chatto raid when his friend Beneactiney died. After he surrendered at San Carlos, Crook had asked him if he could find the Chiricahuas' stronghold in the Sierra Madre. Peaches said he could, and agreed to lead the expedition.

The command traveled southward through a desert overgrown with tropical vegetation. Passing the ruins of abandoned towns, they followed the San Bernardino River until it reached the Bavispe River.[12]

The burning sun scorched every living thing. White men cursed and mules brayed, slipping and stumbling on sandstone, limestone, and jagged-edged lava as they struggled up and down steep hills, only to be torn by sharp-thorned vegetation when they reached the valley floors. In contrast, the Indian scouts traveled without complaint, laughing and joking. At night, they cleaned their hair with yucca or Spanish-bayonet roots. Some made flutes, while others carved pipes, from bamboo-like cane. Each evening Gatewood spread his bedroll amidst the scouts' makeshift wickiups, and as in the past he held council frequently with the Indians under his command.

The landscape became increasingly desolate as Gatewood's Apaches led the column deeper into Mexico, where the dense vegetation looked similar to the flora found in southern Arizona. By now the faces and hands of the white soldiers had burned and blistered, and deep tans appeared under peeling skin. With Peaches and the Apache scouts leading the way, the general, Gatewood, Crawford, and the rest of the soldiers plodded onward. They passed the mud-plastered towns of Bavispe and Bacerac (Basaraca), finally reaching Tesorababi. Each town seemed worse off than the one before. Although the inhabitants greeted the soldiers cordially, their squalor did not sit well with the Americans. "The condition of the inhabitants was deplorable," Bourke later recalled. "Superstition, illiteracy, and bad government had done their worst."[13]

On May 7 the column turned eastward, moving higher into the Sierra Madre. Grama grass and scrub oak covered the foothills, but soon gave way to cedar as the climb became steeper. A soldier caught an owl and tied it to his saddle. Then, scouts discovered the trail left by the Chiricahua raiders when they drove the herd of captured cattle back to their village. The pace of Crook's army quickened.

As the command advanced, Apache eyes kept turning toward the soldiers. Finally, the scouts halted. Crook asked what was wrong and they told him that *Bú* (the owl) was not a good omen. The one the soldier had caught would bring them bad luck. When they insisted they could not hope to destroy the enemy with the owl in their midst, Crook agreed and the bird was set free.

The march continued upward, always upward. Trails seemed to go every which way. They passed cattle; some idly roaming, others butchered. On the ground they found dresses, bags of flour, saddles, letters, and other goods strewn where the Chiricahuas had dumped them.

Medicine men accompanying the column gathered on the night of May 8 to sing and see the Chiricahuas. While the group chanted, the leader dropped off into a trance. After rejoining the living, he pounded his chest, then muttered:

> Me can't see the Chilicahuas yet. Bimeby me see 'um. Me catch 'um, me kill 'um. Me no catch 'um, me no kill 'um. Mebbe so six day me catch 'um; mebbe so two day. . . . Mebbe so tomollow catch 'um squaw. Chilicahua see me, me no get 'um. No see me, me catch him. . . . Me catch 'um, me kill 'um.[14]

Next day the journey turned more perilous, the trail narrowing and becoming steeper. Carcasses of dead and broken mules, horses, and cattle lined the canyon floor far below. During the trek that day, five mules lost their footing and plunged to their deaths.

Peaches led Crawford and Gatewood and their scouts across a ridge and then down into a narrow gorge. It widened somewhat, becoming an amphitheater, a veritable fortress, with flowing water giving the spot life. He halted. Scattered everywhere, the newcomers saw bones of ponies and cattle. Obviously a large group had lived there for some time. Peaches said this was the main encampment when he was last with the Chiricahuas.

Knowing that Chiricahuas were close, Crawford and Gatewood sent scouts out in all directions. Everywhere they looked they saw Chiricahua sign: "extinct fires, the straw of unused beds, the skeleton frame-work of dismantled huts, the play-grounds and dance-grounds, mescal-pits and acorn-meal mills . . ."[15] But the scouts spotted no Chiricahuas. Orders outlawed fires that night.

Feeling the pinch of almost continuous warfare, Geronimo decided to obtain prisoners to swap for his people taken by the Mexicans at Casas Grandes. Unaware that White Eyes hunted him, he led a raiding party in a southeasterly direction until he reached his destination—a road between Carmen and Chihuahua. Here he ambushed a small caravan near the town of Carmen, killing two men and capturing six women, one of whom was nursing a baby. The haul could not have been better: the women were wives of soldiers stationed at Casas Grandes. Geronimo released the oldest captive, telling her to tell the Casas Grandes officials that he wanted to trade for Chiricahuas taken by the Mexicans.

Next day the raiders again failed to snare any captives. They did, however, find some cattle. That night around the campfire, Geronimo ate with his companions. He sliced off a hunk of beef with his knife, but before chewing the morsel he dropped his knife. "Men, our people whom we left at our base camp are now in the hands of U.S. troops!" Geronimo said. "What shall we do?"[16]

Everyone in the war party believed him. They were 120 miles from their base camp and knew they had to return to it immediately. The shocking revelation demoralized the warriors.

That night, after abandoning three hundred head of cattle, Geronimo led his followers back toward their village. The women captives slowed the pace, and the next morning, when the party halted to eat, the captives refused the beef. Geronimo urged them to eat, saying that they were in a hurry and that the women needed to keep up their strength. Still, they refused. Suddenly, an unnamed warrior stomped before the women, brandishing his weapons and screaming at them. The threats worked, the frightened women ate.

May 10 was like the previous day, as the command continued to climb. Gatewood and the other soldiers struggled and slipped as they pulled their mounts and pack mules up perilous inclines. In contrast, the scouts moved with amazing agility—leaping from precipice to precipice without effort.

A low cry—more whistle than whisper—from far above froze all who heard its urgent call. Word quickly passed back to the panting troops: two Chiricahuas had been seen. Scouts stripped for battle—down to their loin cloths, leggings, and moccasins. Leaving their calico shirts and loose cotton drawers on rocks, twelve moved out to attack.

Everyone waited. They could hear the sounds of the mountain and nothing else.

An hour passed. The Indian scouts returned. It had been a false alarm. Two packers, looking for stray mules, had drifted to the front.

The scouts talked among themselves, then with Crawford and Gatewood. Together, they approached Crook. The white troops and pack trains impeded progress. If they had any chance of catching the Chiricahuas, they had to move quickly. They proposed that the soldiers remain in camp and thereafter follow a day behind the scouts.

Crook agreed. His orders were simple: spare the women and children, while killing as many warriors as possible. All prisoners would be returned to the reservation.[17]

The camp came to life. Small fires were lit under rocks where telltale smoke could not give them away. Scouts baked bread and ground coffee, everyone checked their weapons and cartridges, moccasins were repaired, and sweat-baths were taken. To the south, soldiers and scouts found the remains of a canyon ambush the Chiricahuas had sprung on Mexican troops. That night, the medicine men predicted the scouts would find the enemy in two days, engaging in a big kill on the third day.

At daybreak on May 11, Crawford, Gatewood, Mackay, Sieber, Free, Severiano, MacIntosh, Bowman, and 150 scouts moved out on foot. "Each carried on his person four days' rations, a canteen, 100 rounds of ammunition, and a blanket."[18]

For three days, Crawford, Gatewood, and the scouts moved farther into the Sierra Madre. They passed caches of hides, dried meat, calico, buckskin, and clothing. Coming upon a deserted Chiricahua village, they counted ninety-eight wickiups. Close examination showed that the Chiricahuas had many horses and cattle. It was obvious the Indians had no idea that Indian scouts were hunting them because they did not abandon the camp in haste. Crawford called a halt until Crook could forward more rations.

The next morning, May 15, Crawford and Gatewood's scouts began finding stray cattle, horses, and mules. Then, without warning, an advance guard came upon two men and a woman. Instead of waiting to attack in unison, the excited Indian scouts fired at the Indians, setting the as-yet-undiscovered village to flight.[19]

Too late to plan an attack, Crawford, Gatewood, and the scouts rushed forward. Firing as they advanced, they moved across a small valley and into the ranchería, which was "situated half-way up the face of a precipitous mountain gashed with ravines and arroyos."[20] The Chiricahuas fled, and Crawford, Gatewood, and the scouts quickly took the encampment. The one-sided fight continued as the scouts chased Indians "across a fearfully broken country, gashed with countless ravines, and shrouded with a heavy growth of pine and scrub-oak."[21]

Scout bullets killed a Chiricahua woman. Seeing his mother die, Speedy, a warrior who had remained with the village, grabbed Charlie McComas—a white boy captured during Chihuahua and Chatto's raid the previous March—and bashed in his head with a stone.[22] Speedy hid the corpse and fled.

Nine Indians died in the assault; and one young woman, two boys, and two girls were captured. Crawford and Gatewood quickly learned that the encampment belonged to Chatto and Benito. As most of the warriors were out raiding, the village contained mostly women, children, and old people. Two clusters, totaling thirty wickiups, were destroyed. Forty-seven of the captured animals were piled with plunder, including gold and silver watches, a lot of Mexican and American gold and paper money, four breech-loading Winchester repeating rifles, and a new Colt revolver. The attacking force suffered no casualties in the fight, which lasted several hours.

The young captives remained calm, stoic. Through interpreters, the young woman, who was Bonito's daughter, told Crawford and Gatewood: "[My] people [were] astounded and dismayed when they saw the long line of Apache scouts rushing in upon them." She went on to say that "the Chiricahuas would give up without further fighting, since the Americans had secured all the advantages of position. 'Loco' and 'Chihuahua,'" she said, "would be glad to live peaceably upon the reservation, if justly treated; 'Hieronymo' and 'Chat[t]o' she wasn't sure about."[23]

The next morning, the sky clouded and it poured, only to clear quickly. Crook, who had again joined Crawford and Gatewood, set the young Chiricahua woman, along with the oldest boy, free to meet with her people and attempt to talk them into surrendering.

Geronimo continued his hurried retreat. Prodding the captives onward, his war party moved as quickly as possible to return to their loved ones. South of Galeana, warriors captured a herd of cattle. That night, in council, Geronimo again foretold the future: "Tomorrow after noon as we march along the north side of the mountains we will see a man standing on a hill to our left. He will howl to us and tell us that the troops have captured our base camp."[24]

The next day, Geronimo and his warriors hustled through oaks and pines as they raced to find their families. Suddenly, that afternoon as predicted, they heard a howl from above. They halted. A warrior dropped down to them, carrying bad news. American troops and Indian scouts had attacked and captured one of the villages, and their loved ones were on the run. This was devastating news: never before had their sanctuary in the Sierra Madre been invaded.

Geronimo's world always seemed to dissolve into hell. If he loved someone and took them into his life, their future existence became uncertain. That night, around the campfire, Geronimo and his companions talked. They could only make one decision—find out what had happened.

The Crawford/Gatewood-led Indian scout attack destroyed the Chiricahua resistance. The taking of the encampment sealed the fugitives' future. As the invading force waited, refugees began filing into their encampment. Beginning with just six women on May 17, the flow increased. Chihuahua, who had not yet appeared, was said to be gathering his people. It was reported that he was tired of war. On the morning of May 18, four women, one warrior, and a boy surrendered; then another sixteen, including Chihuahua. The refugee count grew from just a few to 121.[25]

The war neared an end. But what about Geronimo? Gatewood did not need to remind the scouts to be wary. Everyone knew that Geronimo, the driving force behind the hostilities, was not far away. Though no one knew just where he was, everyone believed the old warrior was within striking distance.

As Crook commented: "we could never hope to catch them in the rugged peaks . . . the effort would surely cost the lives of many men; each rock being a fortress from behind which the Chiricahuas could fight to the death with their breech loading guns."[26]

No one relaxed their guard.

Geronimo and his thirty-six raiders reached cliffs a thousand feet above the white encampment. He had been right. Americans and traitorous Apaches had captured their belongings; the people had scattered, and some had surrendered. From above, he and his brethren looked down at the hated soldiers and Apache scouts. He turned and directed some of his warriors to take defensive positions on the mountainside. Then he, and the rest of his warriors, climbed down toward the Americans.

Armed warriors anxiously ran and leaped about from crag to crag. They began yelling to the captives below.

Something had to be done. Still, Geronimo had no intention of walking into a trap. When he got as close as he dared, he sent two old men forward to meet with the soldiers. If they did not return, he intended to attack.[27]

Gatewood's scouts grabbed their rifles and raced for cover behind trees, where they began shouting up at the enemy. The women and children who had surrendered joined the din, screaming to their brethren above.

When the two emissaries appeared, one of the Apache scouts and one of the captives walked up to them. When the Indians asked if they would be harmed if they came down to talk, the scout assured them that they would not be hurt. The two old men said Geronimo wanted to talk. The scout told them that until all of Chihuahua's people had surrendered, there would be no hostilities. The old men turned back toward Geronimo.

Nothing happened. Gatewood, his scouts, Crook, everyone waited. It seemed the Chiricahuas had no intention of talking. Then, while the officers ate supper, a couple of Indians climbed down from above and crossed to Crook's tent. In small parties of two or three, others followed. They advanced warily, approaching from different directions. "Each [warrior] was armed with a breech-loading Winchester; most had nickel-plated revolvers of the latest pattern, and a few had . . . bows and lances."[28]

Geronimo stepped forward, said he wanted to talk with Crook. Crook refused:

[I do not want] anything to do with him or his party beyond saying that they ha[ve] an opportunity to see for themselves that their own people [a]re against them; that we ha[ve] penetrated to places vaunted as impregnable; that the Mexicans [are] coming in from all sides; and that 'Hieronymo' c[an] make up his mind for peace or war just as he cho[oses].[29]

Geronimo heard the message, but for once, he did not know what to do and he hesitated. Then he and his warriors moved to a safe distance. An hour passed, nothing happened.

Unsure of what he should do, Geronimo slowly dropped down to the soldiers' encampment a second time, with others following him. Geronimo and his warriors talked with the scouts who came out to meet them, but he was not pleased that he had to deal with Crook. News that Mexican soldiers were close also bothered him. He went to Crook and said: "[I have] always wanted to be at peace, but [have] been as much sinned against as sinning; [I have] been ill-treated at . . . San Carlos and driven away."[30]

Crook said nothing.

Geronimo continued. He complained about Mexican treachery, then returned to his main purpose. He would gladly return to the reservation, walk the road of peace, and work for his living—but only if the general would guarantee him just treatment. If not, he and his warriors would fight to the end.

Crook's reply was curt: "'Hieronymo' could make up his mind as to what he wanted, peace or war."[31]

The meeting ended. It had not gone well. *Nantan Lupan*—as the Chiricahuas called Crook—did not offer anything. Geronimo and his warriors returned to the cliffs above the encampment and talked over what they should do.

It did not take long to reach a decision. Geronimo immediately sent some of his warriors off to gather their people. The old warrior then waited for dawn.

At first light, May 21, Geronimo returned to Crook. He got right to the point: he wanted peace. He said he would change. Putting pride aside, Geronimo begged Nantan Lupan to take him back to San Carlos.

Crook had the upper hand and did not relinquish it. "I am not taking your arms from you, because I am not afraid of you. You have been allowed to go about camp freely, merely to let you see that we have strength enough to exterminate you if we want to."[32]

Geronimo listened, knowing that his and his peoples' lives hung in the balance.

Crook continued: "You must remember that I have been fighting you for our people, and if I take you back and attempt to put you on the reservation the Americans and Mexicans will make a hard fight of it, for you have been murdering their people, stealing their stock and burning their houses. You have been acting in a most cruel manner, and the people will demand that you be punished. You see, you are asking me to fight my own people in order to defend your wrongs."

Geronimo waited. Finally Crook said he would accept the surrender. Suddenly, the burden lifted; his people would live. Geronimo relaxed.

The refugee numbers increased daily. By May 28 the figure had grown to 374 (123 warriors and 251 women and children). Crook did not have enough supplies to feed everyone.[33]

The camp came to life. Chiricahuas busily cut and roasted mescal, while others killed and butchered cattle and horses. "The ring of axes against the trunks of stout pines and oaks, the hum of voices, the squalling of babies, the silvery laughter of children at play, and the occasional music of [a] flute, combined in a pleasant discord which left the listener uncertain whether he was in the bivouac of grim-visaged war or among a band of school-children."[34]

The campaign over, Gatewood could not wait to return to Georgia. As in the past, the rigors had been harsh, but unlike previous times, his body had not rebelled and he would not have to go on extended leave to recuperate. Although he knew that Georgia was not lonely—she had not only their infant son, Charles, Jr., to keep her occupied, but also a young female friend visiting from Virginia—he was.[35]

The homeward journey began May 30. Only 52 warriors and 273 women and children made the trip. Geronimo had asked for, and received, permission, to remain behind to gather the remnants of his people and their belongings. Nana, Loco, and Bonito made the trip, but Chatto and Chihuahua did not. Juh, who had not negotiated with Crook, remained in the wilds of Mexico.[36]

During the homeward march, Gatewood placed Henry Daly, an Irishman, in charge of his pack train. The journey was slow, and he did not reunite with his young family until the middle of June.[37]

CHAPTER FOUR

Gatewood's Stand for Justice

Crook shared the success of the campaign with the Apache scouts and the *Indian men* (Crawford and Gatewood) who led them.[1] Astonishingly, crowds of thankful civilians did not welcome the veterans home. Instead, trouble brewed as the command and its armed hostages returned to Arizona.

> Crook was . . . made the target of every sort of malignant and
> mendacious assault . . . The telegraph wires were loaded with
> false reports of outrages, attacks, and massacres which had never
> occurred; these reports were . . . broadcast with the intention
> [of doing] him injury.[2]

Although such a reception was unfair, it was understandable, for whites lived in terror of the Chiricahuas and did not want Geronimo and his brethren back. The press backed the settlers and clamored for removing all Apaches from the territory.

At the same time, an internal disruption broke out at the arrival of the Chiricahuas. Those who should have been allies and strong supporters of the recent conquest proved to be otherwise.

Agent Wilcox, who admittedly "knew nothing about Indians,"[3] began a campaign of disruption nine months after he had promised to support the military regime. On June 14, Wilcox held a council with the reservation Indians, which was actually a protest rally. He did not want the warring Chiricahuas back on the reservation. With his superior's backing, the agent did everything he could to incite his wards—many of whom already hated the Chiricahuas—to mutiny. Crook sent Crawford to San Carlos to investigate.

This rift—actually a struggle for dominance—between the civil and military authorities was exactly what Crook had tried to eliminate when he assumed command. Wilcox and his superiors had declared war: clearly, they would not give up control without a struggle. The secretary of the interior ordered Wilcox to only receive Chiricahua women and children on the reservation. Crook quickly voiced his concerns: "If these Indians are not fed they must either starve or go back to the warpath."[4] In the same report, he succinctly described the situation: "When the Chiricahuas reach the reservation they will be . . . nervous and distrustful. Any attempts to hold them responsible for their acts before their surrender will drive them back to the cliffs and gorges of the mountains, and we shall then have to fight them till the last one dies."

Amid the swirl of political tension and social unrest, the military triumvirate of Crawford, Gatewood, and Davis tried to perform their duties and maintain peace among their wards.

After reuniting with his family, Gatewood went back to work with the White Mountain Apaches. He did what he could to quiet the disruptive forces that permeated the reservation, and at the same time, he picked up where he had left off. The White Mountain, Cibicu, and Coyotero Apaches were shown how to improve their plots of vegetables, while others, who had done little, were stimulated to begin. As crops began to ripen, the Indians were shown that they could sell them at a profit.

During 1883 the White Mountain Indian Reservation harvested 2,625,000 pounds of corn; 180,000 pounds of beans; 135,000 pounds of potatoes; 12,600 pounds of wheat; 200,000 pounds of barley; 100,000 pumpkins; 20,000 watermelons; 10,000 muskmelons; 10,000 cantaloupes; along with small patches of cabbage, onions, cucumbers, and lettuce.[5]

More and more white men allowed their herds of horses, cattle, and sheep to graze illegally on the reservation. The White Mountain Apaches wanted the White Eyes to remain on their side of the reservation boundary, and Gatewood agreed. The invading animals ate grass in meadows that the Indians planned to harvest to sell to the government or needed for their own stock.

Bay-chen-daysen posted notices, all along the northern perimeter of the reservation and in the nearby towns, prohibiting illicit grazing. The signs carried the warning that those violating the law would suffer confiscation of their stock or a fine. The signs were ignored.

Tired of the invasion, Gatewood allowed his police force to begin seizing livestock found on Indian land. Gatewood recorded what the whites usually yelled when informed that their stock had been confiscated: "What! Fine a *white* man for allowing his cattle to destroy an *Indian's* corn crop, or consume & trample down an *Indian's* hay field? Preposterous!"[6] The loss of money brought about the desired result, and fewer non-Indian animals were found on Indian land.

While Gatewood administered to his wards, Crook traveled to Washington, D.C. The Interior and War departments, caught up in the Arizona uproar, argued over the disposition of the Chiricahuas. Crook had been ordered to give his side of the controversy. He met with the secretaries of both departments, along with the commissioner of Indian affairs. On July 7,

Secretary of War Robert Lincoln and Secretary of Interior Henry Moore Teller signed a joint memorandum that gave Crook control of the feeding, care, and policing of the recently "captured" Chiricahuas. This *control* encompassed the entire San Carlos Reservation, but somehow did not include Indians near the agency buildings without Wilcox's permission.[7]

The Chiricahuas would stay at San Carlos. Crook had his victory, but unfortunately, he did not completely think through his needs. Although he considered the San Carlos and White Mountain reservations one and the same, the memorandum only referred to the recently captured Indians, and did not specify any Indians living at the White Mountain Indian Reservation. Gatewood's wards had not been on the warpath; they did not come under the memorandum's jurisdiction. This glaring omission left the chasm gaping wide that Crook wanted to close.

General Orders No. 13,[8] issued on July 24, placed Crawford in overall control of policing and feeding the Indians on the joint reservations. He chose to keep his base at San Carlos, which left Gatewood, who would report to Crawford, in control at White Mountain. Apache scouts were responsible for all of the police work, a task they liked, especially when the law breakers happened to be Chiricahuas. Arrests were made and Apache juries quickly convicted guilty offenders. "This system of trial by Indian juries has been introduced with happy results," Crook reported, "and offenses committed within the tribe are tried and punished with certainty, promptness and justice."[9]

In spite of the positive results, the divided authority remained a thorn to military agents Crawford and Gatewood. Civilian administrators, led by Wilcox, resisted every effort Crawford and Gatewood made toward Indian self-sufficiency, and the friction quickly escalated.

In September, a disgruntled Wilcox complained that he had been stripped of his authority. Gathering support from his superiors, prominent citizens, and politicians, he lashed out. The key to his assault was the July 7 memorandum Crook had secured in Washington, part of which Wilcox and company interpreted to read: "with the express understanding that the military officers were to have the supervision of the police regulations on the reservation under the *direction* and with the *approval* of the Indian agent."[10] Wilcox wanted his way or to have the memorandum terminated.

As the two factions jockeyed for position, days became weeks and then months. The Chiricahuas who had remained in Mexico with Geronimo to gather their bands had said they would return to the reservation within two moons. The anticipated date of arrival came and passed. In October, Crook ordered Britton Davis to the border to look for Indian stragglers. He would escort all he found to the reservation.[11] Davis did not find any returning Indians.

A week passed and then another. October became November. Davis sent scouts into Mexico, but they could not find the missing people. It looked as if the Chiricahuas had no intention of keeping their promise. Then, on December 20, Naiche appeared with about twelve warriors, over twenty women and children, and some ponies. Davis quickly escorted them to San Carlos. A month and a half later, on February 7, 1884, Chatto, Mangus, a Chihenne leader, and somewhere between fifty and sixty other Chiricahuas crossed the line. Fearing an attack by civilians, Davis made the second trip to the reservation just as quickly as the first.[12]

While everyone waited anxiously for Geronimo to cross the international boundary, Gatewood's administration of the Apaches at White Mountain continued to produce dividends. His wards had become self-sufficient in July. Four months later, in November, they were still self-sufficient and had received no government rations. But this did not mean they did not need other supplies, such as clothing, blankets, or tools. Gatewood's Indians used money earned from the sale of their crops to buy what they needed—items like flour.

Seeing a way to again pad the pockets of its employees, the Interior Department stepped in. Even though Gatewood's wards could purchase flour at .041/2 cents per pound in Holbrook, Arizona, the Interior Department forced them to buy flour from their trader at twice the price (.09 cents per pound).[13]

Near the end of February 1884, Geronimo, fifteen or sixteen other warriors, and about seventy women and children rode up to the border, a large cloud of dust billowing behind them. As soon as the old Bedonkohe warrior saw Davis, he rode up to him and demanded to know why soldiers met him. He had made peace, he should be safe.

Davis said "there [a]re some bad Americans just as there [a]re some bad Indians."[14] He explained that some of these men might come gunning for Geronimo.

Geronimo accepted this, shook Davis's hand, and announced that they were brothers.

Davis, nervous about the approaching cloud of dust, asked what it meant, expecting Geronimo to say that the Mexican army was in hot pursuit.

"Ganado," Geronimo said. He had a herd of 135 Mexican cattle that he intended to take to the reservation. The cattle were tired, Geronimo explained, and he wanted to rest them for three days. This bothered Davis, who knew that in the open he and the Indians were sitting targets for the good Arizona citizens; but he gave in to the request.

When they finally started the drive northward they only covered eighteen or twenty miles a day, and each night Geronimo went to Davis. "[You are] running all the fat off the cattle," he complained, "and they [will] not be fit for trading when we [reach] the Reservation." Geronimo announced that he planned to rest his cattle for several days. Davis tried to scare him into moving on by saying that Mexicans might be following. "Mexicans!" Geronimo said with disgust, "Mexicans! My squaws can whip all the Mexicans in Chihuahua."

"But the Mexicans have plenty of cartridges and you have practically none," Davis countered.

"We don't fight Mexicans with cartridges," Geronimo said. "Cartridges cost too much. We keep them to fight your white soldiers. We fight Mexicans with rocks."

The trip continued. The next day they reached Sulphur Springs, about thirty miles west of Fort Bowie. Here, they compromised: they would camp for a day.

As they were pitching camp, two men from a nearby ranch house walked up to Davis. One was a U.S. Marshal and the other was a customs official from Tombstone, John E. Clark. They wanted Geronimo's cattle and horses, and they also wanted Geronimo for murder. They threatened Davis with ending his career if he did not help them. Then they said they were going to get a posse at Willcox, some forty miles to the north.

A short while later, Lieutenant J. Y. F. Blake (Sixth U.S. Cavalry) rode into camp to visit Davis. He carried a bottle of whiskey that he intended to share with Davis. However, Clark and the Marshal returned, and Davis and Blake proceeded to get them drunk.

After the officials stumbled back to the ranch house, Davis summoned Geronimo. When the Bedonkohe war leader arrived, Davis told him a lie, saying that the two men wanted a thousand dollars or the cattle to sell in Tucson.

Geronimo did not like what he heard. Davis remembered: "As I talked to him he stood staring me straight in the eyes, his anger mounting and his lips twitching as he shifted his rifle from arm to arm."

Davis suggested that Geronimo start for the reservation.

"No!" Geronimo exploded. Controlling his temper, he said he wanted peace, but all he found was trouble and threats. "If these men [think] that they [can] take [my] cattle away from [me], let them try it tomorrow." Finished talking, Geronimo said he was going back to bed. Why, he asked, had he been disturbed for such trivial talk? He turned to go.

Before Geronimo got far, the sergeant of Davis's Apache scouts yelled after him. The unknown words had the desired effect: Geronimo halted and turned back to Davis. "[My] people could leave [you] standing where [you are] and [you] would not know that they were gone."

Davis wondered aloud: "what a joke it would be on the officers in the ranch if they woke up in the morning and found that the Indians with all the cattle and ponies had disappeared."

"Geronimo almost smiled," Davis recalled, "hesitated for a moment, looked inquiringly at his men, saw no opposition from them, and the battle was won." Less than an hour later, Geronimo, his people, and his herd were gone.

Neither Clark, the marshal, nor any of the cowboys at the ranch heard the old warrior move out. The next morning when the officials discovered they had been duped, they exploded. But by then it was too late. Geronimo completed the rest of his trip safely.

The old warrior's efforts came to naught, however. Crook confiscated his herd when he reached the reservation. The cattle were sold, and $1,762.50 was sent to Mexico to compensate the original owners. Geronimo had a problem with this. Batsinas remembered that Geronimo "felt that he was only providing a good supply of food for his people."[15] This was logical, since the constant threat of starvation had been one of the main complaints of all the Indians on the reservation.

Chiricahuas were good with livestock, but they had no interest in becoming farmers. San Carlos was a desert with little arable land and not much game, and even those who wanted to till the land found it difficult. However, the land was good for grazing, and Crawford and Davis proposed to make the Chiricahuas pastoral rather than agricultural. The idea appealed to the Indians, but the Indian Bureau rejected the idea immediately.[16] *All* Apaches would become farmers.

The Chiricahuas had returned to the reservation. Although they lived at peace, they kept a wary distance from the other bands. Unhappy with their current situation, they refused to farm the land. This was not men's work. Leaving the work to the women, they loafed, hunted, and gambled, and soon trouble began to brew among the bands. Problems were usually caused by a young woman, a gambling game, or tizwin. The tizwin problem got so bad that drinking it was banned altogether. If caught with tizwin, the culprits were punished with ten days to two weeks in the Fort Apache guardhouse. Wife beating, although on the decline with Gatewood's White Mountain Apaches, became a major problem with the Chiricahuas.

In a move to avoid trouble, while at the same time quenching the Chiricahuas' craving for higher country, Crook agreed to move the band north to Turkey Creek, seventeen miles southeast of Fort Apache. On the crest of a spur of the White Mountains that was surrounded by low hills to the north and south, their new home boasted giant pines, a mild summer climate, crystal-clear water, and plentiful game. Over five hundred Chiricahuas made the trek.[17]

Soon the Indians' population increased from 512 to more than 550 as Coyoteros and other Chihenne joined the Chiricahuas already at the higher altitude. Of that number, 127 men and boys were capable of bearing arms.

In June 1884, orders reassigned the Sixth U.S. Cavalry Regiment from Fort Apache to Fort Stanton, New Mexico Territory. As the Sixth was Gatewood's regiment, he too should have been reassigned, but he was too valuable to lose. In Gatewood, Crook not only had an officer who performed his duty well, but a white man the Apaches trusted. The general had no intention of losing Gatewood. Knowing in advance that the Sixth would be reassigned, he put in for a retention of the lieutenant's services, a request Sheridan approved on May 24. Bay-chen-daysen remained at Fort Apache.[18]

Neither Gatewood's retention nor the Chiricahuas' move were enough to curtail mounting tensions. Although Crook wrote the adjutant general of the U.S. Army, "The Chiricahuas are now all on the Reservation and are doing their best to cultivate the soil; they are orderly and contented and if unencouraged and treated with fairness will give no further trouble,"[19] unrest continued to escalate as the summer wore on.

But the picture was not that simple. Gatewood and Davis were treading a precarious path.

During this time an Apache scout named Dutchy drew unwanted attention. Territorial Marshal Z. L. Tidball accused Dutchy of murder, and demanded that he be turned over to face a civil court. Crook stalled. Time passed and Tidball became more insistent. Still, Crook refused. His reasons went beyond Dutchy's service as a scout or crimes against humanity. Dissension continued to plague the reservation, and if Dutchy were arrested, Crook surmised, "the whole condition of affairs would be immediately changed: the Indians would become suspicious, and knowing that all had been engaged in depredations, the good effect of the policy of the year past would be wiped out." He would not allow this to happen.

Although Gatewood must have been pleased that Crook respected his ability and did not want to lose his services, he had financial problems that were beginning to get out of hand. Supporting his family on a second lieutenant's salary was not easy, and by the summer of 1884 Gatewood found himself in debt. To save on expenses, Georgia returned home to Frostburg, Maryland, with their son Charley, Jr., to spend time with her father, Thomas McCulloh, and then visit other relatives and friends.

Georgia confided her money woes to her father. Although he did not have the resources to help them financially, he worked on securing a loan for his son-in-law.

The summer did not pass tranquilly, for Georgia's health bothered her during the entire trip. She got sick with nervousness when her uncle, Tom Huddleson, got mad at her father and made a scene in public. She also suffered through an attack of malaria. To make matters worse, Georgia's teeth bothered her. She knew she needed to see a dentist, but kept putting it off because she could not afford the expense.

The trip was not a total disaster, however, for Georgia did enjoy herself at times. Redesigning one of her old outfits, she turned a number of heads when she appeared at church one Sunday, which made her feel good. That same day she sang a solo before the congregation, and everyone expressed surprise at how good a singer she was, making her feel even better. Still, the money situation hung heavy with her, as heavy as it did with her "dear, old, unselfish hubby,"[20] as she called Gatewood. Both scrimped: they owed eight hundred dollars.[21]

At the beginning of August, Thomas Zuck, who had a contract to deliver mail between Holbrook and Fort Apache, approached Gatewood. Zuck wanted to build a stage station and eating house on the White Mountain Indian Reservation, but Gatewood told him no. Although he did not realize it, the stance he took that hot summer day would have far-reaching consequences for his career.

Zuck protested, but Gatewood would not budge. Apparently, the extras that Zuck requested along with the buildings, such as grazing and hay cutting, bothered Gatewood. Besides, he questioned Zuck's character. Nevertheless, he duly reported the proposal to Crook.

Crook did not back his subaltern. Instead, he immediately told Gatewood that he found the enterprise "a desirable one, both for the convenience of such travelers as pass over the route and for the interests of the mail service thereon."[22] Although Crook did not say it, Zuck, a judge who was not a Mormon but had strong political ties with them, was running for the upper house of the Thirteenth Territorial Legislature.[23] Crook had not reached his current position without knowing how to play the political game.

Overruled, but still in command, Gatewood retained the power to set how much grazing and hay cutting, along with any other benefits, Zuck would be allowed on Indian land. On August 28, he wrote Zuck that he could build an eating house next to a mail station at the Forks of the Road, which was about twenty-two miles north of Fort Apache. He asked Zuck to give him all the details regarding the operation, including the amount of hay required and who would cut it. Gatewood then asked Zuck: "What guarantee [can you] give in regard to the non-violation of laws and orders affecting Indians, soldiers[,] and Government property[?]"[24]

Gatewood had no intention of taking this guarantee lightly. He still burned over Crook's decision to grant the eating house to Zuck, and though he obeyed Crook's wishes, he refused to drop the issue. His reasoning was simple: the route normally took 23 1/2 hours to run between Holbrook and Apache. "If [Zuck] runs his mail on time[,]" Gatewood reasoned, "he will pass the Forks of the Road about midnight or a little after, and an eating station is not wanted."[25]

Zuck and his associate, Joseph C. Kay, traveled to Fort Apache to see Gatewood and ask him how they could obtain the hay they needed for the station. Gatewood told them they had to deal with the White Mountain Apaches, it was their land. The hay could be purchased for "a reasonable price, or by giving [the Indians] a fair compensation for the right to cut hay upon their meadows,"[26] Gatewood said. However, he did not limit the area for the cutting of the hay to the vicinity of the Forks of the Road.

Sensing trouble, Gatewood "distinctly & particularly warned [Zuck and Kay before they left] that a failure to pay for the hay after it was stacked, duly measured, & the quantity estimated by the usual rules for such measurement & estimation, seizure of [themselves] & haystack would surely follow, & legal proceedings against [them] would be instituted."[27]

During the last week of September Gatewood traveled to Forest Dale, one of the White Mountain villages, to determine how the Indians were doing with their crops. When Kay, acting as Zuck's agent, arrived at Fort Apache to negotiate the contract, Second Lieutenant Hamilton Roach, Gatewood's assistant, told him where he could find the lieutenant. Kay rode to the village and met Gatewood and Pedro (*Hacke-yanil-tli-din*), chief of the White Mountain Apaches, near noon. Pedro was decrepit, his hearing so bad that he used an ear trumpet. Gatewood had two interpreters he liked and respected with him: John ("Old Jack") Conley (English-Spanish) and Severiano (Spanish-Apache). Alchesay was also present.

"This man has come here to buy, or bargain[,] for the privilege of cutting hay from certain ciénagas, or places [on the reservation],"[28] Gatewood told Pedro and Alchesay. He then told Kay "to say what he wanted."

The negotiations lasted several hours. Gatewood defined the terms: "An ox and ten dollars down, or before he should begin to cut, and $15.00 within one month."

At first Kay hesitated, fearing that Zuck would not agree to the terms. However, he did not want to go away empty-handed. Kay pulled out a wad of bills and flashed them before everyone. He then accepted the terms for himself.

Even though Gatewood paid close attention to the proceedings, he did not see Kay hand any cash to Pedro. Nor did he realize what Kay meant when he accepted the terms for himself.

Almost immediately, Thomas Jones, who managed the mail station, began cutting the grass. Pedro had not yet received the agreed-upon ox. A few days passed. The harvesting continued. Finally an ox was delivered, but the animal was not in the physical condition that Pedro expected. The chieftain complained to Gatewood.

Not pleased, Gatewood, who had tried to avoid the entire situation in the first place, rode to investigate the White Mountain village and the two ciénagas in question, which were five or six miles south of the northern boundary of the reservation. Old Jack Conley rode with him.

Gatewood found the steer's carcass. It had been butchered on the roadside.

Next, Bay-chen-daysen met with Alchesay. Kay had offered the chieftain a pair of cast-off Mormon canvas pants. Alchesay considered the discarded clothing an insult and had refused the payment. Incensed at being taken advantage of by the White Eyes, Alchesay told Gatewood he wanted payment in full. If not paid, he threatened to begin taking livestock from the nearby ranches.[29] The situation did not look good.

Instead of returning to Apache, an angry Gatewood rode to Holbrook with Conley to kick back and lift a mug or two. While they shared a drink in a saloon, Kay appeared and joined them. The three drank together, and "one word led to another."[30] Undoubtedly they spoke of the current hay situation. "[Gatewood] when crossed had a violent temper, and did not hesitate to act in the impulse of the moment." Gatewood grew livid when he became convinced that Kay bought the hay at a lower price to sell to Zuck at a higher price, cutting the White Mountain Apaches out of money that was rightfully theirs. Gatewood saw the man's actions as a clear case of fraud.

Not wasting any time, Gatewood informed the Third Judicial District, Territory of Arizona, of the offense, and on October 1, warrants were issued for the arrests of Zuck, Kay, and Jones. The warrants charged that the defendants "on or about the 1st day of October A.D. 1884 and on divers other days, before and after said date did then and there, wrongfully and unlawfully and feloniously cut, steal and carry away grass and hay from the White Mountain Indian Reservation being the personal property of the United States, of the value of fifty dollars, contrary to and in violation of the Laws of the United States."[31]

Two weeks passed, and no arrests were made. On October 15, Gatewood, disgusted with the lack of action in the matter, decided to act. Assembling an escort of Indian scouts, he rode to the Forks of the Road mail station. The corral contained a year's supply of stacked hay. All three white men were present. Judge Zuck was about to leave to preside over his court and was not pleased by the interruption. Gatewood got right to the point, stating that his Indians had not been paid for the hay.

An outraged Zuck said: "Why should a white man of [my] standing be made to pay for the property of a lot of ragged Indians?"[32]

It was the wrong thing to say. Gatewood knew that Zuck hired thugs, and was aware of his Mormon connections. Nevertheless, he had no intention of being denied. Bay-chen-daysen told Zuck to pay up or be arrested.

"Arrest!" Zuck said. "Arrest me[?] I'm a United States mail contractor; Justice of the Peace . . . ; candidate for the legislature & an American citizen." Zuck pounded his chest. "I will not pay & no one dares to arrest me."

His Indians cheated, Gatewood had but one course to follow. "[W]ith force and arms,"[33] he arrested Zuck, Kay, and Jones.

Gatewood returned to Fort Apache with his captives in tow. He probably expected hearty congratulations for exposing the swindle. Instead, an outraged Crook blew up. The general knew just how powerful Zuck's political friends were, and Crook, who was next in line to become one of five major generals, wanted nothing to endanger his chances. He asked Gatewood to drop the charges, but Gatewood refused to back down. He had made the arrest and it would stick.

When the Post Office Department (Washington, D.C.) initiated an investigation, Crook traveled to Fort Apache to look into the trouble, again asking Gatewood to drop the charges. Gatewood again refused, asking the general to support him. Neither gave in to the other's request. Bay-chen-daysen became as livid as his superior when he realized that he was out on a limb and the person whom he thought was on his side was instead antagonistic.[34]

Zuck, Kay, and Jones spent six days in the Fort Apache jail. During this time, Gatewood interviewed Kay in his office. Kay admitted that the hay in question was cut on the reservation.[35]

On October 21, U.S. Marshal Tidball arrived at Apache. He carried with him a summons for Gatewood, Roach, and interpreter Conley[36] to appear in Prescott in six days as witnesses for the prosecution. Tidball then took the three prisoners into his custody, and delivered them three days later to the Third Judicial District of Arizona Territory in Prescott to await trial.[37]

The trial began at 10:00 A.M. on October 27. Presiding was the Honorable H. McGrew, whom Gatewood described as "an old, gray-haired, partially bald, man [who shared Zuck's political connections]. . . . His spectacles emitted rays of the wisest & most serenely judicial effulgence, inspiring an awe that made the beholder conscious of the presence of a mighty mentality that could convert a dictionary into an encyclopedia of legal knowledge."[38]

Charles Gatewood was the only witness, sitting through two days of testimony and reciting the events as he remembered them. At times the counsel for the defense, E. M. Sanford and J. T. Bostwick, attempted to get him to agree that Zuck did or said something that would be detrimental to the prosecution's case. On the second day, the defense asked: "In that conversation, in July or August [between Gatewood and Zuck] did not Mr. Zuck say to you, that he would make no personal contract with the Indians, as he wanted to be free and independent of them, or words to that effect[?]"[39]

"I do not remember any such language," Gatewood responded.

After failing to show that Zuck and Kay were not in collusion to buy the hay at a cheaper price, the defense counsel altered course. Next, they tried to demonstrate that Gatewood had an ulterior motive for making the arrest.

"What has been your relations with Mr. Zuck, friendly or unfriendly?" The assistant U.S. district attorney, Edward W. Wills, immediately objected and was sustained. The defense then asked: "Have you or not any ill feeling toward these defendants, or either of them[?]"

"I have not," Gatewood stated. "I acted in this matter on account of the dissatisfaction of the Indians, as their agent."

The defense pressed forward. "Did you not write or telegraph to the U.S. Marshal Tidball, or any of his deputies, to have the parties arrested[?]"

"I did not. I had them arrested myself."

After failing to establish that Gatewood tried to get Kay to sign a paper that perjured himself and made the arrest for personal reasons, the defense introduced several letters that were marked as exhibits. They were from

Gatewood to Crook's office and back: mainly Gatewood stating his objections to a stage station and eating house and Crook overruling him on the matter.

The prosecution asked a number of questions that referred to information in the letters, then queried: "Was the contract made between Mr. Kay and Indians for the sale of the hay in writing?" The defense objected and was overruled. Gatewood answered: "It was not in writing."

The prosecution began attacking in earnest, showing that the Indians did not get a fair price for the hay: "You state that the Indians made a complaint to you of a violation of contract by Kay. State what they complained of."

The defense objected on the grounds that the answer was immaterial, and was overruled.

"That Mr. Kay had agreed to take this hay for his own use," Gatewood answered, "and not compete with them in selling hay to Mr. Zuck or to the Government. That they had to wait several days for the ox, and take one not as good as the one promised, and that they believed, that Mr. Zuck wanted to get his hay for nothing and this to deprive them of the market, for the amount required."

Gatewood's testimony ended at 4:30 P.M. on October 28. The court recessed until 7:00 P.M. After the session resumed, the defense closed with:

> Your honor sees before you here a man who's on the bench himself.
> He ought now to be holding court in his own precinct & running
> that mail line. The other candidate for the legislature is making
> capital out of this arrest, & if my innocent client don't soon get back
> to his county, he'll be beaten & our Territory will lose his valuable
> services. Then, Sir, look at that technicality! There it is, big as life,
> staring out of the statute book, & your Honor can't get around it.[40]

Judge McGrew pondered the statement for a moment, then said: "It's only necessary to state that there's a technicality here in this statute book which the accused is justly entitled to the benefit of."

A shocked Gatewood could not believe what he heard. "Where's the technicality, Judge?"

McGrew glared at Gatewood, his face reddening. "In the law, Sir."

The defense attorney leaped to his feet. "I submit, Your Honor, the witness has no right to ask questions, not being a lawyer."

"You're right, Sir, witnesses don't ask questions," McGrew bellowed.

The defense then moved for a discharge of the arrest and charges against their clients, "for the reason that it has not been shown that any offense has been committed . . . and that there is not reasonable grounds to believe that said defendants or either of them have committed any offense against the laws of the United States."[41]

Perhaps a mite too easily, the defense prevailed—giving credence to the earlier warning that Zuck had strong political ties. The defendants were discharged and the case was closed. But it was not over for Gatewood: he had not heard the last of Messrs. Zuck, Kay, and Jones.

Frustration and Discontent

The day after the trial, Gatewood, Roach, and Conley collected their mileage from U.S. Marshal Tidball. That afternoon, before beginning the journey from Prescott to Fort Apache, they met Kay on the street.

Kay told Gatewood he had spoken with his attorney and had been informed "that he was entitled to $20.00 damages for false imprisonment."[1] He said he would be satisfied with less if Gatewood could work out a deal. "[I] would like half of that amount right away if there [i]s government money available to pay it, & the check might be drawn before we le[ave] town[.]"

Gatewood told Kay to expect delays while government paperwork was filled out.

"Well, I reckon that it'll take too long, so you'll have to pay me whatever you can. You ain't got no property but a hoss, but if you'll give me that & the ten dollars, I will give it to the lawyer . . . to retain him in my case for damages, & we'll call it square."

Gatewood must have smiled openly as he considered the "poor simpleminded Mormon" before him. He had no intention of giving Kay his "hoss." And he was not about to hand over ten dollars to pay "for professional advice & 'retainment'" against himself. He simply bid Kay adieu.

The elections were held a few weeks after Gatewood returned to Fort Apache, and Zuck lost. The defeated candidate, his toughs, and the Mormon Church were irate. They not only blamed the setback on the arrest, but claimed that Gatewood had been *put up* to make the arrest. Gatewood, they claimed, acted in cahoots with the Gentile candidate.

Zuck had no intention of dropping the matter, and called a meeting in Show Low with his cronies. They decided that Gatewood should be tarred and feathered, and printed pamphlets that stated as much. They also sent Gatewood a note daring him to step off the reservation and receive said coat of tar and feathers.

Other citizens along the northern border of the White Mountain Indian Reservation, disgusted with Zuck, signed a petition in which they stated that Gatewood had acted properly and had probably prevented an Indian outbreak.

Gatewood thought little of the threat. Then he was summoned to St. Johns, the county seat of Apache County, to appear before the Grand Jury, while they determined if Zuck, Kay, and Jones had a case against him for false arrest. His rheumatism must have been acting up, for this time he chose to ride in a stagecoach. There was an all-night stopover in Show Low, and the coach would not depart until 3:00 P.M. the following afternoon.

Zuck's crowd moved to the hotel where Gatewood took up residence. The landlady, with her own mob backing her stand, came to Gatewood's rescue, cowering the rabble which hurried to a barroom and changed their punishment from tar and feathering to hanging. The threat turned out to be all talk, however, and Gatewood got out of town unmolested the following afternoon.

In St. Johns, the Grand Jury—which consisted of a fair mix of Jews, Mexicans, Gentiles, and Mormons—met to decide if the former defendants had a case. With the Honorable Summer Howard, an ex-army officer, presiding, the Grand Jury, after hearing Zuck's side, decided against indictment.

Howard, the chief justice of the territory, happened to be Zuck's friend. He also resented soldiers. Not satisfied with the decision, he recalled the Grand Jury and delivered a lecture that came down to: "Now is your chance to cinch Shoulder Straps that are trying to run this country." Returning to their chamber, the Grand Jury deliberated a second time. This time they voted to indict Gatewood on three felony counts of false imprisonment.

The warrant for his arrest not yet issued, Gatewood hot-tailed it back to the reservation. When he informed Crook of the development, his superior again refused to back his subaltern. As the governor of the territory also happened to be Zuck's friend, Gatewood felt he had no hope for a pardon, and figured he most likely faced eighteen months in the county jail.

Gatewood waited for the warrant to be served, but nothing happened. The days of fall became short; winter was not far off. Bay-chen-daysen attempted to put his pending trial and the rest of his problems behind and go about his duties of running the reservation.

Realizing he needed additional medical supplies for his wards, he forwarded a requisition; but the disbursing officer never filled the order and the supplies never arrived. Now, more than ever, the inefficiency bothered Gatewood, and he quickly vented his anger at Crook.[2] The entire reservation seemed to be strangling in red tape. Even the simple task of obtaining supplies had become a major ordeal.

While Crawford, Gatewood, and Davis struggled to improve the Apaches' situation, Agent Wilcox continued to agitate the various bands, with his lone objective seeming to be to regain dominance. By November 1884, he had tired of the fight, and realizing he would not get his way, he resigned in disgust. C. D. Ford, who replaced Wilcox as agent, "promised full co-operation as outlined in the memorandum of July 7."[3] Ford assumed his duties in December.

Almost immediately, Ford disagreed with Crawford, clashing over Crawford's fight with contractors who did not want the Indians to become self-sufficient. Ford backed the Indian agency chief of police, who refused to allow Crawford to arrest an Indian policeman suspected of committing a crime. Ford then backed the Indian agency's chief farmer, who gave Yumas tools to dig an irrigation ditch and then took the tools away the next day. The friction became so heated that even the Indians were aware of the infighting.

Ford would not give an inch, and his stubbornness caused the Indians to suffer. When a shipment of Chiricahua and White Mountain annuities arrived at San Carlos, Ford refused to distribute the goods. On December 2, Ford telegraphed the commissioner of Indian affairs:

Lieut[enant] Gatewood asks for annuity goods for his Indians at Fort Apache, the White Mountains. [T]hey receive no rations nor are they under my control. I do not understand that I have any authority to issue [annuity] goods to them. Am I right[?][4]

Gatewood and Crawford complained to Crook, who immediately fired off a telegram to the adjutant general:

Instructions requested . . . from Interior Department to Indian Agent [at] San Carlos either to turn over annuities for Chiricahuas and White Mountain Indians to . . . one of the officers connected with the charge of those Indians, or that . . . one of those officers be designated to witness the issue of such annuities to those Indians.[5]

The strife quickly initiated an investigation into Crawford's administration of Indian affairs on the reservation.[6] Although the military board of inquiry backed Crawford, he had had enough of a bad situation and wanted out. The Third U.S. Cavalry that transferred to Texas during the winter included Troop G, Crawford's troop, which served at San Carlos. Crawford saw his ticket to get away from the governmental power play and asked to be relieved of command. Permission was granted, but he was not able to immediately rejoin his regiment in Texas.

One day turned into the next, and the next, and then eleven days. The weather turned harsh, stormy, and the first snow of the 1884–1885 winter season pelted the earth. The Indians needed supplies, but Ford continued to turn his back on their welfare, and would do so well into the next year.[7]

Turmoil continued as the new year began. Britton Davis decided to move his camp once again. After completing the trek through the falling snow, Davis and his wards made camp, with the lieutenant camping three miles above Fort Apache and the Chiricahuas farther above him on the White River or in the foothills.

Gatewood took advantage of Davis's proximity that winter and visited often. During his visits he made a point of going among the Chiricahuas and speaking with their leaders. Undoubtedly, Geronimo's fierce history, combined with his aloof countenance, compelled Gatewood to seek him out. He had met Geronimo at the conclusion of the Sierra Madre campaign, and now he got to know the war leader.[8] For his part, the old warrior was curious about the respect the White Mountain Apaches had for Bay-chen-daysen. They often spent time together, and apparently both men felt comfortable—to some degree—in each other's presence. Perhaps Geronimo saw the man William Harding Carter (Sixth U.S. Cavalry) would later describe: "[Gatewood's] simple mode of life, his dependableness in all things and his unflinching courage won for him the friendship of his comrades and the unquestioning devotion of the Indians."[9] Henry Daly wrote: "[Gatewood], who next to Captain Crawford[,] was both respected and beloved by Geronimo and his band."[10]

Whatever it was, something must have clicked between the two men, for their short acquaintance grew into a friendship. Exactly how or why the relationship grew is not clear. However, George Wratten, Gatewood's interpreter in 1886, attested to the fact that the two men were friends.[11] This short acquaintance would prove to be the determining factor when fate brought them together one final time in 1886.

On January 3, 1885, Gatewood received his promotion to first lieutenant.[12] Like Crawford, he found that he had an increasingly harder time performing his duties as administrator of the White Mountain Indian Reservation.

More often than not, Crook seemed to be his adversary. On January 13 Gatewood wrote his commander, complaining about delinquent annuity shipments. The medical supplies, ordered the previous fall, had still not arrived.

Crook wrote back:

> You seem to consider that I have no trouble beyond myself in dealing
> with this Indian problem. To give one instance, it took over one
> month's vigorous telegraphing to get authority to buy Indian pro-

duce direct, although I thought the whole matter had been arranged. This was with the War Dep[artmen]t where everything is comparatively plain sailing, but this difficulty is increased tenfold when the Interior Dep[artmen]t is concerned. Whenever your people do anything that can be used against me it is at once taken advantage of & worked for all it's worth. I was officially informed, several months ago, that the annuities for Chiricahuas & White Mountains would be given to them at once & notwithstanding my constant prodding they haven't got there yet. It is always safe not to promise Indians anything which is not in your power to grant.[13]

Gatewood must have been getting quite frustrated with the responsibility of making his wards self-sufficient when they lacked the necessary tools and supplies. Toward the end of his letter, Crook warned: "always [be] careful not to let any personal feelings mix up with your official affairs." Good advice, but advice Gatewood was not capable of following.

By January 18, the Indians' annuities still had not been issued. Both Crawford's and Gatewood's wards suffered. Still, Ford refused to turn the supplies over to either officer or to dole out the supplies himself. The officers again complained to Crook. The general, in turn, wrote the adjutant general: "I request that instructions be given [to Agent Ford] to either turn over the goods to the officer in charge for issue by him or that the Agent be sent with them to Fort Apache to issue them there in presence of the officer in charge."[14]

On February 7, three separate indictments for false imprisonment were drawn against Gatewood. Indictment No. 49 read:

The said Charles B. Gatewood on or about the 15th day of October A.D. 1884 and before the finding of this Indictment at the County of Apache, Territory of Arizona, the said Charles B. Gatewood then and there being, with force and arms at the County and Territory aforesaid, in and upon one T. M. Zuck, in the peace of the Territory of Arizona then and there being, did, him, the said T. M. Zuck then and there unlawfully and injuriously, and against the will of the said T. M. Zuck and against the laws of the Territory of Arizona and without any legal warrant, and without sufficient legal authority, or lawful cause whatever imprison, confine, and detain him, the said, T. M. Zuck for a long period of time, to wit: for the period of six days next following.[15]

Indictment No. 50 (Jones) and Indictment No. 51 (Kay) were almost verbatim repeats of Zuck's. All three were presented to the Grand Jury on February 10 and filed as records of the court. Eight days later, the Territory of Arizona issued a warrant for Gatewood's arrest.[16]

Sheriff J. L. Hubbell attempted to serve the warrant. When he reached the northern boundary to the White Mountain Indian Reservation, he found Gatewood's Indian police patrolling the perimeter. Well-armed and presenting a militant attitude, the Indians made it obvious that attempting to enter their domain would be a foolhardy mistake. Hubbell had no desire to become a dead hero, and decided not to go after Gatewood.

Upon hearing of the sheriff's failure to serve the warrant, an angry crowd demanded his resignation. Not wanting to lose his job, Hubbell sent his brother to Fort Apache to meet Gatewood. Hubbell's brother explained that Gatewood would do the sheriff a favor that would never be forgotten if he turned himself in.

Gatewood figured that he could use some goodwill and decided to surrender, appearing at the county seat on the first day of the new court session. He paid a fifteen-hundred-dollar bond to remain free, then looked about St. Johns for a lawyer. Surprisingly, he was able to secure one of Zuck's former defense lawyers. Satisfied, Gatewood became a man about town as he killed time. He did not have long to wait; his case was one of the first on the new session's docket.

Knowing he would be virtually alone in a very hostile atmosphere, Gatewood concealed a gun on his person before he stepped into Judge Howard's courthouse, which was filled with heavily armed cowboys, Mexicans, Mormons, and toughs.

Gatewood was arraigned. Then Howard ordered him to stand while the felony charges of falsely arresting Zuck, Kay, and Jones were read.

"How say you, guilty or not guilty?"[17]

"Not guilty."

Gatewood's answer caused a commotion. Some cheered, while others hissed. A fight broke out in the back of the room, and others joined in. Howard yelled for the room to be cleared and waited in silence until the sheriff succeeded in emptying the room. As soon as the multitude was outside, Howard allowed them to reenter. The judge then lectured his audience, threatening to jail anyone who interrupted his proceedings again.

The prosecution was ready to proceed, but Gatewood's counsel was not. Unhappy with what he heard, Gatewood told his lawyer to proceed. Counsel refused, then demonstrated that he could be "just as zealous now as then

& transferred his apparent feelings from one side to the other with great ease." As a result, the case was continued until the next term of the court, six months in the future.

Before Gatewood was set free, his bond was raised to eighteen hundred dollars. For the second time in his life, he got out of town as quickly as possible. Frustrated, angry, Gatewood returned to Fort Apache.

As winter neared spring, Captain Francis Pierce (First U.S. Infantry) reported to San Carlos as Crawford's replacement. He received this assignment on February 22, 1885, reported at San Carlos on March 4, but did not assume command until March 28, when Crawford left for Texas.[18]

Unexpected relief came from the civilian sector. At the beginning of March, a Mr. J. Armstrong Chanler, who had political influence, raised five hundred dollars and offered to donate it to Crook to use as he saw fit to improve the Indians' lot at the White Mountain Indian Reservation.

The spring planting season was at hand and the money could be well used immediately. On March 2, Crook asked Chanler to send the money directly to Gatewood. "Lieutenant Gatewood is so thoroughly in sympathy with the White Mountain Indians," Crook wrote, "and so intimately acquainted with all their wants, that he can be relied upon to expend the money sent him in a manner most advantageous to the Indians."[19] Knowing of Gatewood's need for a mill, Crook asked if Chanler could use his influence to get a mill built.

The Apaches continued to be restless. The proximity of the Chiricahuas to the White Mountain Apaches added to the growing turmoil, for the two bands were not getting along.[20]

Gatewood, too, was restless. For all his efforts and supposed success on the reservation, not much had been accomplished. He succinctly summarized the current state of affairs:

> [The Indians] still maintain most of their aboriginal customs and loy-
> alty to their nomadic habits. Nothing can be more mistaken than to
> endeavor to crowd upon them in quick succession the customs of
> civilization, and coerce them to their observance. It is as unreason-
> able to expect them to realize all at once the benefits of law and
> order and industrial pursuits . . . [21]

He knew exactly what needed to be done. But why bother? No one listened. His relationship with Crook had deteriorated to the point of no return. Red tape continued to block his every effort to help his wards.

And now his never-ending problem with Zuck had grown to nightmarish proportions. He was fed up with his entire situation. The Nantan Bay-chen-daysen wanted out, and he wanted out now. He sent his resignation from Indian command to Crook, citing his trouble with Zuck as the reason. Crook, who could never forgive his subaltern for making the arrest, flatly refused to accept the resignation.[22]

The guardhouse at Fort Apache served a dual purpose: it housed soldiers who were delinquent or who had broken the law and it confined Apaches who had been sentenced by a native court. During the spring, one of the inmates was a White Mountain renegade named Gar (*Nah-de-ga-ah*). On March 7, Good-en-na-ha, a White Mountain Apache scout was standing guard with four other scouts. All five had been on guard for six continuous days, had worked hard, and had had little sleep during this time. As sergeant of the guard, and feeling everything was secure, Good-en-na-ha placed the key that locked Gar's cell on a nail on the wall. Then he and his companions promptly fell asleep.

Almahar, one of the scouts on guard duty, feigned sleep. When he was certain the others were asleep, he got up, retrieved the key, and silently opened the lock to Gar's cell. "Now is your time, be quick and get away,"[23] he said.

A third scout, Eshe-jar, heard the commotion and woke. He saw Almahar and Gar leave the building and followed them, not catching up to them until they reached a ravine. Almahar, who was Gar's cousin, turned and fired two shots, with one hitting Eshe-jar.

The shots woke Good-en-na-ha and another guard, Ta-gar-Kloé, who was Eshe-jar's brother. They were getting up when Almahar reentered the building. When Good-en-na-ha asked him which way Gar had gone, Almahar said he did not know. All three went outside. A fifth guard, Pi-cosh-cou-ge, slept through the incident.

A messenger ran to awake Gatewood.

While Good-en-na-ha and Almahar went in one direction; Tar-gar-Kloé went in another direction. They confined their search to the perimeter of the guardhouse. Good-en-na-ha suspiciously watched Almahar as he went through the motions of looking for sign. Tar-gar-Kloé frantically looked about in the dark, but found nothing. He wandered about the jail a second time, but still found nothing. Returning to the guardhouse, he heard a groan and turned toward the ravine. Eshe-jar stumbled out of the blackness, pleading, "Hold me, brother, I am dying. My 'brother sentinel' has shot me. Let me lie down."[24]

Gatewood ran up to the dying man, with the post doctor accompanying him.

"I am dying," Eshe-jar said to Gatewood, "look out for me and watch over me; take me to the hospital." Gatewood did. At the hospital, Eshe-jar asked Gatewood to "bury [me] like an American soldier."

The next morning, Gatewood ordered Almahar's gun taken from him and arrested him, pending a general court-martial. After seeing the turncoat behind bars, Gatewood went to visit Eshe-jar in the hospital.[25] Eshe-jar died that night.

Gatewood's time began to be consumed with Gar. The outlaw, a former Apache scout, now harbored a grudge against Gatewood and threatened to kill him. Knowing Gar's record of murders, Gatewood set about trying to arrest him, but without success.[26]

Several weeks had passed when Britton Davis came up with an idea. Since Gar was a known ladies' man, why not set a lure? Davis asked the Chiricahuas to hold a dance and they readily agreed.

On the appointed day, Gatewood and Roach rode out from Apache to attend the party. Apache scouts infiltrated the crowd. Gatewood waited, hoping the target might appear. Day became night. Gar did not show.

A huge bonfire lighted a grass-covered glade in an orange glow. Giant pine trees circled the clearing; beyond them, blackness. Painted, scantily clad Apache dancers, urged to a frenzy by five hundred onlookers, moved to the rhythmic beat of drums. Gatewood and Davis watched the eerie spectacle from the duskiness of the surrounding forest.[27]

About midnight two scouts reported seeing Gar. He stayed in the shadows at the rear of the line of dancers, where the scouts flanked him. Before he was aware of the danger, they jumped him and manhandled him to the ground.

Gatewood and Davis ran up to the captive. "Done shoot me, Lieutenant! Done shoot me!" Gar cried. "I be good Injin, I do what you say, you done shoot me."[28] Gatewood escorted Gar back to the Fort Apache jail the next day.

Davis concluded that Gar had learned his lesson and had become a "good Injin." But he was mistaken, for Gar continued his evil ways. Finally, Apache scouts laid a trap for him with a pretty woman, and again Gar's weakness for women did him in. He walked right into the snare. The scouts appeared while he indulged in sexual intercourse and killed him.[29]

Gar was simply a bad man; he was not a warrior who craved his freedom and a return to the old ways. The Gar incident had nothing to do with the Chiricahuas' hatred for their incarceration on the reservation. Nonetheless, his capture marked the beginning of trouble.[30]

At Gar's arrest the Chiricahuas, and especially Geronimo, became suspicious. He meant nothing to them; but when his situation was combined with the fate of the Chihenne war leader Kaytennae (*Kaatenny, Kaahteney, Ka-atena, Looking Glass,* and *Jacob Ka-ya-ten-nae*), who had come into the reservation for the first time after Crook's 1883 invasion of the Sierra Madre, they feared what the future held for them. The moody Kaytennae had been accused of plotting to kill Britton Davis. He had been arrested, tried, and shipped to the white-man prison, Alcatraz, in California.

One night, Chihuahua passed by the tent of the Fat Boy (Britton Davis). He heard Chatto and Mickey Free's voices, and paused to listen. What he heard must have curdled his blood. Although the two scouts told Davis that Chihuahua planned to kill him, their tale did not stop with the lie of the proposed murder. He "heard many more lies and knew that they were trying to get him sent to that island like Kaytennae was."[31] Chihuahua did not remain silent, but told his companions what he had heard.

Free and Chatto did their best to agitate a deteriorating situation. "Each time a chief appeared," Kaywaykla stated, "Mickey and Chat[t]o drew their hands significantly across their throats. They kept the leaders constantly expecting that they would be taken and their heads cut off."[32]

Geronimo survived because of his suspicious nature. Chihuahua's news must have put him on edge, alert to the slightest incident that might be construed as treachery. Geronimo may have returned to the reservation, but that did not mean that he would turn his back on the world that surrounded him.

When Free came to Geronimo, he listened. The interpreter made no mention of the so-called plot to kill Davis. Instead, he filled the old Bedonkohe warrior's ears with stories the Arizona press had printed about him. Geronimo knew he was a marked man and guessed that it would not be long before he became the target for a white man's bullet or was locked in chains and shipped to a jail cell in a foreign land.

Although Geronimo would later claim that Free had not told him the truth and had lied to Britton Davis about him, he was concerned that he would be handed over to the white population and either stuck in a cell or murdered. Along with Chokonen leader Chihuahua and Chihenne leader Mangus, he began drinking tizwin.

Yes, the Apache-made drink had been outlawed. But it must be remembered that the Apaches always drank tizwin, which was a traditional part of their culture. The alcoholic beverage relaxed them, but at the same time it led to intoxicated talk.

Mickey Free and others played one side against the other. Employed by the soldiers and not really accepted by the captives who yearned to be free, he related what he heard and saw to the military authorities. At the same time, he played on the fears that Geronimo and others harbored.

Geronimo and his companions began thinking about bolting. However, some of their fellows reneged on the idea—mainly Chatto, Loco, and Benito (*Bonito*). This was not good, especially since more than half of the people were content to remain prisoners.[33]

The drinking increased.

Geronimo knew his actions were leading to a showdown with the military agents. He had tried to walk the white-man's road: he had tried to farm. The old warrior proudly showed the blisters on his hands that his labor had garnered to anyone who would look. But the attempt at pacification was superficial and he knew it. Often he spent his time at his plot of land with one of his wives fanning him while his other two wives hoed Mother Earth. He was not blind: he was not a farmer but he could see that the corn looked sickly and would not turn a profit. He also knew he yearned to be free. This rape of the land was not the Apache way.

He continued to drink, and talk, and plan for the day of decision when there would be no turning back.

Not many of his brethren agreed with him; no more than fifteen warriors listened to his words. The situation escalated. On May 13 Geronimo and thirty other Chiricahuas congregated at Turkey Creek, where that night they drank tizwin and talked. The warriors discussed tizwin drinking and the age-old Apache practice of controlling their women. They had not agreed to a ban on tizwin and wife beating when they surrendered to Crook in 1883. What right did the White-eye government have to make them outlaws for doing what they and their ancestors had done for centuries?

Combined with what Geronimo heard from Free and others, it was obvious that a serious problem existed. Geronimo and his companions had three choices: submit to the whites and turn their back on their culture, speak out for what was right and most likely be locked in a cell, or bolt.[34]

An Apache girl on the San Carlos Apache Reservation, Arizona.
Courtesy of the Southwest Museum, Los Angeles. Photograph No. N 42645.
Related ID: A.80.70

Lieutenants Charles Gatewood (right) and M. F.
Goodwin at Fort Bayard, New Mexico, March
1880, during the Victorio campaign. Evident here is
the toll on Gatewood's already slender body result-
ing from his extended time in the field.
Courtesy: Arizona Historical Society/Tucson, AHS No. 19615.
Gatewood Collection, No. 34-19615

Company A, Apache scouts, after a very hard patrol during the Victorio
campaign. This photo was probably taken on October 30, 1880, two days
before the scouts' November 1 discharge. Lieutenant Charles Gatewood
(Bay-chen-daysen) sits at center, wearing a white hat. White Mountain
chieftain and First Sergeant Alchesay's head is to the left of Gatewood's
hand. Interpreter Sam Bowman stands behind (and above) Gatewood.
Lieutenant Thomas Cruse (a barely visible blur) stands at extreme left,
back row, with Dr. McPherson to his right.

Courtesy: Arizona Historical Society/Tucson, AHS No. 19765.

Gatewood Collection, No. 19763

Lieutenant Britton Davis, pictured here,
was Gatewood's lifelong friend—the two
men drawn together by the dangers they
shared as military agents to the Apaches.
Courtesy: Arizona Historical Society/Tucson,
AHS No. 19621. From MS 441

Charles Gatewood with his wife Georgia in 1882.
Courtesy: Arizona Historical Society/Tucson, AHS No. 19550.
Gatewood Collection, No. 19550

Studio portrait of General George Crook by an
unknown photographer (1880s). Crook, who
recognized the value of good press, models the
clothing he wore while serving in the Southwest.
Courtesy of the Southwest Museum, Los Angeles. Photograph
No. N 42641. Charles F. Lummis Scrapbook: MS1 S5,
opposite page 1

Chihuahua, the Chokonen Chiricahua war leader
during the 1880s.
Courtesy of the Southwest Museum, Los Angeles.
Photograph No. N 42643. Related ID: A.80.29

This bronze panel of Geronimo's 1883 surrender to Crook—which
undoubtedly was also the first meeting between Gatewood and Geron-
imo—is on display at the Crook Monument, Arlington Cemetery, Virginia.
From left: Captain Emmet Crawford, Lieutenant William W. Forsyth,
Lieutenant James O. Mackay, Lieutenant Charles Gatewood, (behind
Geronimo's right shoulder), Geronimo, Chihuahua, Al Sieber (standing),
Chatto, Benito, Loco (standing), Captain Adna R. Chaffee, Alchesay
(standing), Captain John G. Bourke, either Lieutenant Frank West or
Lieutenant Gustav J. Fiebeger, General George Crook, and Peaches.
The Apache behind Peaches is unknown.

Courtesy: Arizona Historical Society/Tucson, AHS No. 19772. Gatewood Collection,
No. 19772

Kaytennae, the Chihenne war leader, shown here
(right) wearing his cartridge belt and knife, pre-
pares to make the journey to San Carlos to stand
trial, charged with plotting to kill Lieutenant Britton Davis shortly after coming to the reservation
for the first time following Crook's invasion of the
Sierra Madre. Benito (left) guaranteed his safe
delivery in order to spare him the humiliation of
arriving there without his weapons.

Courtesy of the Southwest Museum, Los Angeles.

Photograph No. N 42642. Charles F. Lummis Scrapbook:

MS1 S5, opposite page 55

This photograph of Mickey Free (by Baker and
Johnston) dates to the time of the last Apache war.
Courtesy of the Southwest Museum, Los Angeles.
Photograph No. N 42639. Related ID: P.9353

Studio portrait of Chihenne Chiricahua leader Mangus.
Courtesy of the Southwest Museum, Los Angeles. Photograph No.
N 42644. Related ID: A.80.34

This 1885 studio portrait belies the turmoil that dominated Charles Gatewood's life at this time. The impact of his civil difficulties, brought about by standing up for Indian rights, cannot be understated. The year saw the end of his relationship with George Crook, the termination of his tenure as military commandant of the White Mountain Indian Reservation, and his banishment from the last Apache war.

Courtesy: Western History Collections, University of Oklahoma Libraries. Rose Collection, No.1194

Geronimo supposedly requested this C. S. Fly photo at Canyon de los Embudos in March 1886. From left: Perico, holding Geronimo's son, Robert Geronimo; Geronimo (mounted); Naiche (mounted); and Tsisnah.

Courtesy: National Archives. 111-SC-83615

C. S. Fly took this photograph at Canyon de los Embudos during the
surrender talks with Crook in March 1886. From left to right: Yahnosha,
Chappo, Fun, and Geronimo, who holds a Model 1873 Springfield
Infantry Rifle.
Courtesy: US Army Military History Institute. FH 430 (C. S. Fly No.174)

General Nelson Miles, who took over command of the Department of Arizona in April 1886.
Courtesy: Arizona Historical Society/Tucson,
AHS No. 22235

Captain Henry Lawton, commander of Miles's primary seek-and-destroy mission in Mexico during the summer of 1886.
Courtesy: National Archives, 111-SC-87410

Leonard Wood, Lawton's medical officer during the summer 1886 seek-and-destroy mission.
Courtesy: National Archives, 111-SC-94965

The train that took Geronimo, Naiche, and their people to San Antonio, Texas (1886). First row from left: Fun, Perico, Naiche, Geronimo, Chappo, and the boy Garditha. Second row from left: Kanseah; Yahnosha; unknown; Ahnandia; the rest unknown until the third person from the right, She-gha (often misidentified as Ih-tedda); at far right, Beshe. Much confusion surronds the identification of the women in the back row, from left: Naiche's wife Haozinne, Perico's wife Biyaneta (sometimes named as Lozen or Dahteste), Chappo's wife Nohchlon (sometimes named as Lozen), and Ahnandia's wife Tahdaste.

Geronimo, at Fort Sam Houston, San Antonio,
Texas (1886), shortly after surrendering.
Courtesy: Western History Collections, University of Oklahoma
Libraries. Rose Collection, No. 854

George Wratten (standing), Gatewood's interpreter in
1886, is seen here with Ahnandia (who surrendered with
Geronimo) at Fort Pickens, Florida.

Courtesy: Arizona Historical Society/Tucson, AHS No. 73379,
Wratten Collection, PC 159 f.2

First Lieutenant Charles Gatewood in dress uniform,
shortly before his death in 1896.

Courtesy: National Archives, 111-SC-87684

Charles Gatewood in 1896. Contrary to the portrait,
in which he is wearing a helmet, this photograph
shows how emaciated he was near the end of his life.
Courtesy: Arizona Historical Society/Tucson, AHS No. 19610,
Gatewood Collection, No. 19610

Geronimo, nearing the end of his life, is here dressed in a suit
with a headdress, symbolically depicting his desire to carry his
lifeway, now long gone, into a modern world that he never
dreamed existed.

Courtesy: Western History Collections, University of Oklahoma Libraries.

M. R. Shumard Collection, No. 60

Still a prisoner of war, a guarded Geronimo decided to tell his life story to Stephen M. Barrett (left), the superintendent of schools at Lawton, Oklahoma (1905–1906). Asa Daklugie (right), who as a boy rode the war trail with his uncle, translates.

Courtesy: Western History Collections, University of Oklahoma Libraries.

Phillips Collection, No. 1445

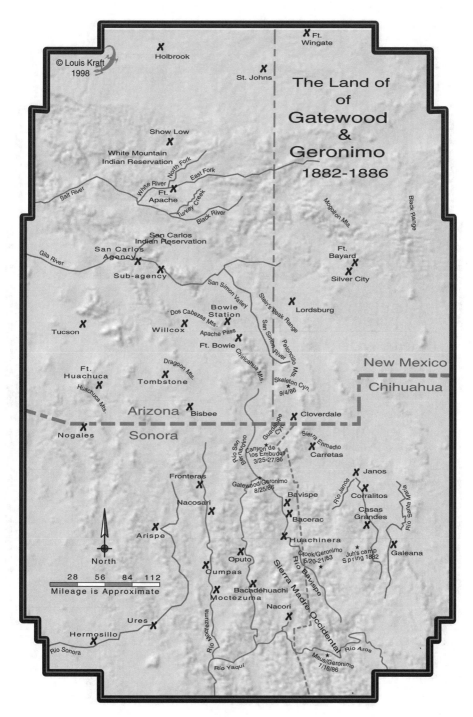

The Land of
of
Gatewood
&
Geronimo
1882-1886

© Louis Kraft
1998

Ft. Wingate

Holbrook

St. Johns

Show Low

White Mountain
Indian Reservation

North Fork

East Fork

White River

Ft. Apache

Turkey Creek

Black River

Salt River

Mogollon Mts.

Black Range

San Carlos
Indian Reservation

San Carlos
Agency

Sub-agency

San Simon Valley

Gila River

Ft. Bayard

Silver City

Stein's Peak Range

Lordsburg

Bowie
Station

Dos Cabezas Mts.

Tucson

Willcox

Apache Pass

Ft. Bowie

San Simon River

Peloncillo Mts.

Dragoon Mts.

Chiricahua Mts.

Ft. Huachuca

Tombstone

Huachuca Mts.

Skeleton Cyn.
9/4/86

New Mexico

Chihuahua

Arizona

Bisbee

Sonora

Nogales

Cloverdale

Rio San Bernardino

Guadalupe Cyn.

Sierra Enmedio

Carretas

Canyon de
los Embudos
3/25-27/86

Fronteras

Gatewood/Geronimo
8/25/86

Janos

Rio Janos

Corralitos

Nacosari

Bavispe

Casas
Grandes

Bacerac

Rio Santa Maria

Arispe

Huachinera

North

Oputo

Crook/Geronimo
5/20-21/83

Juh's camp
Spring 1882

Galeana

28   56   84   112
Mileage is Approximate

Cumpas

Sierra Madre Occidental

Rio Bavispe

Bacadéhuachi

Moctezuma

Nacori

Rio Moctezuma

Ures

Hermosillo

Rio Sonora

Rio Yaqui

Rio Aros

Maus/Geronimo
7/16/86

Map by Louis Kraft

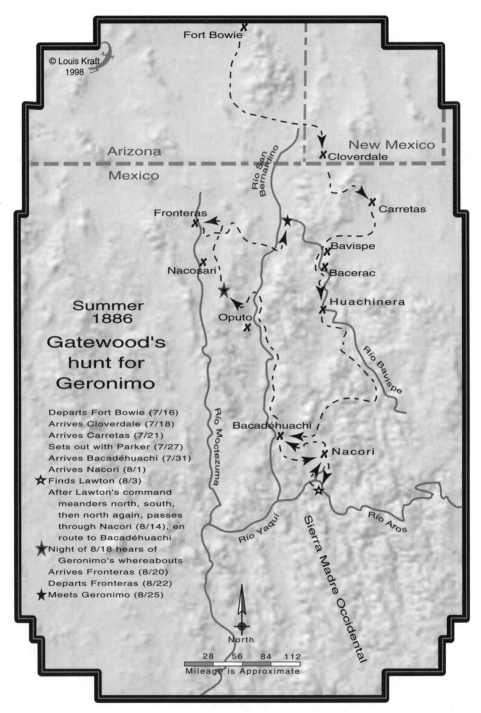

Fort Bowie

© Louis Kraft
1998

Arizona

New Mexico

Río San Bernardino

Cloverdale

Mexico

Fronteras

Carretas

Bavispe

Nacosari

Bacerac

Summer
1886

Huachinera

Gatewood's
hunt for
Geronimo

Oputo

Río Bavispe

Departs Fort Bowie (7/16)
Arrives Cloverdale (7/18)
Arrives Carretas (7/21)
Sets out with Parker (7/27)
Arrives Bacadéhuachi (7/31)
Arrives Nacori (8/1)
★Finds Lawton (8/3)
After Lawton's command
  meanders north, south,
  then north again, passes
  through Nacori (8/14), en
  route to Bacadéhuachi
★Night of 8/18 hears of
  Geronimo's whereabouts
Arrives Fronteras (8/20)
Departs Fronteras (8/22)
★Meets Geronimo (8/25)

Río Moctezuma

Bacadéhuachi

Nacori

Río Yaqui

Río Aros

Sierra Madre Occidental

North

28   56   84   112
Mileage is Approximate

Map by Louis Kraft

CHAPTER SIX

Outbreak and Pursuit

That fateful night of May 13, Mangus, egged on by his wife Huera, spoke out against government rule. Although well behaved and industrious since returning to the reservation, he now voiced the "dissatisfaction [that grew] out of their own worthlessness and a determination . . . not to be punished for offenses committed on the reservation."[1] Word had it that the White Eyes intended to turn Apache offenders over to civil authorities for punishment. Just when or for what offenses was unclear. What was clear was they wanted nothing to do with the citizens of Arizona.[2] Mangus played on Geronimo's fears of being locked in a cell—much as Mickey Free had done—throughout the long night as they, Chihuahua, Naiche, and twelve or fifteen warriors guzzled tizwin.

Geronimo and Mangus watched the growing predawn light with red-rimmed eyes. Their heads felt unsteady and the hangovers fueled their anger. Life on the reservation was no good. Geronimo had been here before. There was no turning back. It was time to take a stand.

The leaders ordered the women and children to leave their wickiups and keep out of sight. Sentries stood guard on hilltops, watching for troops from Fort Apache. Then, together, Geronimo, Mangus, and Chihuahua strode to Britton Davis's tent, with thirty warriors following them. Darkness still blanketed the land when they reached their destination, so they waited for daylight.

At sunrise on May 14, Davis stepped from his tent. "Apparently all of the remaining Indians, except the Scouts, [stood] in little groups or squatt[ed] on the hillside. All were armed. My scouts were mostly in a group by themselves."[3] Chihuahua said they wanted to talk. Davis sent for Free, then invited the leaders into his tent.

After everyone sat, Chihuahua told Free: "we agreed on a peace with Americans, Mexicans, and other Indian tribes; [we said] nothing about [our] conduct among [ourselves]."[4] Drinking and wife beating were not a part of the surrender to Crook. Chihuahua continued: "[Tell Fat Boy] that [I] and all the other chiefs and their men, except the scouts, ha[ve] been drinking Tizwin the night before and now . . . [we want] to know what [he] is going to do about it—whether or not [he is] going to put [us] all in jail."[5] Chihuahua added that he did not think the soldiers had a jail that was large enough.

Davis replied that he wanted higher authority to act upon the problem, saying that he would telegram Crook and meet with them as soon as he had an answer. Davis made sure they understood that it might take several days for an answer, as the telegraph line was not dependable. When the council ended, everyone stepped outside. The leaders told the others what Davis said. Then they all disappeared, except for a sentry who watched for soldiers. Davis rode to Fort Apache and sent the message to Crook.

The telegram had to pass through civilian hands before reaching the general. To avoid leaks, messages were kept to simple facts. Davis's telegram did not go directly to Crook; instead it went to Pierce, Crawford's replacement. Before forwarding the telegram to Crook, Pierce showed it to Al Sieber. Sieber himself had drunk the night away and his judgment was not at its best when he read the message. It had been "just an ordinary Tizwin drunk,"[6] Sieber proclaimed, and Pierce accepted Sieber's conclusion. Crook never saw the telegram.

Gatewood, who was at Fort Apache when Davis appeared, had also heard that the government considered making the Apaches subject to arrest and trial in civil courts. The news of the brewing trouble did not surprise him. He would later write:

> There is not a doubt in my mind that this act of Congress was the moving cause of [Geronimo running]. Simplicity of administration is quite as important as uniformity and fairness. The authority to administer at once upon any matter which may arise, and [the Indians'] confidence in the power and the justice of the one exercising that authority, are the prime elements of their control, and it is the conflicts of authority, delays of redress and the accumulation of small things . . . [that lead] to outbreaks and ultimate disaster.[7]

A day passed; then two. Tensions grew as everyone waited. Finally, on the third day, Geronimo decided to return to Mexico. He talked to all who would listen to him, but could not find many recruits. Chatto, Loco, Benito, and their people refused to return to the war trail. Even Naiche and Chihuahua saw the futility of fighting another war.

Geronimo claimed that Davis planned to kill him. He talked three Apache scouts into deserting, then plotted to have these men assassinate Davis and Chatto. The plot thickened, with Geronimo again approaching Chihuahua and Naiche. As Mangus had played on his fears, he played on theirs. Soon, they too feared white treachery. Still, less than a quarter of the Chiricahuas wanted anything to do with Geronimo and his planned escape.

Davis and his men played baseball. There was no sign of the soldiers Geronimo knew would eventually come from Fort Apache to punish them for drinking tizwin. Geronimo knew that if he and his band were going to be able to run, they had to do it before the soldiers surrounded them. Gathering their stock, Geronimo and the fugitives prepared to leave. Before departing, an angry Geronimo visited some of the tribe members who refused to join him. He threatened to return to the reservation some time in the future to kill them.[8]

While waiting for an answer from Crook, Davis kept his eyes open, anxious because he knew something was up. At 4:00 P.M. on May 17, a runner from the Chiricahua encampment interrupted his baseball game to announce that Geronimo was preparing to leave the reservation. Davis sent a hurried message to Gatewood, apprising him of the situation; then called for his scouts to assemble.

Gatewood sent a message back to Davis; he and his scouts, along with two companies of cavalry, would come to Davis's aid as soon as possible. Gatewood immediately gathered as many scouts as he could find. Speed was essential; the only chance of success was to stop the outbreak before it began. He knew it would be hell to corner Geronimo once he got free.

As soon as he learned that Gatewood would support him, Davis sent a report to Pierce, who was at San Carlos. "They will have probably 20 or 25 men of whom not more than two-thirds are armed."[9] Davis assumed that he would follow the trail and that Gatewood, his scouts, and the soldiers would support him. "I will have about thirty Scouts with me and if it comes to a fight[,] Gatewood will be near enough to come to my assistance."

That night at 7:00 P.M., Gatewood and his scouts accompanied Captain Allen Smith and two companies of Fourth U.S. Cavalry (ninety soldiers) out of Fort Apache. Lieutenant James Lockett commanded Troop A. Lieutenant James Parker, with Lieutenant Leighton Finley (Tenth U.S. Cavalry), commanded Troop K. The pack train carried rations for fifteen days. Intending to move quickly, they took no tents. Gatewood rode a mule, his scouts walked, and the troops rode horses.

Smith and Gatewood found Britton Davis at Turkey Creek. Geronimo was long gone; perhaps as far as fifteen or twenty miles away. Davis and his Indian scouts joined the pursuit. Daylight began to fade, dusk became night, and as the sky turned darker, the advance slowed. Following an uncertain trail, caution became the keyword, for no one wanted to walk into an ambush. Soon the command found where Geronimo had cut the telegraph wire that connected Fort Apache with Department Headquarters. Just beyond the severed wire, the forest had been set on fire, but apparently the blaze had died out or presented little threat. Continuing the pursuit, Smith and Gatewood reached Bonito Canyon, but the dark sky made travel dangerous. A number of riders fell during the descent and ascent on the opposite side.[10]

It took over an hour to reassemble the command, and during the halt, fires were lighted. One trooper had a broken leg; several horses had to be abandoned. Again, they set out in pursuit. A few miles beyond the canyon, Smith called another halt when scouts who had been out in front of the command returned. The scouts reported that Geronimo was not too far ahead; they had seen the fleeing Indians crossing the Black River.

Gatewood and Davis discussed the feasibility of continuing and decided that it would be better to attempt the same crossing early the next morning. Smith agreed.

The next day, Crook sent a telegram to the commanding officer of Fort Bayard, New Mexico:

> About fifty Apaches under Geronimo are reported to have left reservation near Fort Apache about dark last night and are thought to be making for Mexico. Troops from Thomas, Grant, Bowie and Huachuca are out endeavoring to intercept them. Would it not be well to send out a detachment from your post to their usual point of crossing the border[?][11]

He also sent telegrams to Chihuahua, Mexico; to Sonoran governor Luis Torres; to the editor of the *Clifton Clarion*; and to the adjutant general of the Division of the Pacific (San Francisco, California).

Reports on the number of Chiricahuas on the warpath ranged from 42 men and 96 women and children to 40 warriors (including boys over twelve years of age) and about 103 women and children to 143 of the 550 Chiricahuas under Davis's charge to "Geronimo, Mangus, Chihuahua, and [Naiche], with about 50 bucks . . ."[12]

Geronimo and his party moved out quickly. After crossing the Black River, they hurried southeastward toward the Mogollon Mountains in New Mexico. The Chiricahuas traveled ninety-five miles that night and first full day. When they reached the Mogollons, they climbed up into them and hid. Sentries watched for pursuit while the others rested. The fugitives knew soldiers and scouts would soon be on their trail, and their only hope to remain free was to reach Mexico before the soldiers caught them.

Trouble arose when Chihuahua and Naiche claimed that Geronimo and Mangus had lied to them to get them to join the outbreak. The men argued, causing a rift between them. Geronimo moved his camp farther away from the others. That night Chihuahua, his brother, and another warrior prepared to kill Geronimo. Geronimo and Mangus heard of the plot, and not wanting a confrontation they led their bands from the safety of the mountain hideout at first light.

Geronimo and Mangus forced Naiche, who made the mistake of spending the night in Mangus's camp, to go with them when they set out. Before leaving, Naiche sent word to his wife and child, who were with Chihuahua, to return to the reservation. They tried to do as instructed, but seeing Apache scouts in pursuit, they returned to Chihuahua's band.

After Geronimo left, Chihuahua planned to hide in the Mogollons, commit no depredations, and return to the reservation at the first opportunity. Unfortunately, Davis's Apache scouts dogged his trail, which forced him to also run for Mexico.[13]

Geronimo wanted to head straight for the international border, but for some reason Mangus did not like this idea and they split up. While Geronimo headed south, not stopping again until he had covered another 120 miles, Mangus remained in New Mexico.[14] Most likely Naiche now traveled with Geronimo.

Although the plan was to ford the Black River at dawn the next morning, Smith encountered delays. Some of the horses had lost shoes on the lava rock the previous evening and had to be left behind. The command did not reach the river until broad daylight. Gatewood and his ten Apache scouts remained with Smith, as did Davis and his scouts. As they were making the crossing, scouts ran back to the command shouting for everyone to hurry. They had seen Indians crossing the Prieto Plateau six miles ahead; the plateau was fourteen miles long.

Parker immediately led his troop out at a trot, and just as quickly Smith ordered him to slow the advance to a walk. Smith and Gatewood traveled as fast as they deemed wise. Although they knew that lives depended upon their reaching the settlers at Eagle Creek and the ranches on the Gila before

Geronimo did, they also knew they could not run their animals into the ground. The trail—which led east toward New Mexico—was at times very rough, slowing them considerably.

When Smith, Gatewood, and Davis reached a ridge above the valley of Eagle Creek, which was at the far end of the plateau, scouts pointed to the opposite side of the valley. Looking through field glasses, Gatewood and the other officers could see several fugitives ascending the mountain slopes in the distance. The Chiricahuas were now somewhere between eight and ten miles ahead.

Everyone knew they were in for a long campaign. Davis returned to San Carlos to enlist more scouts, while Smith and Gatewood continued the pursuit, marching down the valley of Eagle Creek. When they camped at 2:00 P.M., everyone sat around, hungry. The rations were with the pack train, which did not arrive at the bivouac until 9:00 P.M. Although Gatewood and Smith had covered about sixty-five miles that first day, it was not enough. The long, exhausting chase produced no results: Geronimo had escaped.

The next day riding became impossible. On foot, soldiers struggled to lead their mounts over mountainous terrain. Covering twenty-five miles, they camped near Blue Creek.[15]

On May 20, Smith and Gatewood crossed Blue Creek and again climbed through the mountains. As Gatewood and his scouts approached the settlements near the San Francisco River and the New Mexico border, signs showed that Geronimo had begun killing settlers. After traveling eight miles through the mountains, they found the bodies of a white man named Lutter and his horse. When the command reached his ranch, a short distance further on, they found it ransacked. Lutter's brother and some livestock had also been killed. Gatewood and Smith pushed on, knowing that every hour decreased their chances of catching anyone. After traveling another three miles, they reached a spring where they found a dead man named Smith. Four miles farther on, they found Jim Montgomery, also dead. Soldiers covered each corpse with stones.

Even if Gatewood did not worry about his scouts deserting, he probably heard an earful on this possibility from Parker, who did not have anything good to say about Indian scouts. He even accused most of Gatewood's command of desertion. Certainly, memories of the Cibicue mutiny had to be fresh with anyone who dealt with scouts. This was a fear that at least subconsciously hung with the Indian men—would their Indian allies become caught up in the fervor to be free and turn against them? Gatewood's scouts remained loyal.[16]

By May 20 Gatewood had traveled 115 miles from Apache. The fleeing

Apaches were long gone, perhaps fifty miles ahead of him. The late-spring sun streaked through the trees, casting deep shadows but little else; the mountains seemed devoid of human life. It was as if Gatewood followed ghosts.

After marching ten miles the next day, Gatewood and Smith reached the San Francisco River, where they found settlers terrified of an enemy who was nowhere near.[17] They covered a total of twenty-two miles that day, but by now the Chiricahuas had stolen fresh horses and were either high in the Mogollons or in Mexico. To date, they had killed only to obtain weapons and horses, a condition that would not last long and certainly would change after they had sustained some losses themselves. It looked as if the Chiricahuas intended to head for the Black Range before turning south for Mexico, and Gatewood knew that the chances of catching them now were slim. It did not help that Smith still refused to increase the speed of their pursuit.[18]

On May 22, Gatewood followed what he thought was Geronimo's trail as it crossed the San Francisco River and headed east into New Mexico and toward the Mogollons. Gatewood and his scouts led Smith's two companies of troops up a long slope and into the roughest part of the mountain range. The scouts did not spread out far in the lead anymore, for they feared an ambush. After traveling twenty-five miles that day, Gatewood found that the trail dropped down into the six-hundred-foot canyon of Devil's River. At that point, they were twenty miles east of Alma, New Mexico.

When they entered a narrow valley, some forty feet wide, Smith ordered his men to make camp. After placing Parker in charge, he and Lockett left camp and went to bathe in a nearby creek. The time was 1:30 P.M.

Although the camp seemed secure, Gatewood sent his scouts to the top of the canyon to reconnoiter. Half an hour later he sat down under a tree with Finley and Parker. They were on the east bank of a creek, while the troops, except those with the pack train, were on the west bank of the creek. Suddenly Indians attacked from four directions; up and down the canyon, and from both canyon walls. Gatewood and his companions found themselves in a very precarious position—they had no cover. At the first shot, they leaped to their feet.

The main attack came from up the canyon. Parker rallied his men and led them into the firestorm. Gatewood raced after Parker's charge, yelling for his scouts to rejoin him. The White Mountain scouts scrambled back from the clifftop to Gatewood. He immediately led them to the summit, where, refusing to stand and fight, the attackers fled. Within a matter of minutes, Gatewood, Parker, and Finley captured the enemy position at the crest. A mere five hundred yards farther on they took the Indians' now-deserted camp, which included some horses, along with their belongings, and a lot of beef. Two soldiers (Private Haag, Troop A, and Private Williams, Troop K) and one Indian scout (shot through the left arm) were wounded, one horse was killed and another wounded, and several Chiricahuas were reported wounded.

After the fight ended, Smith reappeared. Dressed in his drawers and top boots, he began giving orders as if he had been there the entire time. Not only did Smith's report imply that he was in the thick of the action; he gave little credit to Gatewood, Parker, or Finley, all three of whom were disgusted with him. "To the best of my recollection," Gatewood later wrote Parker, "Captain Smith appeared after the firing had ceased, and had nothing whatever to do with the fight."[19]

Scouts reported that the fleeing Chiricahuas headed due east toward the southern end of the Black Range. Gatewood informed Smith that the Indians' trail "led into a wild country where [Smith] would be likely to run out of food before he could get back."[20] This did not please Smith.

Nevertheless, the next day, Gatewood again led his scouts after the Indians. However, after traveling some six miles beyond the site of the fight through very rough terrain, Smith called a halt. He wanted nothing more to do with the chase. Claiming that he needed supplies and the White Mountain scout needed medical attention, he left the trail and rode toward Fort Bayard, New Mexico.

It looked like Gatewood's pursuit had ended, but this did not mean that he had abandoned the field—at least not yet. Nor did it mean that the hunt for Geronimo and his companions was over. Other soldiers and Indian scouts converged on Stein's Pass and Guadalupe Canyon "to intercept [the] hostiles if they should double back to go into Mexico by usual trails."[21] The Fourth and Tenth cavalries congregated at Fort Bayard and points east in an effort to support troops from New Mexico. Everyone knew the outbreak had to be crushed quickly or face another war.

Geronimo had hurried to Mexico. However, Chihuahua and his people had stayed in the mountains north of Silver City, New Mexico. On May 23, after killing a prospector, they split into small groups. Keeping well away from the usual roads and trails, they approached whites only when they needed horses or supplies. Six days later they were east of Duck Creek.

After hiding the women and children deep within the desolate crags of the Black Range, the warriors broke into smaller groups and began attacking solitary whites who were scattered throughout the mountains. Striking at will, Chihuahua's Chokonen Apaches continued to avoid troops from the Fourth and Tenth cavalries while terrorizing the area.

By the end of the month, the various groups of Chiricahuas had changed their direction. They now followed Geronimo's lead and headed south toward Mexico.[22]

On the night of May 26, Gatewood and Smith, who had been informed that Davis was back in the field, found him six miles above the Gila River. Davis had sixty-eight Chiricahua scouts with him. His pack train carried three thousand pounds of rations.[23] The pursuit had been given new life.

After marching just six miles from the Gila on May 27, Smith went into camp. During the day, a small Indian trail had been found, one that led into the Mogollon Mountains of New Mexico. That night, Gatewood, Davis, and sixty scouts set out in pursuit. Before departing, however, it was decided that Gatewood would direct Smith's movements by sending back messengers. Later that evening, the trail grew in size, and Gatewood immediately sent a runner to Smith, informing him to return to the Gila. He then followed the trail farther into the Mogollons.

The next night, certain that the Indians sought the high ground, Gatewood divided his force, keeping half of the scouts on the trail. With Davis and the remainder of his command, he returned to Smith to discuss a plan of attack.

With offensive strategy decided, Gatewood and Davis set out to catch up with the rest of the scouts. After reuniting his command, Gatewood again split it in two. While he moved to the north, Davis moved to the east. Smith would move to attack from his current position.

Scouts reported the Chiricahuas were now high in the Mogollons. Gatewood hoped that he or Davis would find and attack the Indians, who would then run into one of the other independent commands. But again, the pursuit was too late.

When he reached Sapillo Creek, about forty-five miles north of Silver City, and at the point where he anticipated catching the Chiricahuas, Gatewood found nothing. All signs indicated that the Indians had left the high mountains and were now moving west. On May 30, he sent word to Smith that the plan had failed.[24]

At Crook's request Crawford was ordered to report to Deming, New Mexico, to take command of the troops and scouts then en route to that location. Britton Davis and fifty-nine Indian scouts were among those ordered to report to Crawford. Crawford would be ordered to drop into Mexico and hunt Geronimo. Crook made it clear that he could leave the white troops at the international boundary if he felt he had enough native strength to confront the Chiricahuas.[25]

With his men drooping in their saddles, Smith now rushed them toward the San Francisco River to get food and water. By June 3 he was at the mouth of Duck Creek. A disgusted Gatewood and his scouts ranged far out in front of Smith's soldiers. He still had with him ten White Mountain scouts, all of whom were on foot. Everyone was bone-weary. Following the scouts, Gatewood slumped forward on his mule's saddle, his brown nonregulation clothing stuck to his skin and his joints undoubtedly aching. He was close to Alma, a small mining community about sixty miles northwest of Silver City, plodding along the Eagle Creek trail.

Suddenly someone yelled: "Halt! Don't try to run!"[26] Gatewood pulled the mule to a stop and quickly called to his scouts to remain still. "Who are you?" the voice demanded.

"I'm Lieutenant Gatewood, and these men are Indian scouts," Gatewood yelled.

A white man with a bushy mustache stood on a hill about one hundred yards from Gatewood. He pointed a 40–90 Sharps rifle steadily at Bay-chen-daysen and ordered: "come nearer; the Indians stay where they [a]re." Gatewood rode forward until he was about thirty yards away; then he asked the man to identify himself. When he did, Gatewood said: "[Are you] Jim Cook, the hunter and guide of whom [I have] often heard Captain Emmet Crawford speak[?]" Cook said he was, then added that he and his companion, Charlie Moore, had considered ambushing Gatewood and the scouts because they thought they were raiding Indians.

Gatewood told Cook that he and his scouts had been trailing Geronimo, who had broken out from the reservation. He nodded over his shoulder at Smith and the two troops of cavalry that were now plainly visible in the distance.

When Smith and the troops arrived, Cook invited everyone to the WS Ranch, which he managed, and there everyone ate, then rested for an hour. Smith and some of his command remained at the ranch to search for bodies of recently murdered whites, while Parker, with the rest of the command, and Gatewood, and his scouts, pushed on to Fort Bayard. They reached Bayard on June 5 and Gatewood immediately met with Crook. After discussing what Gatewood had seen during the pursuit, Crook ordered him back to Apache to enlist additional scouts. Gatewood and Parker left that evening for Albuquerque and then Fort Apache.[27]

On June 3 a well-mounted group of Chiricahuas raced past the town of Duncan, Arizona, on their way into Mexico. Knowing that soldiers were hunting them from all directions, the warriors became more aggressive. They attacked Captain Henry Lawton's (Fourth U.S. Cavalry) camp near Guadeloupe Canyon at noon on June 8, killing five soldiers and capturing two mules and five horses. Within days, the main body of the Chiricahuas were either in Mexico or very close to the international border. At this time Geronimo had only six or seven warriors and a few women and children with him.

Mangus, with six or seven warriors and a few women and children, was the only leader who had not crossed the railroad, not dropped down through Stein's Pass, and not attempted to reach Mexico. Instead, he moved east of the Black Range.[28]

On June 9 Crook obtained the go-ahead to enlist two hundred additional Indian scouts. As Gatewood hurried back to Fort Apache to oversee conscription and outfitting of these scouts, Crook chose Fort Bowie, Arizona, to serve as his headquarters during the uprising. Crawford's command of cavalry and scouts headed toward Mexico in the hope of cutting off the Chiricahuas before they reached the Sierra Madre. At the same time Crook prepared a second command to move into Mexico, and once again struggled with the same interminable delays and impediments he had faced in 1883.[29]

Gatewood would not take part in the invasion of Mexico. Instead, Crook ordered him "to take the scouts you enlist at Apache, particularly those acquainted with that country, and destroy"[30] Mangus, whom reports placed in the mountains near Sapillo Creek. Crook warned Gatewood to avoid any trouble between his scouts and the whites.

Crook also said: "I do not intend to take you in the field unless you have strong reason for wishing to go, preferring that you should return to Apache and attend to matters there, but shall need your scouts." This seems to refer to Gatewood's rheumatism (or maybe even the Zuck problem). If so, it was considerate of Crook to give Gatewood the option, if he wanted it, to avoid the painful hardships of campaigning in Mexico.

Taking Smith's pack train, Gatewood left Fort Apache on June 16 with seventy-five Indian scouts, fifty-five of whom were White Mountain Apaches. The other twenty were Chokonen and Chihenne Apaches, who knew the mountains near Sapillo Creek well. Gatewood's mission was to "destroy or drive out any Indians who may still be lurking"[31] in the mountains bordering the upper Gila River.

Crook intended to hide troops at all the water holes along the international boundary to prevent Chiricahuas from reentering the United States. Indian scouts would patrol the border and report any enemy movements they detected, but he had no intention of doing this until after Gatewood reported that New Mexico was free of warring Indians. Crook did not want any lagging Chiricahuas to become aware of the troops on the border and warn Geronimo.[32]

The mountains surrounding Silver City, New Mexico, and running all the way east to Hillsboro were rugged and wild, containing fertile meadows, deep canyons, and plenty of game. Mostly unknown by white men, the place remained a favorite haunt for the Chiricahuas. This was Gatewood's destination.

Although a number of his scouts knew the terrain, Gatewood marched first to a cabin midway between Silver City and Fort Bayard. Old Black Joe lived there. Gatewood did not know Joe's real name and sometimes referred to him as Joe Black. Joe, an old, grizzled-haired, and dark-complexioned half-breed Mexican hunter and trapper, knew the country intimately, and Gatewood not only knew this but also knew that Joe often hired out as a military guide.

"Then we proceeded to scout laboriously through the Black Range," Gatewood wrote, "visiting all the known water holes and searching out all other sources of water we could find, observing carefully at each place for the tell-tale signs of hostile Indians."[33]

Each succeeding day melded into the next, and the heat sapped the men's strength. Ten days, then twelve passed, but nothing changed, "for Geronimo and his gang of land pirates were already far down in Old Mexico," Gatewood would later write, "though none but themselves then knew it."[34]

Gatewood and his scouts turned back toward the rough towns and camps in southwestern New Mexico. Even though he had found no sign of Mangus, he refused to let his guard down. Gatewood wrote:

> On the march, each day, a number of the Scouts would spread out for miles in front and to each side of the main body, spying out the country in advance in every direction. To keep in touch with them and to get the first possible news of anything they might discover, I usually rode with the small advance party half a mile or more ahead of the main body.[35]

By June 30, Gatewood's patience began to wear thin. From Sapillo Creek, twenty-three miles north of Fort Bayard, he wrote Georgia: "We are still aimlessly wandering around these mountains hunting for Indians that are not, & examining all sorts of rumors that have no shadow of foundation of truth in them."[36]

As Gatewood and his Indian scouts moved closer to civilization, he found the settlers and miners experiencing a mixed bag of emotions. Some were wild with fear and did everything in their power to convince him to remain in camp near them. But even more than the safety Gatewood's presence meant, he provided them with what they saw as an opportunity to make a buck, offering hay and grain for sale at high prices. Others viewed the entire outbreak with calm detachment, laughing at those who were frightened.

Gatewood found the whites' attitude toward both the Chiricahuas and his scouts ludicrous. One prospector came upon tracks left by his scouts and hightailed it to parts unknown. Another stated he intended to kill Indian scouts but changed his story when Gatewood and the scouts appeared. "Few are friendly towards the troops," Gatewood realized, "unless they can sell things."

He summarized the patrol for Georgia: "Our trip has been without interest. Up one hill and down another would sum up the whole thing." He intended to send a report to Crook, detailing his fruitless search. Gatewood expected a reply by July 2, ending the scout; "and that can't be too quick to suit this chicken," he confided.

In the meantime, Crawford's invading force ranged ever deeper into Mexico. By June 19, he was at Huasaras, where he received word that Chiricahuas had been seen near Oputo. The next day he set out for Oputo and two days later he found their trail leading up into the Bavispe Mountains. Crawford immediately sent Chatto, who now served as a sergeant, and the scouts in pursuit.

The next day Chatto and his scouts found the Chiricahuas' ranchería—Chihuahua's—northeast of Oputo and attacked. When the Indians fled, Chatto and his men set out after them, but due to rough terrain they did not make good progress. The scouts, however, did have some success—they killed a woman and wounded several others. Fifteen women and children were captured, including Chihuahua's entire family, while eight warriors, four boys, and three women escaped.[37]

Crawford had hoped for a communication from Gatewood, detailing the warring Indians still remaining in New Mexico, but by June 25 he had still not heard anything.

Gatewood's blasé pursuit of shadows continued. By now he was three days' march from Fort Bayard, but there still was no sign of Mangus.[38] The next day Gatewood and his scouts set out for Bayard. Shortly after arriving at the post orders came through for Gatewood and his scouts to return to Fort Apache, where the scouts were disbanded.

The war in Mexico dragged on. Gatewood forgot it. Reservation management again demanded his complete attention. At the same time his own private fight swirled about him, surrounding him. A growing number of real or imagined enemies took pot shots at him. Surely he had to have been aware that most of his problems were of his own making. Still, it is doubtful that he could have surmised that he would soon be yanked from the war and his career put on hold.

CHAPTER SEVEN

The Outcast

Gatewood would fight the war on the home front. His experience with the White Mountain Apaches, and his compassion for them, made him a key player in ensuring that the reservation would continue to function properly. His active participation in tracking down Geronimo and the rest of the Chiricahuas had ended.

Bay-chen-daysen kept the reservation Apaches productive. Well aware that Crook wanted him "to create disaffection among the refugees and disintegrate them,"[1] Gatewood worked to eliminate the reservation Indians' sympathy for the Indians riding the war trail. By helping them prosper from their small plots of crops, he showed them that they did not have to follow the old ways to survive. At the same time, he prepared to convert any prisoners delivered to him to the farming life.

As in the past, Gatewood found himself exempt from the usual military chain of command. This did not mean he was cut off from the military establishment. Crook had made it clear that he could request the assistance of post commanders in Arizona and New Mexico at any time.

Gatewood's orders regarding the recalcitrants returning to the reservation were straightforward. He, in turn, passed Crook's dictum along to the peaceful Indians: "If any of the Chiricahuas return [you] must kill them or capture them all and turn them over as prisoners."[2]

The inner battle for control of the reservation had yet to be resolved, for the dual Interior/War department control did not work. Crook firmly believed: "The same hand that feeds should punish."[3] He wanted complete control, and if he did not get it he wanted out. The general was tired of the in-fighting. His private war with the Interior Department, and ultimately the political quagmire that had a stranglehold on military advancement, now began to seriously undermine his capability to sustain his Indian men. Although Crook demanded that Gatewood and his other subordinates be supported, he ignored their needs more and more—especially Gatewood's.

The general did not realize this, . . . or, if he did, did not care. Defeating the Chiricahuas dominated Crook's list of priorities. Watching all his hard work of the previous thirty months slowly disintegrate before his eyes, and with it his chances for advancement, did not sit well with him.

Crook's negative attitude, combined with the Zuck affair, continued to undermine Gatewood's outlook. He realized his Indians needed him, and he made every effort to see to their welfare, but he had had it. He had to get out of an impossible situation, and again put in for a transfer back to his regiment.

The request was denied. Gatewood refused to accept Crook's answer and resubmitted the request. Perhaps tiring of his subaltern's antagonistic persistence, Crook asked Gatewood to name his replacement. Caught off guard, Gatewood could not think of a suitable replacement. Then, more as a joke than as a serious consideration, he named an officer he considered a fool—Lieutenant James Lockett.[4]

Intent on destroying the Chiricahuas, Crook instructed Crawford to stay east of the San Bernardino River, hoping his positioning would force them westward toward the Abispo country. On July 7 he ordered a second expedition into Mexico. Led by Captain Wirt Davis, the command consisted of Lieutenant Matthias Day, Lieutenant Robert Walsh, Troop F, Fourth U.S. Cavalry (forty men), one hundred Indian scouts, and two pack trains, with Day commanding the Indian scouts. Davis had been forced to wait until Gatewood returned from his patrol because his scouts were the only ones available who knew the Sierra Madre. With rations for sixty days, Davis crossed the international boundary and entered Mexico on July 13. His destination was the Abispo.[5]

Growth in Gatewood's White Mountain Indian Reservation was uneven: some areas saw an increase in acreage under cultivation, while others experienced a decrease. Still, it appeared that 1885 would end with a slight gain over the previous year. He found that the Indians living farther out from Fort Apache had little incentive to till the land as they had a plentiful supply of game. Since hunting was much more to an Apache's liking, Gatewood was not surprised to find that some Indians ignored their plots, or in some cases abandoned them altogether, to feed their families in what they considered to be a manly manner. Another problem that his wards living on the edge of the reservation had to face was the lack of transportation to haul their produce to the post to sell.

Contrary to some reports, Gatewood's Indians had yet to become totally self-sufficient. Even so, Gatewood was pleased with the steady improvement he saw on the cultivated plots. But, as in the past, he knew his Indians lacked the necessary tools to become efficient farmers. "I believe that if they were properly supported and aided by the introduction of farming implements and tools," Gatewood reported, "they would soon become not only self-sustaining but a source of help to the country in developing its agricultural interests."[6]

Gatewood made sure that charitable contributions made to the reservation were put to good use, seeing to it that all donated monies were spent on sheep. Both the White Mountains and the Chiricahuas thrived with sheep herding and were accumulating sizable flocks, and although both bands were considered troublesome by the Interior Department and the general populace, Gatewood viewed them in a different light. As far as he was concerned, the White Mountain and Chiricahua Apaches were the only two tribes on the reservation that approached self-supporting status—in spite of a large handicap. "[They] are the only Indians discriminated against in encouragement in their efforts," Gatewood reported. "This has retarded their progress to a very considerable extent."[7] Contractors charged inflated prices for inferior goods they supplied to the Indians.

Characteristically, Gatewood refused to ignore items he felt were owed to the Indians. The mill to grind corn that he had requested the previous year still had not materialized, and Gatewood would not sit still on this matter: the Indians had to harvest their corn while it was still *in the milk* and dry it for winter. "I am quite sure that their manner of using it is productive of disease," he wrote, "and I believe a mill erected and run under proper condition would not only advance them in health but that it would be a great source of encouragement to them to raise wheat as well as corn."[8]

Although completely disgusted with his current state of affairs, Gatewood remained an efficient administrator. His morality, combined with his absolute refusal to back down when he considered himself right, had always been a pain in Crook's posterior. This gift, or curse, suited him well for another function he performed as military commandant of the reservation. An Indian judicial system had been set up to punish native lawbreakers. Gatewood presided over the court as judge, while White Mountain Apaches served on the jury.

Even though the corruption and inefficiency of his own entanglement within the web of the American judicial system continued to gnaw at him, the simplicity of the aboriginal version gave him satisfaction. Apache juries were honest, quick to act, and harsh. Most of the cases Gatewood presided over consisted of wife beating and the production and consumption of tizwin—crimes and transgressions that were on the decline. However, once in a while, a more heinous offense, such as rape, would be committed, and when this happened, the criminal would usually be quickly apprehended and brought to justice.

Gatewood's jury always sat on the floor against a wall. Everyone "solemnly smok[ed] cigarettes,"[9] he recalled, "for without smoke, nothing of importance c[ould] be done." Gatewood supplied the tobacco and *makings* for cigarettes. Usually the cases and judgments were cut and dried with both judge and jury agreeing upon the punishment.

But this was not always the case. Sometimes Gatewood and his jury found themselves worlds apart in what they considered a fair punishment. When this happened, the jury—which sometimes advocated a much harsher punishment than Gatewood felt the crime warranted—became stubborn, refusing to budge. To break the deadlock, Bay-chen-daysen usually gave in to his wards' will—providing he could oversee the punishment to ensure that the convicted felon did not receive more than the agreed-upon judgment.

While Crawford and Wirt Davis continued to scour the vast and rugged Sierra Madre for Geronimo and the Chiricahuas, Crook set in operation a systematic monitoring of all the known water holes and lines of entry into the United States from the Rio Grande westward. He chose the locations with care. Eight troops of Fourth U.S. Cavalry patrolled Copper Canyon, Song Mountain, Solomon's Springs, Mud Springs, Willow Springs, San Bernardino, Skeleton Canyon, and Guadalupe Canyon; two companies of the Tenth U.S. Infantry guarded the San Luis Pass; and three troops of Sixth U.S. Cavalry rode the line in New Mexico. Each detachment of troops had an auxiliary of Indian scouts to use exclusively as their eyes. Finally, Crook placed the Tenth U.S. Cavalry on call to intercept any Chiricahuas who broached the defensive line and reentered Arizona Territory.[10]

Conflicting reports reached Crook from Mexico. More Chiricahuas were being counted as dead than American bullets had found. Nonetheless, Crawford and Wirt Davis did have some success.[11]

As the days of summer passed, Gatewood continued to perform his duty at Apache. Although Bay-chen-daysen still ruled the reservation, still commanding White Mountain scouts, his tenure was limping toward its end. All attempts at an amicable relationship with Crook had ended. Estranged, almost like a jilted lover, Gatewood had no more use for his commander; all he wanted was his release.

The general showed Gatewood just as stiff a back. Still, he stalled, refusing to set his disgruntled lieutenant free.

Gatewood's position, although supposedly special, had deteriorated to the pits of hell. He was all too painfully aware that no matter what he did for the Indians, there would be no recognition, no rewards. Anxious over his next appearance in court, and tiring of waiting for Crook to make a decision, Gatewood decided to act in his own behalf. On August 5 he wrote the adjutant general of the army requesting "to be relieved from my present duties in connection with the management of Indian affairs" and "returned to duty with the troop to which I belong—'D' 6th Cavalry, Fort Stanton, N[ew] M[exico]."[12]

To avoid the American soldiers hunting them, Geronimo and the Chiricahuas split into small groups and dispersed ever deeper into the hidden reaches of the Sierra Madre. Keeping to rocky areas, they disguised their movements as much as possible. Mother Nature chipped in: throughout July and into August it rained almost constantly, obliterating their trail almost as soon as they made it.

Whenever Geronimo, Chihuahua, or Naiche became aware that the soldiers and turncoat Apaches lost their spoor, they immediately sent out small raiding parties to strike their tormentors. The hunted became the hunter. Raiders struck quickly, stealing food and horses. Then, ranging far from the clefts and arroyos where their loved ones hid, they left new trails that led their pursuers farther into the maze of deep canyons and cliffs.

Almost as if Geronimo had used his powers to call upon Ussen, Mother Nature remained a stout ally—torrential rains continued to hide the Chiricahuas' trail. When it became obvious that the soldiers had once again lost the scent, Chiricahua warriors quickly circled about and slunk back to their camps.[13]

But Geronimo's luck did not hold. His band was camped west of Casas Grandes, Chihuahua, when on August 7 Wirt Davis's scouts attacked. Davis claimed a major victory, announcing that Nana and Chappo—Geronimo's warrior son—were dead and that Geronimo had been wounded. This was not true: Nana, Chappo, and Geronimo escaped without harm.[14] Although Geronimo claimed: "One boy was killed,"[15] actually a woman and two boys died.

This did not mean Geronimo had scored another moral victory over the White Eyes, for he had not. Although his casualties were low, this skirmish proved devastating to the old warrior. Thirteen horses and mules, along with saddles, blankets, and dried meat were taken. Mangus's wife, Huera, was captured, as was Perico's wife, Hah-dun-key, and children.

Geronimo stated that "nearly all of our women and children were captured."[16] The attack wiped out his family. Two of his wives, Zi-yeh and Shegha, were seized, and a third wife who soon disappeared from history, Sht-sha-she, may have also been taken. Five children from Geronimo's family were apprehended, including Zi-yeh's infant son; Dohn-say, a girl who had just reached womanhood (her mother, Chee-hash-kish, was captured during the Casas Grandes treachery in 1882 and was now a Mexican slave); and a three-year old girl. The other two may have been Geronimo's grandchildren, for Dohn-say had recently married a warrior who followed Geronimo named Dahkeya.[17] This was the third time Geronimo had lost wives and other loved ones. Each succeeding loss compounded his hatred for the Mexicans and Americans. There is little wonder why he struck back with such ferocity—the invaders of his land wanted everything. When he refused to hand over his land and live as a prisoner, he became a hunted outlaw, a scourge of society.

The old warrior's entire lifeway revolved around the hunt. Be it beast or man, be he the hunter or the hunted, he was superb at it, for his desire to survive was matchless. In Native American culture, the young participated in war, and a warrior was usually considered old when he neared the end of his thirties. Geronimo was about sixty-two years old.

By August 9, two Chiricahua women who had been held captive by the Mexicans at Mexico City reached Fort Bowie. They, along with seven other women and some children, had been freed and sent north. The others had tried to enter the United States through New Mexico but had disappeared.

Crook forwarded the two women to Gatewood at Fort Apache, along with the request that Gatewood query them about Chatto's son. Bay-chen-daysen welcomed the women back, then asked them what they knew about Chatto's son, but apparently they knew nothing of the boy's whereabouts.[18]

Days passed slowly as Gatewood continued his tasks as administrator. Then, on August 14, Crook wrote to Headquarters, Division of the Pacific, requesting that Gatewood's transfer be granted.[19]

Early in August, Britton Davis, who had been with Crawford's command, split off and moved eastward into Chihuahua. His task was to follow Geronimo. His command consisted of Al Sieber, Mickey Free, Chatto, and forty scouts. The trek over the next twenty-four days proved to be rough, and he lost Geronimo's—or whomever's—trail. Deprivation haunted Davis and his companions as they tramped five hundred miles following leads that led nowhere. Filthy and worn-out, they limped across the international border at Texas, reaching Fort Bliss on September 5. Having had enough of the war and Crook's bad attitude, Davis submitted his resignation and requested a leave of absence until it became official.[20]

❖❖❖

Anticipating his pending transfer, along with the uncertainty of his next court appearance, Gatewood went about putting his administration in order. As the summer drew to a close, he rode across the reservation to make a personal inspection, and comparing what he saw with the figures already at hand must have pleased him. In all, some 2,120 acres were under cultivation. His wards had raised 80,000 pounds of barley, 65,000 pounds of which they had already sold to the United States Government. Before year's end he estimated they would sell Uncle Sam another 15,000 pounds. Although he did not know the exact amount of hay grown, he knew the government had already bought 700,000 pounds, and guessed they would buy another 1,000,000 pounds in the near future. The Indians also produced 3,500,000 pounds of corn.[21]

September arrived, and with it the uncertain future that Gatewood had lived with for the past six months. Although he had collected all the necessary information to complete the report on his last year as commandant of the reservation, he had to put the task on hold. His next court date, September 7, was approaching and he left for St. Johns.

Completing the seventy-five-mile trip in two days, Gatewood met with his lawyers, who told him they wanted to increase his bond. Gatewood found the reasoning—a higher balance meant more dignity and thus a greater chance of acquittal—absurd. He told them to drop this approach, or he would complain to the court. The threat worked.

On the appointed day, the case was called. With the Honorable Summer Howard again presiding over the third judicial court of Apache County, the prosecution began matters by asking for a continuance. They needed more time to prepare. This did not please Gatewood: he wanted to end the farce, and at his request the defense counsel made an appeal for the trial to proceed, telling the court of the strain the postponements had caused his client. "Either he should go to jail for 18 months," he said, "or he should be free & able to hold his head up among his peers in this sun-kissed land."[22] The words fell on deaf ears, however, and Howard continued the case for another six months.

There was nothing Gatewood could do but return to Apache and wait for another six months to pass. He sarcastically commented: "It looked as if this business would never end till the surplus in the treasury was exhausted . . ."[23]

Before leaving St. Johns, Gatewood completed his report on the reservation. He pointed out that most of the White Mountain males now served as scouts, which directly affected the year's crop yield. Although this stage of his career was about to end, Gatewood did not turn his back on his wards. Under adverse circumstances he had seen his Indians make something of their new world. "In conclusion," he wrote, "I desire to state that these Indians evince a zeal in the way of improvement worthy of encouragement and in my opinion with proper help at just this time they will in a short period advance to such a degree that their future government will only be a matter of decent treatment."[24]

Gatewood also recognized the Indians' profound understanding of their situation, remarking that "they would be equally quick to resent anything savoring of imposition of what they know to be their rights."

The loss of one-third of their women and children was a tragedy for Geronimo and his group. "Apaches were devoted to their families," historian Angie Debo wrote. "Also, in their well-structured division of labor a man without a wife to prepare food and clothing was as seriously handicapped economically as was a woman without a male provider."[25]

Geronimo and four warriors set out on foot to recapture their families, . . . if possible, and if not, to steal new wives. They quickly reached the United States border, slipped past Crook's line of defense, and, after passing through the mountains, reached the reservation. Geronimo and his companions easily avoided the White Mountain Apaches who patrolled the area, and found that the Chiricahuas who did not return to the warpath had been moved closer to Fort Apache.

After stealing some horses, the raiders caught a White Mountain woman, whom they forced to take them to where Geronimo's family now camped. At one o'clock in the morning of September 22, Geronimo rescued She-gha and their three-year-old daughter. Another woman was also freed.[26]

Gatewood heard about the raid soon after Geronimo disappeared into the night. He dressed and sent for Alchesay. Although Bay-chen-daysen had no idea what the future held, the raid had set in motion a series of events that would put a strain on his close working relationship with the White Mountain Apaches. Again, Gatewood's morality would come to the fore, and again he absolutely refused to deviate from what he knew to be the proper course of action. As in the past, his decisions would once again pit him against an ally, but this time, instead of being his commanding officer, it would be his wards—though the result would be the same.

When Alchesay appeared at his quarters, Gatewood swapped information with the chieftain, then ordered him to lead a party of scouts in pursuit of the raiders. The White Mountain leader set out before dawn.

At first light, the Nantan Bay-chen-daysen parleyed with the Chiricahuas camped near Fort Apache. They denied any knowledge of Geronimo's appearance. He then met with White Mountain Apaches. Several told him they saw Geronimo approach the reservation on foot, but had not bothered to report the sighting. An opportunity—so close, and yet never realized.

Gatewood wired Crook that the only way to prevent Geronimo—or someone else—from raiding the reservation a second time was to place the Chiricahuas in confinement.

There was nothing to do but wait for the results of this latest pursuit. In the meantime, Bay-chen-daysen beefed up reservation security. Horses and mules were corralled to make them harder to steal, and sentries watching the Chiricahua camp were increased in an effort to prevent any communication between the reservation Indians and Geronimo.[27]

The rescue of his wife marked just the beginning of Geronimo's raid. Like a famished wolf amidst a flock of sheep, he struck swiftly and frequently as he raced eastward, and puddles of White Mountain blood marked his passing. Frantic White Mountain families abandoned their homes, and after scrambling toward Fort Apache, they huddled together in large groups. As fear terrorized the reservation, most were lucky and escaped Geronimo's wraith—but not all.

An old Coyotero warrior returned from an unsuccessful hunt, and as he crested the ridge above his isolated home, he saw one of Geronimo's warriors bash in his grandson's head with a stone club, then toss his small body into a bonfire that the raiders had made of his wickiup. A glance quickly told the story: his family had been butchered, their torn, broken bodies haphazardly littering Mother Earth. With nothing to fear and no reason to continue living, the devastated man cocked his Sharps, took deadly aim, and the murderer fell, dead.

Refusing to turn and run, the Coyotero calmly reloaded and recocked his ancient rifle. Taking aim a second time, he wounded his target. Only then, as the raiding party scattered and began to stalk him, did he turn and race for his life. The worst day of the old man's life ironically turned out to be a lucky one—he escaped. The next morning he reached Fort Apache.

White Mountain Apaches quickly gathered at Gatewood's quarters to hear the old man's story, and everyone listened quietly as the Coyotero described the massacre of his family. While those who surrounded him snickered at his supposed heroism, he requested a supply of bullets and to have the firing mechanism on his rifle be fixed.

Gatewood had the gun fixed and the Coyotero supplied with cartridges.

At that point, the old man raised his face and arms skyward and said, "may the great spirits protect me till I have my revenge."[28] Finished, he left.

Murmuring their disbelief in the story, the crowd dispersed. However, they had to know the truth, and a party of White Mountain warriors rode out to investigate. They found the old man's slaughtered family. Sign showed that two of the raiders had been shot. A short distance from the massacre site, they discovered a solitary grave.

Geronimo's group scattered as it fled eastward toward Mount Ord, New Mexico. Passing a Mescalero village, Geronimo halted the flight. In the distance he saw some women and a boy gathering piñon nuts. The raid had not been a success: they had failed to retrieve their families or to capture more women. As evening approached, Geronimo decided to strike. With lightning speed, he and his warriors charged the women, one of whom carried an infant. They grabbed them and pulled them onto the backs of their horses as they galloped past. The boy, who was about four or five years old, was nicked by a bullet in his calf as he ran for safety in some chaparral. A warrior grabbed him.

Although Naiche would have had first choice, he did not want another wife. This gave Geronimo the first selection. He took the youngest of the three women as his wife, renaming her Ih-tedda. Juan-si-got-si chose the boy—who years later would be known as Charlie Smith—and his mother. Another warrior claimed the other woman and her infant.[29]

While Gatewood wrote at the desk in his office, White Mountain warriors filed in and dropped a bloodied cloth-enclosed bundle before him. He opened the package, and to his shock looked at the decapitated head of the Chiricahua that the old Coyotero had killed. Bay-chen-daysen struggled, trying to keep from vomiting. After regaining control of his body, he immediately issued an order that under no circumstances was a severed head to be delivered to him again.

Before the meeting ended, news of other outrages wrought by Geronimo arrived. The White Mountain Apaches burned for vengeance and made no attempt to hide their feelings.

Soon afterward, Alchesay, Sanchez, and other White Mountain leaders presented themselves to Gatewood and asked for cartridges for their warriors who served as scouts. When Gatewood asked why the extra bullets were needed, they simply replied they were necessary to protect the people from another raid. On the surface the request seemed honest, but the more

Bay-chen-daysen thought about it the more he began to think something was amiss. Suspicious, he asked Alchesay and the others what was going on:

> The chiefs when taxed with organizing some scheme for devilment, looked surprised & said that their hearts were made sore to have it tho[ugh]t that they were capable of doing anything not authorized & approved by the Nahn-tahn. All the same there was that unaccountable, uneasy feeling that generally for[e]bodes evil. No bribes, threats nor persuasion could get one man, woman, or child to even hint at what would be the result.[30]

Gatewood remained in the dark. When the Chihenne leader Loco secretly met him and asked if he could move his people to Fort Apache for protection, Bay-chen-daysen asked why. Loco replied that the White Mountain Apaches planned to murder his people. Gatewood immediately granted the old chieftain permission to bring his people to the fort. He then sent runners to the rest of the Chiricahua villages on the reservation, inviting them to move closer to Fort Apache for protection.

When White Mountain warriors saw the Chiricahuas begin to arrive at the fort, they descended upon Gatewood's quarters en masse. Bay-chen-daysen calmly waited while they crowded into his office, sat on the floor, and lighted their cigarettes. As minutes stretched into an hour, the confined space quickly became stuffy, body odors melding with the smell of burnt tobacco. He knew by the length of the smoke that something was really bothering his wards.

Finally, the White Mountains told Gatewood that they did not want the Chiricahuas living so close to the post, for they did not like the favoritism the nantan suddenly displayed. Gatewood told the assembly he knew what they were up to, and he asked them to return to their homes, go back to their work, and forget all thoughts of vengeance. Sanchez leaped to his feet, and, puffing malevolently on his cigarette, said:

> Our homes have been invaded, & our women and children outraged & massacred. Where can we get revenge? Those who committed these crimes are by this time far away in Mexico, & we can't reach them there. By our laws, their kindred here are proper victims, but you have placed them beyond our reach. Yes, more than 200 of our braves had intended to root out their nest of hornets, counting upon your help rather than opposition. We always have looked on you as one of us, a true Coyotero, but now you've joined the Chiricahuas & act like an enemy of ours. The mournful cries of our squaws over the bodies of their dead, seem to make sweet music to your ears.[31]

Bay-chen-daysen replied: "[I am] proud to be a Coyotero, & would gladly put on war paint & a breechclout & join [you] in carrying out just retribution: but [my] orders from . . . the big chief of the soldiers, [forbids] it."

This exchange began a discussion that ended in compromise: the White Mountains could kill any Chiricahuas they found beyond a safe zone that Gatewood would set.

Three days after abducting Ih-tedda, Geronimo approached Lake Valley, New Mexico. He was traveling quickly, taking no time off to kill White Eyes. Seeing soldiers, Geronimo and his people broke up into parties of two or three and headed west, and though the White Eyes gave chase they could not catch them.[32]

A few days after his last meeting with the White Mountains, the warriors returned to Gatewood's office, planting themselves on his floor and smoking for over an hour. Finally they said that they were tired of waiting in vain for a Chiricahua to venture from the safe zone so they could kill him.

"You've gone back on us again," they told Gatewood, "by notifying them of our agreement. Now, we are convinced that you are a Chiricahua. Our hearts are bleeding."[33]

So was Gatewood's. However, he would not allow innocent people to be murdered, and argued with the gathering until they began to understand his view on the matter.

Suddenly, there was a loud commotion outside. Before anyone could react, a Chiricahua boy pulled his pony to a halt outside Gatewood's quarters and dove into the crowded room. A White Mountain war party was right behind him, brandishing their guns and knives over the prostrate boy.

Gatewood heard a mob gathering outside. He yelled for his scouts as he pushed his way to the boy's side.

Outside, the mob began to yell: "Chiricahua! Kill him. Kill him!"

Apache scouts appeared. Although White Mountains, they remained loyal to the Nantan Bay-chen-daysen, and held the mob at bay.

Inside, the scene worsened. Warriors swung their weapons as they clamored to hack the boy to pieces. Gatewood would not have murder, and drawing his revolver he quickly arrested the ringleaders. Gatewood's firm action broke the threat of violence. It also severed his close working relationship with the White Mountain Apaches.

Although his replacement had still not been named, Special Order No. 200 released Gatewood from Indian duty and ordered him "to join his regiment without delay."[34] Gatewood thought he was finally free. However, before he could pack his family and travel to New Mexico, Crook changed his mind: he did not want Gatewood to leave Apache. On October 2, Crook wired Major General John Pope, commander of the Division of the Pacific, of Gatewood's civil problems, explaining that he felt it would "prejudice [Gatewood's] case if he is obliged to leave before [his] trial."[35] Crook received confirmation of his petition on October 3: Gatewood would remain in Arizona until the completion of his trial.[36]

Bay-chen-daysen unofficially remained the military commandant of the reservation. Days passed, then weeks. He was still in control when Crawford and Wirt Davis's exhausted commands limped back to Fort Bowie later that October.

Indian scouts, whose enlistments would soon expire, were mustered out of service, while new scouts enlisted. Davis began refitting immediately, for he planned to take one hundred Indian scouts and return to Mexico in November. Crawford also began preparations for returning to Mexico, but he would not reenter Mexico until December.[37]

On November 14, Gatewood's tenure as military commander of the White Mountain Indian Reservation came to an end.[38] The day before, Crawford had recommended to Crook that Gatewood relinquish control immediately. Crook agreed and ordered Bay-chen-daysen to turn over the management of the Indians to Lockett.

With his Apache connection severed, Bay-chen-daysen now found himself totally separated from the war. Even though warring Chiricahua activities in Arizona and New Mexico were minimal,[39] Fort Apache swirled with activity as Indians enlisted and prepared to continue the hunt for Geronimo. Gatewood's working hours during this time must have been split between making the transfer of reservation management as smooth as possible and preparing for his never-ending civil case.

So far the raids into the United States led by Geronimo and others had not cost many lives, but that changed when Chihuahua's brother, Josanie (*Ulzana, Ulzahuay, Jolsanny*), with nine warriors, entered the Florida Mountains of New Mexico early in November. He struck quickly and frequently, then hid only to resurface on the night of November 23. Just four miles from Fort Apache, he tore through the reservation, killing everyone he encountered except for a few Chiricahua women whom he took as wives. His goal was to devastate and terrorize the Chiricahuas for not going on the warpath and for daring to aid the White Eyes. Five men and boys, eleven women, and four children died.[40]

Waves of fear paralyzed the Southwest as the citizenry of Arizona and New Mexico screamed for an end to Geronimo and the war. In Washington, Sheridan found the news disquieting. Results were all that mattered, and Crook had nothing to show. Not only did the outbreak appear capable of continuing for a very long time, the Chiricahuas were bringing the war back to the homefront. Sheridan wanted results—now. He traveled to Fort Bowie and, on November 29, told Crook to go on the offensive. He wanted Geronimo's band destroyed.[41]

Before the meeting ended, Crook complained about General Nelson Miles, whom he felt was campaigning for his command. Crook's words were persuasive; not only did he keep his job, but on December 1 he assumed command of the District of New Mexico.[42] However, he could not stop Josanie, and the reign of terror continued unhindered until the war leader returned to Mexico on December 27. During the two-month raid, Josanie killed thirty-eight people, stole somewhere between two hundred and three hundred horses and mules, and traveled approximately twelve hundred miles. He lost one man.[43]

Crawford, whose battalion of one hundred Indian scouts were already in the field looking for Josanie, re-entered Mexico on December 11.[44] Wirt Davis continued to hunt the Chiricahuas, who kept constantly on the move. Rumors continually placed ravaging Indians in the Southwest, and when manpower allowed these rumors were quickly checked out. Usually, nothing was found: the soldiers and their Indian allies followed ephemeral trails that ended as soon as they began, . . . without a trace of the quarry. The war droned on and on, with no end in sight.

And Gatewood did nothing. Discarded, forgotten, an outcast, . . . he had all the time in the world to reflect on what should have, . . . or what could have been. His career had flourished. He had gained the respect of both his peers and the natives with whom he worked so closely. And then, in a little more than a year, he had seen all his hard work come to a staggering halt as his career plummeted toward oblivion.

Then in December, although his civil difficulties still had not been resolved, Crook changed his mind once again and released him. Reassigned to troop duty at Fort Stanton, New Mexico, Gatewood packed, anticipating a new beginning for his career and young family.[45]

CHAPTER EIGHT

Courtroom and Conference

The year 1886 marked the dismal end of Lieutenant Charles Gatewood's relationship with Crook and the Apaches; at the same time it gave his floundering military career new life. After years of hard service—years in which his health had been ruined, and for which he had received little praise and almost no advancement—Bay-chen-daysen must have felt as though a heavy load had been removed from his shoulders. Even with eight full years of campaigning and reservation administration behind him, he had little to show for his endeavors.

He had many memories of burning days and freezing nights, of endless marches, of thirst and near-starvation, of the obscenity of sudden death, but mostly of the comradeship and struggle for survival. All these memories melded together, became one—the ancient, harsh lifeway of an Indian people whom most white men viewed with a skeptical, jaundiced eye, a culture that duty had forced him to live and endure. He had walked among a people totally different from himself—sometimes for months at a time—and even if he did not embrace and cherish the experience, at least he gained knowledge and respect for the Indians called Apache.

At thirty-two years of age, Gatewood still had his career before him. He still had time to find his niche in *this man's army*, still had time to climb the military ladder and provide a decent home for his family.

With the bitter taste of accusation and the lack of Crook's support behind him, Gatewood bid the White Mountain and Chiricahua Apaches good-bye. Leaving the Department of Arizona behind, he packed his family off to the Department of New Mexico. With his Indian duty at an end, Gatewood rejoined his regiment at Fort Stanton, which was located on the north bank of the Rio Hondo in south-central New Mexico. He expected to resume his career with garrison duty,[1] but unfortunately, his experience with the Apaches was far too valuable to be ignored.

As Gatewood turned his back on the Apache war, Geronimo felt the pressure of Crawford's scouts in hot pursuit. By January 9, Geronimo camped near the Aros River, about sixty miles below Nacori.[2] Kaywaykla later described the situation:

General Crook put eighty companies of infantry and cavalry in the field. But it was the scouts whom the Apaches dreaded, for only they knew the trails and the hiding places. And only they could traverse the country rapidly enough to be a menace.[3]

Geronimo knew soldiers and turncoat Apaches were near, but did not know their exact location.

Miles openly campaigned for Crook's job. His supporters ranged from the citizens of Arizona Territory to the president of the United States. Surprisingly, Sheridan, who was never impressed with Crook, fought to keep Crook in charge.[4]

On January 10, the dreaded Apache scouts struck, and the sudden attack took Geronimo's camp by surprise. The old warrior and his band scattered into the surrounding mountains. Even though the scouts' bullets did not find their marks, they had dealt Geronimo a terrible blow, for he had lost his stock and his supplies.[5] The realization must have struck home that it would be difficult to escape the Apaches who tracked him.

The night turned cold, and Geronimo moved to a spot high in the crags where he could watch the scouts from Crawford's command ransack his camp. What they did not want, they destroyed. Around midnight, the scouts set up their camp above what was left of his.[6]

The situation was not good. The White-eye camp was too strong to storm, and now he had no camp to recapture. Geronimo returned to where his cold, hungry people huddled. Time was short and the people had to decide what to do. Nana said the women and children should return to Turkey Creek, that some of the warriors also tired of the fight. Geronimo was not blind: he saw how bad his plight was. The old warrior sent the Chihenne warrior woman, Lozen, and a Chokonen woman named Dahteste, to Crawford's camp to set up a meeting.

Crawford agreed to talk, promising Geronimo safe conduct.[7] But before Geronimo could go to him to parley, a force of Mexican irregulars attacked the American Indian scouts at dawn the next morning. Crawford frantically tried to end the firefight, as he and his officers yelled, "Soldados Americaños [sic]," in an attempt to stop the Mexican assault. Geronimo and his band rushed to the bank of the Aros River, about a mile distant, to see what was happening. After about fifteen minutes, the shooting stopped.

Suddenly, another shot rang out and a Mexican bullet hit Crawford, who stood exposed on a rock. The scouts fired a volley, and the shooting became general. When the Mexicans saw Geronimo's people in the distance, the shooting stopped a second time.

Lieutenant Marion Maus, who assumed command when Crawford fell, and Tom Horn, an interpreter who spoke fluent Spanish, used the lull in the shooting to speak with the Mexicans. "They assured me that they took us for hostile Indians,"[8] Maus later reported. He thought they were sincere, until they told him they had tracked the Chiricahuas for days. Maus surmised that it was his trail they had found and followed because Geronimo had come from a different direction.

The unprovoked attack cost the Americans: Crawford would soon die, Horn and two scouts were slightly wounded, and one scout was severely wounded. The Mexicans, in turn, reported four dead and four wounded.

In the meantime, Geronimo did not know what was happening. He could see that the two sides were in communication, and this bothered him. That afternoon he sent a woman—most likely Lozen or Dahteste—to the American camp. She told Maus that Geronimo was afraid to talk while the Mexicans were near. Agreeing, Maus returned to the Mexicans the next morning, only to be made a hostage. This was a mistake. The Apache scouts knew the truth behind the attack, knew Crawford's pending death was no accident, and liking nothing better than to strike back at the hated Mexicans, they stripped for battle and spread out along the mountainside. Seeing the defiant, screaming scouts, and wanting no part of them, the Mexicans released Maus.

On January 13 Maus moved four miles away from the Mexicans, camping by a stream. The next day, with five scouts, he met some of the Chiricahuas, but no Indian leaders were present. Nevertheless, he demanded an unconditional surrender.

Even though Geronimo did not like the demand for unconditional surrender, he and Naiche met Maus a half-mile from his camp two days later. The next day, Geronimo and Naiche said they wanted to talk about surrendering and would meet General Crook near the border south of San Bernardino in two moons.[9]

On January 16, Maus began his homeward march to the United States, accompanied by nine Chiricahuas, including Ih-tedda, Geronimo's sister, Naiche's wife and two children, Nana, a warrior, another woman, and a boy. Crawford's condition never improved and he died on January 18.

Gatewood's thoughts regarding the latest developments in the war are unknown, but it is safe to surmise that he was saddened by Crawford's death. Crawford, Britton Davis, and Gatewood had been joined by their assignment as military agents. They had sustained the brunt of the inner conflict between the War and Interior departments, suffered through the lack of support whenever the heat from Washington became excessive, and withstood the blatant hatred that the Arizona citizenry harbored toward Apaches and the soldiers who controlled them. First Crawford and then Gatewood had been called onto the carpet for their administration of the reservation, and tired of enduring a bad situation, all three had gotten out. Unfortunately for Crawford, orders had returned him to the war.

Gatewood's Indian duty had not ended, either. Although he undoubtedly put in for commissary work, as this was a position for which he constantly applied throughout his career, Gatewood's intimate knowledge of Indians prevented it.

The army's need of officers who knew and understood Indians made Gatewood a likely choice to again command Indian scouts. Initially assigned to command a company of scouts at Fort Stanton,[10] Gatewood, who did not want any more Indian duty, soon found himself caught in a difficult situation. Not only could he not escape command of the Indians, but the new assignment soon separated him from Georgia and his children. Undoubtedly, Gatewood was disappointed when he found out that his stay at Fort Stanton would be brief.

Ordered to report to Fort Wingate, New Mexico, Gatewood traveled north to Navajo country, while Georgia and the children remained at Fort Stanton. Arriving at his new station, Gatewood found himself in charge of a company of Navajo scouts. In Gatewood's eyes, the *Diné,* as the Navajo call themselves, ranked a poor second when compared to the Apaches, and after commanding Navajo scouts for only a short time he dismissed them as "loafers."[11]

Geronimo needed a respite for his people and he needed peace. After parting from Maus and the Indian scouts, the old warrior sent two women to Sonora to ask for a council with Mexican authorities. Waiting for an answer, Geronimo and his people remained in camp, but when the women did not return at the anticipated time Geronimo suspected treachery.

Fear of attack kept Geronimo alert, for he had no intention of being surprised. Deciding not to wait any longer, he led his people north toward the American border, but this time there was no treachery. Mexican officials told the women they would meet with the Chiricahuas, but when the women returned to the camp and found it deserted, they were forced to track Geronimo before reporting the good news.[12]

❖❖❖

Gatewood's next trial appearance neared, so he packed and once again made the journey to St. Johns. By this time his views of the American judicial system had become jaundiced: all sides seemed to be out for money and nothing else. As he rode into town, he did not know what to expect, except perhaps another continuance.

St. Johns continued to flourish, the streets overflowing with alcohol-guzzling humanity. One glance was all Gatewood needed: he could see the town was *red hot*. Gentiles and Mormons, cowboys, thugs, sheepmen, and even businessmen moved about with thinly veiled hostility. The uneasy mix of races, religions, and politics added to an atmosphere that seemed on the verge of exploding.

Hamilton Roach, Gatewood's former assistant on the reservation was in town, subpoenaed to testify; as were others who would be friendly to his cause. Familiar faces must have eased his anxiety over once again being center stage in what had become a farce without end.

Gatewood's case was called on March 24. The Honorable Summer Howard no longer presided over the Third Judicial District; he had been replaced by the Honorable John C. Shields, who had recently arrived from the East. The change in tenure, however, did not mean that Gatewood had heard the last of Howard, not by a long shot, for Howard had joined the prosecution.

As soon as the court was called to order, Zuck tried to exert his political influence, telling Shields that he would see to it that His Honor heard a true recounting of events. He hinted that it would be in Shields's best interest to place himself on the *popular side* when deciding upon the case. Zuck's words outraged Shields.

Suddenly Gatewood's outlook brightened. For the first time since being charged with felonious false arrest, he felt he had a chance of an impartial judgment.

Next, the district attorney announced that all his witnesses were available. He "was anxious to go ahead & finish by placing [Gatewood] where he belonged—in gaol."[13]

At recess, Gatewood met with his attorneys. "We have examined the list of jurors to be drawn," the good counsel said, "& you are sure to be convicted. We propose, when the court [reconvenes], to ask for a continuance."[14]

Gatewood had had enough. "And I propose to be tried," he snapped, "even if I have to conduct my own case, & will state to the court that we are ready." This brashness was not without reason, for Gatewood had had eighteen months to ponder the problem. He had arrested Zuck on the reservation, and as this was a territorial court he began to question the legality of the charges. He made it clear he wanted his counsel to pursue this angle.

Recess ended, the jury was sworn in, and the prosecution began their case. Defense conceded that Gatewood had made the arrest. Next, witnesses testified to the suffering and hardship endured by Zuck, Kay, and Jones. During the recital, someone in the back of the court shouted: "Liar!"[15] This brought an angry retort from another member of the gallery, a scuffle broke out, Sheriff Hubbell restored order, and the prosecution continued. The first day ended with the conclusion of the evidence against Gatewood.

On March 25, Gatewood's counsel began their argument regarding the jurisdiction of a territorial court in the matter, which led to a barrage of insults between the prosecuting and defense attorneys. When tempers flared to the point of blows, Sheriff Hubbell stepped between the lawyers and prevented them from coming to fisticuffs.

Howard had been retained by the Mormons, who sought revenge for Zuck's defeat in the 1884 election. Promised a handsome bonus when Gatewood was put behind bars, Howard attacked Gatewood's character when quiet in the courtroom had been restored. Not satisfied with this onslaught, he added the defense counsel to his assault, and this, in turn, resulted in an insult directed at Zuck.

Zuck sprang to his feet screaming to be heard; and so did Gatewood. The lawyers from both sides, Sheriff Hubbell, even the witness on the stand leaped to their feet, yelling. The mob in the gallery joined the bedlam, screaming their view. Only the jury remained aloof, calmly watching the madness that surrounded them.

Shields pounded his gavel, demanding silence, and when he did not get it he threatened to jail everyone in the room. This restored order.

Taking control, Shields told both benches: "The point to be argued, gentlemen . . . is purely one of law, & that is, [i]s the trial of this case in this court legal?"[16]

Howard argued that he could try this case anywhere, and to prove his point he began to quote the law. After listening to him for half an hour, the court again began to deteriorate. One insult led to another, prompting Shields to again take control and stifle tempers. Howard continued his recitation of the law and soon half an hour passed, then an hour. The gallery lost interest and began to filter out of the courthouse. After two hours, the pontification ceased.

Before allowing the defense to call their first witness, Judge Shields delivered an instruction to the jury: "the evidence introduced on behalf of [the]

Plaintiff discloses that this court has no jurisdiction of the offense charged in the indictment and you are therefore instructed to render a verdict discharging the defendent."[17] And the jury did, ending the trial. A bitter Gatewood found himself free—finally free after eighteen months of hell, and all because he dared to defend Indian rights.

At about this time, Geronimo's scouts told him that Crook had entered Mexico and camped in the Sierra de Antunez. Geronimo's choice was simple—Americans were less treacherous than Mexicans.[18] He found Maus at the location he had previously specified for the meeting with Crook (in the northeast corner of Sonora, about twenty miles south southeast of San Bernardino Springs, Mexico). The lieutenant camped "in the Cañon de los Embudos, in a strong position, on a low mesa overlooking . . . water."[19] Crook had not yet arrived.

Always wary, Geronimo set up his ranchería "in a lava bed, on top of a small conical hill surrounded by steep ravines, not five hundred yards in direct line from Maus, but having between the two positions two or three steep and rugged gulches which served as scarps and counter-scarps."[20] Sycamores, ash, cottonwoods, and willows coexisted with Spanish bayonet and yucca, amidst the volcanic outcroppings and basalt boulders. The desolate, broken terrain could not have been better suited for defense. His small group of warriors—Chihuahua, Naiche, Fun, Eyelash, Chappo, Yahnosha, Kanseah, Zhunne, Ahnandia, Matzus, Bishi, Bihido, Lozen, Hanlonah, Nahpeh, and Perico—could easily hold off an army. The impregnable location made it impossible for the Americans to launch a surprise assault.[21]

Crook had left Fort Bowie with a small party that included Bourke, Kaytennae (who had been released from Alcatraz) and Alchesay, along with Tombstone photographer C. S. Fly.

Geronimo intended to keep a safe distance from the White Eyes. On March 25, he, Chihuahua, Naiche, along with a few others carefully approached the soldier camp. The rest of his warriors fanned out, watching, waiting. They were "[s]o suspicious," Crook reported, " . . . that never more than from five to eight of [them] came into our camp at one time."[22] According to Crook, the old warrior and his brethren "were in superb physical condition, armed to the teeth, with all the ammunition they could carry. In manner they were suspicious and at the same time independent and self-reliant."[23]

Everyone sat under large cottonwood and sycamore trees. Crook had Bourke, Maus, a few other officers, along with Kaytennae, Alchesay, and interpreters Concepción, José María Montoya, and Antonio Besias (or Brasseas). Geronimo insisted upon Concepción doing the interpretation, to which Crook agreed as long as the other interpreters could remain to ensure that the words were translated correctly.

Photographer Fly and his assistant, a man named Chase, flitted about during the proceedings. Fly had inquired if he could photograph the meeting, and Geronimo readily agreed, even moving whenever Fly asked him to. Only Chihuahua did not want his picture taken, and he constantly moved away from the camera lens.[24]

Geronimo explained why he ran from the reservation. He then said: "I don't want what has passed to happen again. Now I am going to tell you something else. The Earth-mother is listening to me and, I hope that all may be so arranged that from now on there shall be no trouble and that we shall always have peace."[25]

He spoke of the lies men had told about him:

From this [time] on I hope that people will tell me nothing but the truth. From this [time] on I want to do what is right and nothing else and I do not want you to believe any bad papers about me. I want the papers sent you to tell the truth about me because I want to do what is right. Very often there are stories put in the newspapers that I am to be hanged. I don't want that any more. When a man tries to do right such stories ought not to be put in the newspapers.

Crook, having had his own problems with the Arizona press, should have commiserated with Geronimo on this point, but he did not.

Geronimo then addressed the reason for the meeting:

There are very few of my men left now. They have done some bad things but I want them all rubbed out now and let us never speak of them again. . . . Sometimes a man does something and men are sent out to bring in his head. I don't want such things to happen to us. I don't want that we should be killing each other.

He must have paused, anticipating the Nantan Lupan to reply. When Crook remained silent, Geronimo, sensing something was wrong, said:

What is the matter that you don't speak to me, and look with a pleasant face? It would make better feeling. I would be glad if you did. I'd be better satisfied if you would talk to me once in a while. Why don't you look at me and smile at me. I am the same man. I have the same feet, legs and hands and the sun looks down on me a complete man. I want you to look and smile at me.

Crook's hostile attitude did not make it easy for Geronimo. Having lived with treachery his entire life, he most likely began to grow suspicious. Years later he commented on Crook: "It was hard for me to believe him at that time [March 25–27]. Now I know that what he said was untrue, and I firmly believe that he did issue the orders for me to be put in prison, or to be killed in case I offered resistance."[26] Geronimo's summation of Crook's thoughts is inaccurate.

At the same time, his words illuminated his firm grip on the position from which there did not appear to be any escape. His angry view toward the unsavory end to his entire lifeway is not uncalled for. Unfortunately, Crook's firm stance at the beginning of the parley unwittingly set Geronimo to revolt at the slightest provocation. Geronimo continued to speak:

> I think I am a good man, but in the papers all over the world they say I am a bad man. . . . it is a bad thing to say so about me. I never do wrong without a cause. Every day I am thinking how am I to talk to you to make you believe what I say . . . There is a God looking down on us all. We are all children of the one God. God is listening to us. The sun, the darkness, the winds are all listening to what we now say. To prove to you that I am telling you the truth, remember I sent you word that I would come from a place far away to speak to you here, and you see us now. If I were thinking bad, or if I had done bad, I would never have come here.

Crook did not attempt to work out a peaceful settlement; instead, he verbally tore into Geronimo. His main points consisted of: 1) Geronimo lied in the Sierra Madre in 1883 when he said he wanted peace; 2) Geronimo plotted to kill Britton Davis and Chatto, even though Crook had gone out on a limb to get him reinstated on the reservation in 1883; and 3) Geronimo had returned to the warpath and resumed killing innocent people.

In reply to the murder attempt on Davis and Chatto, Geronimo blurted out: "That's not so." However, he must have known that he had been caught in a lie. Surely he could not have forgotten that Chihuahua and others broke away from him in disgust when they suspected he had manipulated the outbreak.

Refusing to admit to anything, Geronimo said: "I am a man of my word. I am telling the truth . . . why I left the reservation." Unfortunately, Geronimo's intonation was not recorded along with his words.

"You told me the same thing in the Sierra Madre," Crook snapped, "but you lied."

The meeting did not progress as Geronimo would have liked. Bourke recorded that Geronimo "appeared nervous and agitated; perspiration, in great beads, rolled down his temples and over his hands; and he clutched from time to time at a buckskin thong which he held tightly in one hand."[27]

"Then how do you want me to talk to you[?]" Geronimo asked. "I have but one mouth. I can't talk with my ears."

"Your mouth talks too much."

"If you think I am not telling the truth, then I don't think you came down here in good faith."

"I came with the same faith as when I went down to the Sierra Madre. You told me the same story then as that you are telling me now. What evidence have I of your sincerity?"

"I was living at peace with my family on the reservation. Why were those stories started about me?"

"How do I know? . . . Who were all the Indians that these stories were started about[?]" When Geronimo ignored the question, Crook demanded: "Answer my question."

"They wanted to seize me and Mangus."

"Then why did [Naiche] and Chihuahua go out?"

"Because they were afraid the same thing would happen to them."

"What made them afraid?"

After further prompting, Geronimo said: "I told them . . . that I heard I was going to be seized and killed."

"But why did you send up some of your people to kill Lieut[enant] Davis and Chatto?"

"I did not tell them to do anything of the kind. [Had] I . . . said anything like that[,] these Indians would say so."

"That's just what they do say." Crook only saw one side to the incident; Geronimo's reputation did not allow him to consider any other interpretation. Crook said, "you reported that [Davis and Chatto] were killed and that's the reason so many went out with you."

Geronimo told Crook to ask others, that they would tell the truth. Crook replied that plenty had already told him what happened. "Whenever I wanted to talk with Lieut[enant] Davis," Geronimo said, "I spoke by day or by night. I never went to him in a hidden manner." Referring to Crook's Indian scouts, Geronimo continued, saying: "maybe some of these men may know about it. Perhaps you had better ask them."

"I have said all I have to say," Crook said. "You had better think it over tonight and let me know in the morning."

The threat could not have been more clear, and the meeting ended as it began—on unstable ground. Crook's unrelenting attack only fueled Geronimo's fears. Uncertainty fogged his mind as he returned to the safety of his camp. Knowing he could retreat into the high peaks to his rear must have offered some consolation.

That night Crook sent Kaytennae and Alchesay to infiltrate Geronimo's camp, where they found Geronimo and everyone else heavily armed and ready to shoot. An agitated excitement permeated the camp. No fools, Kaytennae and Alchesay did not dare talk about surrendering.[28]

The next day, Bourke, Kaytennae, Alchesay, and some of the others visited Geronimo's ranchería. While the Indians mixed with Geronimo and his brethren in an attempt to divide their loyalties, Bourke saw how well Geronimo had entrenched his "'rancher[í]a,' which was situated upon the apex of an extinct crater, the lava blocks being utilized as breastworks, while the deep seams in the contour of the hill were so many fosses [ditches], to be crossed only after rueful slaughter of assailants. A full brigade could not drive out that little garrison, provided its ammunition and repeating rifles held out."[29]

Geronimo took no chances with the White Eyes. Supposedly, he gave orders to "kill all they could, and scatter in the mountains"[30] at the first sign of treachery.

Photographer Fly and his assistant used this time to good advantage: he asked Geronimo and Naiche if they and their people would pose for his camera, and they agreed. The pictures that Fly took during the three days of the conference are marvelous. Geronimo posed standing and mounted. Heavily armed, he looked every bit the warlord he was. Although in his sixties, he was still an impressive specimen.

On the afternoon of March 27 the conference continued. Crook's Indian emissaries had bent the ears of Chihuahua the previous day, filling him with thoughts of distrust for Geronimo. Others wavered too, wanting peace at any cost.

Sensing the change in mood, Geronimo kept to himself, blackening his face with pounded galena. While the meeting convened under sycamores, he and another warrior sat under a mulberry.[31]

Chihuahua told Crook: "If you don't let me go back to the Reservation, I would like you to send my family with me wherever you send me." Naiche seconded Chihuahua, saying: "What Chihuahua says, I say. I surrender just the same as he did." Crook did not antagonize Chihuahua and Naiche as he did Geronimo, and the surrender happened easily.

Geronimo came forward. "Two or three words are enough," he said. "I have little to say. I surrender myself to you." He shook Crook's hand, then continued. "We are all comrades, all one family, all one band. What the others say, I say also. I give myself up to you. Do with me what you please. I surrender. Once I moved about like the wind. Now I surrender to you and that is all." He shook hands with Crook a second time. After saying, "My heart is yours and I hope yours will be mine," he shook Crook's hand a third time.

Alchesay spoke for the Chiricahuas. "They have all surrendered," he said. "I don't want you to have any bad feelings toward them." The surrender became history.

Godfrey Tribolet, who had a contract to supply beef to the U.S. military in the field, followed Crook to Cañon de los Embudos, selling officers and enlisted men alcohol from his wagon. That night he sold the Chiricahuas mescal, and Geronimo, Naiche, and a number of others got drunk. Naiche downed so much of the firewater that he could not stand the next morning.

At daylight on March 28, Chihuahua told Crook what had happened. He promised Crook, who was leaving for Fort Bowie immediately, that everyone would move toward the border with Maus and the Indian scouts that day as planned.

The war had ended. It should have stayed ended. But two things undermined Crook's success. One he could blame himself for: his hard-line attitude toward Geronimo. The other rested with the Chiricahuas: their love of, and weakness for, alcohol.

Maus, the Indian scouts, and the Chiricahuas began the journey toward the international boundary. No one seemed to count the prisoners to ensure that all were accounted for. The prize had gone AWOL, but not for long. Geronimo, with four warriors, waited for the column of prisoners at Cajon Bonito. He and his companions were "drunk as lords."[32] All five sat on two mules, while four or five other mules wandered about, with the grass and woods burning behind them. The blazing inferno, combined with an armed and most likely belligerent Geronimo, could not have made the Americans breathe easily. Geronimo never learned to control his addiction to alcohol, and undoubtedly it now agitated his agony of the past few days with his fears of the future.

Nothing came of the incident. Maus and the scouts, along with Geronimo and the Chiricahuas, continued their march toward the border. When the column reached San Bernardino Springs on March 29, it halted for the night. Although efforts were made to keep the Chiricahuas from getting more mescal, they failed. Under a drizzling rain, Tribolet again sold Geronimo and Naiche booze. As they got drunk a second time, he filled their fogged brains with stories that made them fearful of the future.

Geronimo had seen the changed Kaytennae. He did not want to be locked in a cage on Alcatraz Island. After most had gone to sleep, he, Naiche, and thirty-four of their people (twenty men including the two leaders, fourteen women, and two boys) slipped quietly into the darkness. Geronimo moved southward toward Casas Grandes in northwestern Chihuahua. There was no pursuit. Maus, with Chihuahua, Josanie, and eighty Chiricahuas, reached Fort Bowie on April 2.

Geronimo's escape swept across the Southwest with the speed and intensity of a prairie fire. Outrage and terror gripped the population. The press blamed Crook; and though Gatewood's opinion remains unknown, he may well have been pleased to be far removed from the maelstrom.

Crook had been fighting a war on two fronts: one against the Chiricahuas; the other against Miles and the U.S. Army establishment. He now knew that the outcome of both were a foregone conclusion. Crook was next in line, via seniority, to become a major general, with Miles directly below him, and Crook must have been aware that his advancement in rank was in jeopardy. Sheridan informed Crook that President Cleveland "cannot assent to the surrender of the hostiles on the terms of their imprisonment East for two years with the understanding of their return to the reservation."[33] When Sheridan accused his Indian scouts of being aware of Geronimo's plan to escape a day later, Crook immediately defended them. Knowing the rest of the Chiricahuas would scatter if they knew the truth of what was about to happen, Crook refused to inform the prisoners that their term of incarceration would now be indefinite. Not liking what he must have realized would soon happen, on April 1, Crook requested to be relieved from command.[34] Sheridan could not have agreed more: on April 2 he consented to Crook's request and removed him from command.

That same day, Crook recommended that the Chiricahuas recently returned to captivity be shipped away at once. On April 3, Sheridan and Secretary of War Lincoln agreed to ship them to Fort Marion, St. Augustine, Florida. Two days later, Sheridan informed Crook: "The present terms not having been agreed to here and Geronimo having broken every condition of the surrender, the Indians now in custody are to be held as prisoners and sent to Fort Marion without reference to previous communications and without in any way consulting their wishes in the matter."[35]

On April 11, Nelson Miles assumed command of the Department of Arizona at Fort Bowie. The aggressive Miles knew that he controlled the ultimate destination of the soon-to-be-available star of a major general, and he had no intention of ignoring Sheridan's wishes to go after Geronimo with the U.S. Army. However, he knew he had a very difficult assignment. The day he arrived at Bowie, he wrote his wife: "I can only make the best effort possible."[36]

Miles immediately planned his campaign, which would be completely different from Crook's. Whereas Crook had relied upon his Indian scouts, using his troops as auxiliary and border patrol, Miles dismissed the Indian scouts (except as auxiliary) and deployed somewhere between five thousand and six thousand U.S. troops. His plan was constant pursuit, "putting in fresh relays and finally wearing [Geronimo and Naiche] down."[37] He "organized the hostile field of operations into districts, each with its command of troops, with specified instructions to guard the water holes, to cover the entire ground by scouting parties, and give the hostiles no rest."[38] He intended for his troops "to capture or destroy any band of hostile Apache Indians found."[39]

Before Miles could put his offense into action, Geronimo struck first, entering Arizona on April 27. He and Naiche, with ten to twelve warriors, quickly moved up the Santa Cruz Valley. Supposedly they divided into groups of three or four. Geronimo, however, claimed his group contained six men and four women. The raiders hit as far north as Fort Apache, stealing stock and killing a few people.[40]

Georgia Gatewood, although living in New Mexico at this time, commented on the raid years later: "those Indians came up to Apache, & killed wom[e]n & children & stole stock, & scared the few Inf[antr]y out of their wits."[41] Georgia's opinions were as strong as her husband's: "Only useless men were there [at Apache]."

Geronimo spoke of the raid later: "We ranged in the mountains of New Mexico for some time, then thinking that perhaps the troops had left Mexico, we returned. On our return through Old Mexico we attacked every Mexican found, even if for no other reason than to kill."[42]

There is an inconsistency here: white testimony put the raid into Arizona; Geronimo placed his raid into New Mexico. Since the Chiricahuas had broken into small bands, it must be assumed that they raided both territories at the same time. The raid lasted twenty-three days and fourteen people died.

In 1890 Crook, referring to 1886, asked Naiche: "Why did you kill people after promising me you would not."[43] Naiche answered:

> Because we were afraid. It was war. Anybody who saw us would kill us, and we did the same thing. We had to if we wanted to live.

Early in May, a warrior deserted after his horse was shot from under him.

In forty-five days, he traveled 250 miles north to Fort Apache, where he surrendered on June 28.[44] The defecting Chiricahua has been named both Kayitah (*Kateah, Kieta, Kaytah, Ke-ta, Kayihtah, Keyehtah*), most likely a Nednhi or Chokonen, and Massai, a Chihenne.

Miles's war began in earnest, but with a minimal number of Indian scouts and no Chiricahuas.[45] A series of clashes took place during the next two months.

On May 3, 1886, Captain Thomas Lebo (Tenth U.S. Cavalry) fought with Geronimo's band twelve miles southwest of Santa Cruz, Sonora. Lebo lost two soldiers, one wounded and one dead. He sent three troops southward after the fleeing Indians.

The next day, the man who would become Miles's key player in the effort to subdue Geronimo, Captain Henry Lawton (Fourth U.S. Cavalry), received his orders[46] at Fort Huachuca, Arizona. He would lead a lightly equipped but hand-picked force to track down the Chiricahuas and destroy them. His command consisted of Troop B, Fourth U.S. Cavalry (twenty-five soldiers currently at Nogales), twenty Indian scouts (White Mountain Apaches), twenty men from Company D, Eighth U.S. Infantry, and two pack trains (Henry Daly was one of the packers). His officers included First Lieutenant Henry Johnson (Eighth U.S. Infantry), Second Lieutenant Leighton Finley (Tenth U.S. Cavalry), Second Lieutenant Harry Benson (Fourth U.S. Cavalry), and Assistant Surgeon Leonard Wood. Lawton's command moved out from Huachuca on May 5.

On May 12, Chiricahuas partially defeated Mexican troops, near Planchos, Mexico. Three days later, Captain Charles Hatfield (Fourth U.S. Cavalry), attacked the same band east of Santa Cruz, Sonora, capturing nearly all their equipment, supplies, and twenty horses. The Indians counterattacked him in a canyon while he was en route to Santa Cruz.

The next day, Lieutenant Robert Brown (Fourth U.S. Cavalry) chased and then engaged Chiricahuas near Buena Vista, Mexico, capturing several horses and some rifles and ammunition. At this point the Indians split into two groups: one fled to the west, while the other moved to the north. During the next month and a half, the military documented a "series of outrages, with fatiguing chases by troops."[47] On each occasion, the Chiricahuas avoided a decisive action against them until Mexican forces repulsed them forty miles southeast of Magdalena, Mexico, on June 21, "and recaptured a young Mexican girl."

The war dragged on, . . . and on. The engagements looked good on paper, but did little to end the conflict. To date, all Miles had to show for his massive force in the field was a lot of worn-out mules and horses and some captured supplies. Time had no bearing on the ultimate success of his strategy, and he had every confidence that he would eventually kill or capture Geronimo. However, this same sense of time endangered the elusive star he sought.

As previously stated, Crook was next in line to become one of five major generals, and Miles was second in line for the increase in rank. Most military promotions depended on seniority, and before a major generalcy became available again, one of the current holders of rank had to move up, retire, or die, which could happen in a month, a year, or ten years. Miles did not want to wait: he wanted to be the next major general, to beat the seniority rule and leapfrog over Crook. His ace happened to be Sheridan, whom, he knew, supported him over Crook. Still, Miles had to end the war to win Crook's promotion.

CHAPTER NINE

The Assignment

Far, far away, the distant war droned on. Gatewood could have been stationed in Alaska, for he certainly seemed to be an exile. Separated from his family and no longer a part of the hunt for Geronimo, he had plenty of time on his hands with little to do, and his current mundane assignment held little interest for him. During his waking moments he seemed to focus on the things with which he no longer had contact: Georgia and Geronimo.

The uneventful days passed slowly at Fort Wingate, and bored with loafing, Gatewood found himself lonely. When Georgia's letter of June 10 arrived, he fell further into the doldrums. She worried about him spending too much time with the ladies at Wingate, described her financial situation, which was not good, and then complained that he did not write.

On June 12, Gatewood wrote Georgia, saying that he had sent two prepaid telegrams while traveling to Wingate and two since his arrival, and could not understand why she did not receive them. The idea that he ignored her, and consorted with the ladies at Wingate, bothered him. "I have kept my promises as to dinner parties here," he wrote, adding, "it can be no pleasure to me to fly around knowing . . . of your forlorn condition."[1]

At the same time, he refused to become a recluse. "The ladies invite me to dinner, & there is no reason why I should not accept. Or if they give a hop . . . ain't it better that I should go than that I should sit around the stove?"

After defending himself, Gatewood expressed his true feelings: "My dear wife, I am so sorry that things turn out this way, but it is simply impossible for me to better it. The combination of circumstances as a whole render me far from happy." After telling Georgia he would send his pay as soon as he cashed his pay account, Gatewood returned to the matter that concerned him most: "My poor old woman, you have a right to complain, for you have had a hard time ever since you married me, & my dear, I am behaving myself, though appearances are against me."

Turning to his current status, Gatewood continued: "God knows how long I shall have to be in the field, . . . Luckily[,] I have no board bills here, but will have to provide some rations when I leave. That[,] with a little underclothing[,] will constitute my expenses." Gatewood was referring to a scout with Navajos that he anticipated making. The hold up to him entering the field immediately was arms; the government had not bothered to deliver weapons for the Navajos.

His physical condition was not the best. Surprisingly, it was not the rheumatism that ailed him—a rotten tooth did. His humor easily outshone the pain:

> This morning the Dr. wrestled with that tooth which has threatened for some time [to] create trouble. I mustered up courage to have it taken out, as it began to be sore & sensitive to touch. The Dr.[,] who[,] by the way[,] is a muscular man, braced himself & turned loose his muscle. That tooth would not budge. It had made up its mind to stay there, & the Dr. made up his mind that he'd stay there[,] too. Twice he had to stop to rest. Then[,] he pulled of[f] his coat, got the stewar[d] to hold on to my head, while I [hung] on to the chair. There was the Dr. on one side, the stewar[d], the chair, the tooth[,] & myself, . . . all in for a trial of strength. Just before my jaw gave way, the tooth surrendered & came out. . . . The Dr. said that he never had had such a tussle with a tooth. The side of my face feels as if it has been pounded with a sledge hammer, but the tooth won't cause any more trouble.

Returning to a concern, Gatewood informed Georgia that the baby carriage he ordered would arrive soon. Then he stated he did not want her to pay for it. After again commenting on her unhappiness, he closed with: "Good-bye & God bless you & the boy, kiss him for me."

As June moved quickly toward a close, Gatewood continued to remain grounded at Wingate. A number of officers, including Tupper and Chaffee, had been summoned to meet with Miles, and Gatewood supposed the meetings forewarned a general movement of troops. He also realized, perhaps with a tinge of sarcasm after his acquaintance with the Navajo, "that Gen[eral Miles] has changed his mind in regard to Apaches as scouts, and is going to enlist them again. This may mean the discharge of the bloody Navajo outfit of mine."[2]

Not having any idea what the future held in store for him, Gatewood surmised that the discharge of the Navajos and the enlistment of Apaches would end his active service with Indian scouts. "Probably that will give me a chance to get back home," he wrote Georgia, "for if I am ordered to command Apaches, I shall protest on the ground that they no longer have any liking for me, & the best interest of the service would require that I be not connected with them in any way."[3] Bay-chen-daysen mistakenly thought that the White Mountain Apaches held his refusal to allow them to massacre peaceful Chiricahuas against him, but nothing could have been further from the truth. He would be surprised years later when he returned to Fort Apache. Alchesay, Sanchez, and others came to see him. The Chiricahua incident was long forgotten, and the Indians were still his good friends.[4]

Again, Gatewood hinted at his future. "Imagine my going back to that outfit [commanding White Mountain scouts] after finally succeeding in getting away. However, it is best not to worry over it, for there may be nothing in it."[5] Rejoining the war effort was the last thing Gatewood wanted. "I am not spoiling for a fight," he wrote Georgia, "nor [am I hoping] for a long march down south at this time of year."

Before closing the letter, Gatewood reminisced about all their anniversaries he had missed, along with his children's birthdays. *Tough No. 2,* as Gatewood affectionately called his second son, had arrived on April 6.

"If only Ger[onimo] would come in & surrender," Gatewood wrote in the same letter, "so that a fellow could go home and stay there with no prospective absence hanging over his head, what happiness that would be."

Six days later, Gatewood wrote Georgia again. After asking her not to worry about finances any more than necessary, he indulged himself with his pride in his children:

> And I don't care for him, eh? Well, that's good. It would actually do me lots of good to see a finer baby. Humph! As I have told you already, he bids fair to eclipse Tough 1, & that's saying about as much as can be said of anybody's baby.[6]

Loneliness, combined with yearning, also crept into this letter. "What pleasure is it to retire & wake up alone?" Gatewood asked. "Or to sit in the office Col[onel] Crofton gives me—alone?"

The next day Gatewood wrote Georgia again, this time speaking of the far-off war. He had heard "that an Indian had come in from Geronimo, & others would follow. It is too good to be true, but it sets me off building castles in the air, how I shall return home, what a welcome I shall have, & so on. I do regret having to be away with no chance of watching the development of our babe, & I regretted in the case of the other one."[7]

By July 3, Congress appropriated money for distribution to the military. Gatewood was due 129 dollars, which would ease his monetary difficulties for the present.

One governmental problem ended, but another continued, for the weapons required for the Navajo scouts had still not arrived. No one knew where the arms were currently located. Supposedly, they were en route from San Francisco.

Perhaps due to the recent extraction of his tooth, Gatewood had lost some weight. As he was always needle-thin, weight loss did not bode well for him. This time, however, it did not affect him negatively. "My health is very good," he wrote Georgia, "but I've fallen off a little in flesh."[8]

Gatewood closed this letter with the comment: "There is no news from the Indians." The distance from the far-off war, combined with a lack of up-to-date news of the action, made the conflict appear almost surreal to Gatewood. The Geronimo war almost seemed to be happening in another place and another time. The change of command had not brought about an end to the conflict.

Twenty-three days after beginning the raid into the United States, Geronimo returned to Mexico. Moving through the Janos Plains, the old warrior hustled southward, passed Casas Grandes, and kept going until he came to a town the Chiricahuas called *Gosoda*. The Mexicans operated a thriving freighting business out of Gosoda. Geronimo and his warriors hid in the mountain pass where the wagons had to go through with their shipments.

Geronimo described his activity in the pass:

> whenever Mexican freighters passed we killed them, took what supplies we wanted, and destroyed the remainder. We were reckless of our lives, because we felt that every man's hand was against us. If we returned to the reservation we would be put in prison and killed; if we stayed in Mexico they would continue to send soldiers to fight us; so we gave no quarter to anyone and asked no favors.[9]

In 1909 Georgia Gatewood wrote of "the whole 6th & 4th Cav[alries], the 10th I think, the 12th Infantry and heaven knows who,"[10] saying of Miles's strategy: "That whole country [Arizona and New Mexico] swarmed with troops, guarding water holes, & mountain passes, wandering up & down on the hope of running into the Indians, month after month."

The massive military presence, not to mention the absence of Geronimo, did not ease the white population's fears. Panic reigned throughout the Southwest; terrified settlers demanded the end of the war and the execution of the Chiricahuas. Fearing that the Indians living peacefully on the reservation would be caught up in the war fervor, Miles began plotting the mass emigration of the Chiricahuas. He instructed Lieutenant Colonel James Wade, who commanded Fort Apache, to gain the confidence of the reservation Chokonen and Chihenne so that when the order came to remove them from the territory they could be rounded up easily.[11]

Wanting victory at any cost, Miles began considering other alternatives. At Fort Apache he summoned a Chiricahua named George Noche, who, although not a leader among his people, knew all of Geronimo's haunts. "I want you to organize the Chiricahua Apache Scouts to run down the renegades,"[12] Miles said.

Still uncertain about the loyalty and usefulness of Chiricahua scouts, Miles hunted for another course of action to follow. He sent for Noche a second time, and this time he asked the Chiricahua what he thought was the best way to catch Geronimo. Noche must have been doing some thinking about the question beforehand. "I have two men here for you, Ka[y]itah and Martine,"[13] he said, then explained that they had many relatives with Geronimo, making it "impossible for those bandits to kill [them]." Noche recommended that Kayitah and Martine (*Martin, Martinez, Marteen, Nahteen*) a Nednhi, tell Geronimo "that further resistance can end only in death."[14]

After being wounded in the Hatfield fight and returning to the reservation, Kayitah lived peacefully, caring for his plot of beans and corn. Martine, who as a boy served as Juh's orderly after being set free by the Mexican family that owned him, also lived on the reservation. The next morning, July 1, Noche took Kayitah and Martine to Miles. After Kayitah told Miles that the people with Geronimo were in a weakened state, the general told them his plan, to which they agreed. With the details worked out, Kayitah and Martine enlisted as scouts. Each was given a gun and a mule.[15] On July 9, Miles wrote a safe conduct pass for them.[16]

Miles did not place much hope in the mission, which still had a missing link. The general wanted a white man to lead the negotiation, but did not know who to select. He must have guessed, however, that the officer had to be a Crook man (none of his men knew the Chiricahuas in Mexico). As it turned out, the three men most fit for the duty did happen to be Crook men. Unfortunately, two were no longer available: Crawford was dead, and Britton Davis received his discharge papers on June 1, 1886.[17] That left the Crook outcast—Gatewood.

Uncertain whom to select, Miles turned to Wade, and Wade did not hesitate. He recommended Gatewood, who knew Geronimo, Naiche, and everyone in their band, as well as all their relatives on the reservation.[18] Wade declared that Gatewood's "long and varied experience with the [White Mountain and] Chiricahua . . . Apaches"[19] made him the logical choice.

Gatewood had recently traveled to Albuquerque, New Mexico, on official business. He completed the assignment by July 10 and was ordered back to

Fort Wingate.[20] At this point he had no idea what was in store for him. Just the day before, an official telegram ordered the commanding officer at Fort Bowie to outfit Gatewood with a "string of riding mules and any supplies needed and [to] render [him] any assistance required."[21] Miles wanted Gatewood to follow the enemy trail that Lieutenant James Parker then followed in Mexico.

Gatewood's ignorance did not last long. Before leaving Albuquerque and returning to Wingate, Gatewood was summoned before Miles on July 13. Miles instructed Gatewood "to accompany two friendly [I]ndians, [Kayitah] and Martin[e,] with a message to the hostiles demanding their surrender."[22] Gatewood then understood Miles to be "promising removal to Florida or to the [E]ast. The final disposition of them . . . to be left to the President of the United States."[23] Gatewood believed that Miles wanted "U.S. Troops [to] give [Geronimo] no rest, and when a favorable opportunity occurred,"[24] he would notify Geronimo "to surrender as prisoners of war."

Gatewood balked. He knew his body could not handle the sweltering heat of summer while campaigning in the wilds of Mexico. Also, he wanted nothing more to do with Indians—especially Apaches. Besides, the entire mission sounded like a fool's errand.

Miles probably concurred. Still, he wanted Gatewood and would not accept no as an answer. As an incentive, he offered to make the lieutenant his aide-de-camp.[25] Being an aide must have appealed to Gatewood because he accepted the assignment.

Both men knew Gatewood had little chance of completing the assignment as it currently stood, so Miles insisted that Gatewood take a twenty-five-man escort. The general did not want Gatewood to go near Geronimo with fewer men for fear that the lieutenant would be taken and held hostage. "Written authority was given me to call upon any officer commanding U.S. troops," Gatewood wrote, "except those of several small columns operating in Mexico, for whatever aid."[26] The *written authority* included Fort Bowie and any other post that Gatewood might pass.

Bay-chen-daysen did not record his feelings regarding his new assignment. However, he did not think much of the military escort. "Hell," Gatewood said, "I couldn't get anywhere near Geronimo with twenty-five soldiers."[27] During the following weeks he supposedly got several officers to state they did not have enough troops to spare twenty-five men.

Gatewood met interpreter George Wratten in Albuquerque. This was simply good luck on the lieutenant's part. Wratten, although only twenty-one years old at the time, had been around Apaches for the last seven years. Five feet ten inches tall, athletic, with hair that was described two years later as silvery gray, Wratten spoke all the Chiricahua dialects fluently. Gatewood immediately approached him to join him on the hunt for Geronimo, and Wratten, who currently had charge of twenty-five Indian scouts, accepted the offer.[28] Gatewood and Wratten left for Fort Bowie to prepare for their mission of peace.[29]

Miles played every angle; success was all that mattered to him. "There should be no cessation of hostilities against [Geronimo and Naiche]," Miles declared, "until they surrender or are destroyed."[30]

Lawton's force by now had dropped deep into Mexico. During July, Lawton reported that "the suffering was intense. The country was indescribably rough and the weather sweltering hot, with heavy rains every day or night."[31] The force Lawton had set out with only two short months before no longer resembled a war-ready punitive expedition. His cavalry mounts, no longer fit for service, were left at Oposura, and only the infantry and Brown's Indian scouts remained with Lawton.

As Lawton continued to drop lower and lower into Mexico, and Gatewood rode to Fort Bowie to outfit for the excursion into Mexico, the government decided that a delegation of Chiricahuas should travel to Washington, D.C., to discuss removal of their people from their native homeland. On July 13, Sheridan ordered Miles to send ten Chiricahua Apaches to the country's capital to meet with the secretary of the interior.[32]

The military position on the removal was split. Legalities prevented the removal of the Chiricahuas to Indian Territory (present-day Oklahoma), which rankled Miles, as he considered the territory the ideal location. His reasoning came from the earlier removal of the Chiricahuas who had surrendered to Crook in March and were now incarcerated at Fort Marion. Miles wrote: "They are a mountain race, accustomed to high altitudes and would in a short time, most likely, die, if kept in the lowlands of Florida."[33] As the movement to remove all of the Chiricahuas from Arizona continued to gain momentum, Sheridan held firm in his belief that the prisoners should remain at Fort Apache,[34] but it would not be long before he began to waver from this view.

Although Sheridan stated that he wanted the number of the Indians in the delegation sent east to be ten, Miles sent thirteen[35] with Captain Joseph Dorst (Fourth U.S. Cavalry), "to see the authorities and learn what the Government would do for them and what it would expect them to do, . . ."[36]

Chatto, a warrior who was both fierce and ambitious, served as one of the delegates—making his role during this tumultuous time unique. Before the surrender to Crook in 1883, he had been one of the firebrands of the tribe, but when he finally returned to the reservation following the surrender, he became a different man. This metamorphosis affected people differently, as the multitude of recorded comments attest.

Although Britton Davis claimed that "Chat[t]o was one of the finest men, red or white, I have ever known,"[37] the Bedonkohe, Nednhi, Chokonen, and Chihenne view differed considerably. "Chatto!" Kaywaykla exclaimed, "Turncoat and traitor!"[38] He was "heartily disliked and distrusted by our people." Daklugie believed that Chatto went to the army only after he realized that the recognition he craved among his own people would never happen.[39] Eugene Chihuahua, Chihuahua's son, called him a *coyote,* which was a term of contempt, saying: "Chat[t]o, the traitor and liar, never was a chief."[40]

According to the original plan, the Apache delegation would return to Fort Apache at the conclusion of their business in the land of the White Eyes.[41] This is what they were told and what they were led to believe.

While Miles cleared the path for the banishment of a people from their land, the war plodded on. On July 13, Lawton's rag-tag force found a Chiricahua camp on the Yaqui River, three hundred miles south of the border. The village was hemmed in by mountains. While Lawton and his soldiers dropped down the steep canyon walls and attacked from one side, Brown's Indian scouts flanked the village, which happened to be Geronimo's, and attacked from the river at 9:00 A.M. Lawton killed three Indians, captured all their property and supplies, along with nineteen horses, but the Chiricahuas escaped. With only fourteen able-bodied infantrymen left after the victory, morale plummeted.[42] After the attack, the soldiers vacated Geronimo's camp and returned to theirs, where they remained the rest of the day and all of the next day.

Again, victory looked good—on paper.

The never-ending hunt for a foe who refused to stand and fight continued, and Lawton began to agree with Crook that the Chiricahuas could not be captured in twenty years.

Britton Davis commented on Geronimo's loss: "Being deprived of their ponies and scant camp equipage meant little to the hostiles. Seven times in fifteen months this happened to them, and seven times within a week or ten days they reequipped themselves through raids on Mexican settlements or American ranches."[43] This may have been true the previous year, but now was no longer valid. Geronimo's band continued to shrink. Constantly on the run, with no safe zones to rest up and use as a base while resupplying, the Chiricahuas had almost been pushed to the limit of their endurance. They were shot-up, hungry, worn out. Some were tired of war, blaming Geronimo for all their woes. Cosel, who was a small boy in 1886, remembered hearing his father say:

> If we had only listened to Chatto instead of Geronimo. Geronimo is not a brave warrior. When we attack or are attacked, he is always far away. We should have remembered that he is not a chief among us. He is a medicine-man. He does not help us, but he always tries to save himself.[44]

Undoubtedly, the thought that armed forces from two countries hunted them from all directions played heavily upon their psyches.

Geronimo, Naiche, and their people scattered into the rough terrain, moving northward. Without food the situation had to look bleak. Fortunately, the soldier army did not press the attack, did not follow them. The next day Geronimo, Naiche, and the band continued to put as much distance as possible between themselves and the White Eyes. Warriors hung back, watching for pursuit. They saw Indian scouts hunting for their trail, but no soldiers.

On July 15, the White Eyes and Indian scouts moved northward along a rough trail between the cliffs and the Yaqui River, covering a scant five miles before halting to make camp.[45] By this time, Geronimo and the Chiricahuas were long gone.

CHAPTER TEN

Into Mexico

Gatewood and Wratten reached Fort Bowie on July 15.[1] At Bowie, Gatewood picked up Chiricahuas Kayitah and Martine. He also hired a packer named Frank Huston.[2]

Although the mission may have seemed suicidal, Wratten bragged about what Gatewood and the others might have felt: "No! We weren't *afraid*! . . . I could tell you of several dozen more blood-curdling incidents in our lives than the so-called capture of Geronimo."[3]

Fully outfitted, Gatewood was ready. "Having all that was necessary to our health & comfort," he wrote, "and everybody mounted on a *good* riding mule (do you know that all mules are not good riding mules?), we set out."[4] Considering the assignment—to demand Geronimo's surrender, while promising removal to Florida or to the East—his spirits appeared to be high.

Bay-chen-daysen rode out of Fort Bowie, on July 16, with a much smaller outfit than Miles envisioned. Colonel Eugene Beaumont (Fourth U.S. Cavalry), who commanded Bowie, told Gatewood that he could not supply the twenty-five-man escort, adding that he could get the twenty-five soldiers he needed at Cloverdale (on the Mexican border).[5] Martine, Kayitah, George Wratten, Frank Huston, and three pack mules represented Gatewood's entire entourage.

Keeping to the west of the Chiricahua Mountains, Gatewood and his party proceeded due south, and a three-day ride brought them to Cloverdale. Here, Gatewood found the infantry company, as promised. He also found one of his former West Point instructors in charge: Captain John F. Stretch commanded a company of Eighth U.S. Infantry. Stretch did not have much of a command; in fact, his paltry outfit would have been hard put to field an adequate escort. Gatewood must have inwardly smiled. Certainly he had some fun at his former teacher's expense. "A company of infantry," Gatewood wrote, "about ten broken-down cavalry horses, & a six-mule train— and you could have knocked the commanding officer down with a feather when I showed my order and demanded my escort."[6]

To commandeer twenty-five of Stretch's soldiers would have depleted the captain's command, and Gatewood did not want to do that. After eating with Stretch, Bay-chen-daysen left, as he had arrived, with his four (most likely five) companions. Eventually, Gatewood hired an old rancher, Tex Whaley, to act as courier. All indications point to the fact that Gatewood hired ol' Tex (at a salary of one hundred dollars per month) before entering Mexico.[7]

On July 19 Gatewood's small command crossed the line and entered Mexico. Hoping to find the trail that Lieutenant James Parker supposedly followed,[8] Gatewood traveled eastward in Sonora, Mexico, until he reached the Guadalupe Mountains that separated the Mexican states of Sonora and Chihuahua. He then rode south until he could find a pass through the range and enter Chihuahua.

The trip aggravated Bay-chen-daysen's old ailments. A blazing sun, accompanied by frequent downpours, along with the rugged terrain, played havoc with his health. He was not the only one to suffer, for the mules fared little better. Gatewood and his companions reached Carretas, Chihuahua, on July 21. "Upon arriving here the animals were in such a condition as to be unable to make the usual marches much longer,"[9] Gatewood reported.

As expected, he found Parker—who had received orders from Cloverdale via courier to wait for Gatewood.[10] Parker's command included a troop of cavalry (thirty men), along with infantry detachments (fifteen men) under Lieutenants W. P. Richardson (Eighth U.S. Infantry) and Robert Bullard (Tenth U.S. Infantry), fifteen Yaqui Indian scouts, and a pack train. Parker labeled the Yaquis worthless. Gatewood placed their total strength at somewhere between thirty and forty men, but it is apparent he did not count everyone.

As the momentum grew to remove the Chiricahuas from Arizona, Miles began to seriously plan for it.

Just the month before, in early June, Parker—the same Parker Gatewood had just found—had approached Miles at Fort Huachuca. Knowing of Miles's desire to rid the territory of the Chiricahuas, and most likely trying to get on the general's good side, Parker told Miles about the reservation Indians running to the quartermaster corral at Fort Apache whenever there was a raid. "I would suggest a false report of a raid be spread and when the Indians are in the corral," Parker said, "they be surrounded by the troops, disarmed, taken to the railroad and shipped east as prisoners of war."[11]

Miles may have been a career soldier whose uppermost goal seemed to be reaching the top of the military ladder, but he was not the total beast some writers would have us believe. "Why[,] that would be treachery," he replied to Parker. "I could never do that."

Nevertheless, Miles retreating from one means to an end did not imply he

intended to turn his back on the situation—not when he deemed it a necessary step in the dog-eat-dog fight to become the supreme military commander. He considered the reservation Indians a problem. There were 440
Chiricahuas living near Fort Apache who had never been disarmed and were
in good fighting condition. The general, certain the Indians' camps had been
a refuge for Geronimo, declared: "a more turbulent and dissipated body of
Indians I have never met."[12] He concluded that as the Chiricahuas' numbers
decreased, their animosity toward the whites increased.

As August neared, Miles decided to disarm the Chiricahuas. In a move
to destroy family ties as well as the peoples' culture, he also gave serious
thought to scattering their children throughout the industrial Indian schools.
Legal objections to the removal of the Apaches to Indian Territory made
Florida the logical choice. It did not matter to him that he thought the moun-
tain-living Apaches could not survive in Florida, for that was where he
intended to ship them if he could find no better place. Although Miles originally opposed shipping them there, he wanted them out of Arizona. At the
same time, he did raise valid opposition to the plan: mainly that banishment
for the reservation Indians "would necessitate a war of extermination
against"[13] the warring Chiricahuas for they would fight to the end knowing their fate would be worse.

The Indians remaining on the reservation did so by choice. They had given
their word to abandon the war path, and they kept it. They may have been
unhappy with their situation—who would not be?—but the bottom line is,
they lived in peace. What Miles and the U.S. government plotted for them
was, and forever will be, treachery at its blackest.

Even though Gatewood quickly reasoned that Parker could not spare the
twenty-five men Miles required, he showed the lieutenant Beaumont's order:
"The District Commander directs that you furnish Lieut[enant] Gatewood
with sufficient escort to enable him to perform the duties he is entrusted
with."[14]

Parker was aware of Gatewood's mission and knew Bay-chen-daysen
intended to track the trail he had been following. "But," Parker said, "the
trail is all a myth—I haven't seen any trail since three weeks ago when it was
washed out by the rains."[15]

Parker's comment startled Gatewood. The mustachioed former nantan
must have felt his assignment was doomed to failure: just six days out from
Bowie and only fifty miles into the Mexican interior, his health gone, his
mules worn out, and now no trail to follow. This bit of news must have
destroyed his last visage of strength. Gatewood thought for a moment, most

likely reflecting on the past year—a year that had seen him end his relationship with Crook, then the Apaches, and finally the war. He must have pondered the merit of continuing what now appeared to be another endless goose chase. "Well," Gatewood finally said, "if that is so I will go back and report there is no trail!"[16]

"Not at all," Parker replied. "If Gen[eral] Miles desires that you be put on a trail[,] I will find one and put you on it."

If, indeed, Gatewood had wavered from his task, he did no longer. If the possibility of failure haunted him, it was now gone—along with any thoughts of quitting. Gatewood determined that his best bet now was to find Lawton's command, operating somewhere in the Sierra Madres. Parker's entire command would now function as his escort.

There was still a problem. Gatewood was physically a worn-out wreck: his body had failed him, his joints ached, and he also may have suffered from dysentery at this time. Although he would downplay his health in a report to his superiors back in the United States, Gatewood knew he needed rest. Now. Bay-chen-daysen called the shots and put the mission on hold.

The part of Mexico he was in was not easy on those who invaded it. Temperatures climbed to 128 degrees in the shade, the skies could turn black on any given day, and a torrential rain might pelt the earth for hours turning the land into impenetrable muck. Britton Davis described conditions in northern Mexico in 1885: "we . . . marched over five hundred miles through a mountainous country in driving rains, much of the way in mud so deep that the mules sank above their fetlocks. Seldom were we able to ride."[17] Gatewood, whose body was no longer capable of standing up to nature's constant assaults, undoubtedly experienced similar conditions a year later. A day passed, then two; the third day came and went. Still, "the effects of old injuries revived by my ride to this place,"[18] as Gatewood put it, kept him bedridden.

During his convalescence, when Gatewood talked with Martine and Kayitah, their conversation turned to the Chiricahuas' compensation for the key roles they played. The Indians did not know what they would be paid, but anticipated pay regardless of the final outcome.[19]

The weather remained hot and muggy, raining every night, sometimes torrentially. The soaked ground attracted hordes of mosquitoes and sand flies. Finally, by the sixth day of his forced rest at Carretas, Gatewood decided he could travel. No sign of Geronimo had been found during this time and no reports arrived with even a hint of the old warrior's whereabouts.[20] Lawton's location was also unknown. Gatewood did not have a set plan. Finding Geronimo was a long shot, but that was his goal. He decided to move into Sonora, with his ultimate destination Nacori, or wherever he might find Indian sign. Gatewood decided that if he could not find Geronimo's trail, he could eventually find Lawton somewhere near Oposura, Sonora. With luck, Lawton would have left a trail to follow.

Huachinera, on the Bavispe River, became Gatewood's first destination. The Bavispe, shaped almost like an inverted horseshoe, flows northward from just south of Huachinera until it circles the northern end of the Teres Mountains and then flows southward until it feeds the Yaqui River, about one hundred miles south of the horseshoe. Gatewood set out with Parker's command acting as escort on July 27. Moving westward, he rode over the divide and into Sonora, then dropped down into a valley that was cut off from the rest of Mexico by high mountains—the valley of the Bavispe.[21]

Although Gatewood and the U.S. troops with him entered Mexico legally, they avoided contact with Mexican troops, for Gatewood was very aware that his mission of peace would not please the Mexicans and took care to conceal it.[22] His line of march consisted of: "The scouts with six infantry- men . . . in [the] advance, followed at 200 yards by the cavalry, commanded by L[ieutenan]t Richardson; the pack train in rear of the cavalry, never more than a quarter of a mile distant, with a rear guard of infantry following the pack train."[23]

By the time Gatewood reached the pueblo of Bavispe, on the Bavispe River, Martine and Kayitah had still not found anything. Gatewood's luck did not improve in the town; no one had any idea where the Indians were. The search, however, continued with Gatewood changing directions. Instead of moving into the Teres Mountains, he now moved southward, skirting the river as the massive Sierra Madres loomed forbiddingly just to the east. Mar- tine and Kayitah looked in vain for sign. It was almost as if Geronimo had vanished from the face of Mother Earth.

Lawton summed up everyone's situation: "the suffering was intense. The country was indescribably rough and the weather sweltering hot, with heavy rains every day or night."[24] The terrain and weather represented only part of the tribulation. "In our bivouacs we suffered much from ants and various insects that crawled under our bedclothes," Parker wrote. "Scorpions, taran- tulas and centipedes abounded. Several men and animals were badly bitten."[25]

Gatewood and his escort continued to move southward, passing Bacerac before finally reaching Huachinera.[26] By this time another malady had struck the column, and it worsened at each pueblo. "Mescal, a fiery stuff in taste like gin," Parker wrote, "could be had cheaply, to[o] cheaply, in fact."[27] Parker and his subordinates had trouble controlling their men, who came close to insubordination as they grabbed every opportunity to cut loose. The alcohol only added to the disciplinary problems.

The men discovered that wherever they could buy the cheap drink, they could also obtain sex, sometimes for free. Parker downplayed the situation: "the immorality of the women, who made up for their lack of beauty by their generosity, caused disorders at times among the men." Drunkenness became the order of the day at the pueblos as disobedient soldiers came just short of assaulting the towns, drinking at will and taking any available women. One corporal was broken in rank, while a number of men *walked the pelican* as punishment—leading their horses at the rear of the column.

Still there was no sign of Geronimo.

Gatewood left Huachinera, and after passing the Bavispe's source he changed direction once again. The lieutenant now headed south-southwest toward Bacadéhuachi on the east side of the Bavispe, about thirty miles north of the Yaqui River, and after a march of some thirty-two miles, Gatewood reached his destination on July 31.

"With fresh horses, taken from every ranch they passed," Gatewood claimed, "incredible distances were covered by the hostiles, and it would have required a long time to have overtaken them by following the trail."[28] That is, if he had a trail to follow. He did not. Gatewood still had seen no sign whatsoever of Geronimo, and had no idea if the Indians were anywhere near his current location.

By this time Gatewood had word that Lawton was not too far to the southeast. Knowing Lawton was Miles's primary search-and-destroy column in the field, he surmised that Lawton's "system of gathering information was almost perfect,"[29] and would save valuable time. Undoubtedly, he hoped Lawton followed a trail, no matter how faint. At the same time, he had to be aware that, since his and Lawton's missions were complete opposites, they would not make good comrades. Gatewood must have also been painfully aware that no one had found a solitary Apache footprint. Also, he may not have been happy with Parker's handling of his men. The lieutenant, whose health again began to deteriorate, wrote Lawton from the camp at Bacadéhuachi:

> I presume you are informed of the object of the trip. It is simply to try to open communication with the hostiles, with a view to the sur-render of at least a part of them. If it does not interfere with your plans, will you please wait till I can catch up with you? It is part of the plan of General Miles that I should be ahead of any command.[30]

The next day, Gatewood traveled to Nacori.

❖❖❖

Geronimo and Naiche's situation was not any better than that of the White Eyes who chased them. Forced constantly to keep on the run, no one had time to rest or to regain strength. Although they had once again escaped after the White Eyes had hit their camp on July 22, the constant stress they were under began to take its toll. As Miles put it: "[The attack] reduced the numbers and strength of the Indians and [has] given them a feeling of insecurity, even in the remote and almost inaccessible mountains of Old Mexico."[31]

Hungry, shot-up, and ragged, the hunted had to remain the hunter. There was precious little time to live off the land, and Geronimo needed everything—food, clothing, livestock, bullets. To get them, he had to continue raiding rancherías, and each strike brought the end nearer, as each strike showed the Mexicans and the Americans where he had been.

President Cleveland had wearied of the entire Apache situation in the Southwest. He received a constant flow of letters from outraged citizens who all asked the same question: "Why[,] with over six thousand soldiers here in the Territory, [cannot] seventy or eighty vagabonds . . . be captured[?]"[32] Strong words; words that Cleveland did not relish reading.

The pressure the president felt, he passed down to Sheridan. Sheridan, who had at first wanted the Chiricahuas to remain in Arizona, now decided to do whatever was necessary to ensure that his own position remained secure. On July 31 he wired Miles that Cleveland wanted his opinion regarding forcibly arresting all reservation Chiricahuas and sending them to Fort Marion, Florida.[33]

Gatewood reached Nacori on August 1, then moved southeast toward the Aros River, camping about fifteen miles north of it. Packer Henry Daly, appeared, heading northward after delivering supplies to Lawton. He told Parker that Lawton camped on a stream called Rio Viejo, and after giving directions he continued his journey north to Fort Huachuca.

Daly had an interesting story to tell that he heard from Lieutenant Abiel Smith (Fourth U.S. Cavalry), who had just reported to Lawton. Smith had told Daly that Miles considered court-martialling Lawton in two weeks for drunkenness. Gatewood must have been present at the meeting between Daly and Parker, but Daly—who had packed for Gatewood in the past—claimed he never recognized the lieutenant. If this is true, we can only assume that the rigors of the march into Mexico had so wasted Gatewood that he was little more than a shadow of his former self.[34]

Gatewood's approach did not mean the end of Lawton's offensive, for a message informed Lawton that more reinforcements were on the way. The same message told Lawton that Gatewood would soon arrive at his camp. More importantly it stated: "this need not delay your operations against them."[35]

Gatewood and Parker continued onward, reaching Lawton's camp on the Aros River on August 3. Parker claimed they had marched 200 miles, while Gatewood put the mileage at over 150. "Upon arrival here," Gatewood reported, "the animals [are] in such a condition as to be unable to make the usual marches much longer."[36] Gatewood wrote:

> It was extremely hot, the thermometer registering 117 in the shade, not a breath of air stirring, the river barely fordable, the water of it muddy & almost hot, too warm to drink or even bathe in. The heavy rains in the m[oun]t[ain]s had swollen it so that it was almost out of its banks. To cool the water so as to render it fit to drink, we filled canteens, soaked the heavy woolen covering & hung them in the shade.[37]

Lawton had a surprise for Gatewood. Even though his scouts had hit Geronimo's camp as recently as July 22, he had no idea where the Chiricahuas were. He claimed to "have heard nothing of the hostiles since the 21st of July."[38] An interesting comment, to say the least. Gatewood reported: "There is no information whatever as to the whereabouts of the hostiles, nor are [Martine and Kayitah] able to form any reasonable judgment as to their hiding place."[39]

Parker decided he needed more supplies. This decision did not please his two subordinates, Richardson and Bullard, as they wanted to be in at the end and figured that Gatewood would be the only person to bring it about.[40]

Disappointed as he most likely was over the lack of information, Gatewood did not give up in his desire to remain with Lawton. While Parker prepared to march northward, Gatewood wasted no time. On August 6, he asked Lawton to accompany him, "subject to your orders, until circumstances may favor carrying out the instructions of the Commander of the Department of Arizona."[41]

This did not please Lawton, who said: "I get my orders from President Cleveland direct. I am ordered to hunt Geronimo down and kill him. I can not treat with him."[42] Their talk continued; Gatewood insisted on remaining until the captain relented. "But," Lawton said, "if I find Geronimo I will attack him—I refuse to have anything to do with this plan to treat with him." He told Gatewood that he could treat with him "on his own hook."

Gatewood, now knowing there was no trail, apparently did not relish his

future prospects, and there is good reason to believe that he silently questioned his own mortality. Wood observed Gatewood and Lawton's meeting:

> Gatewood stated that he has no faith in this plan and is disgusted
> with it. Wants to go home. He is not in especially good health. Is suf-
> fering from an old inflammation of the bladder which renders riding
> difficult.[43]

Gatewood did not report his pessimism. Instead, he documented Lawton's
acquiescence differently. "I put myself under Lawton's orders, with the
understanding, however, that whenever we approached the hostiles & circumstances permitted, I should be allowed to execute my mission."[44] At best,
an uneasy partnership began.

Near Ures, approximately 150 miles due west of the Gatewood/Lawton
camp, Geronimo and his warriors attacked a large Mexican pack train that
carried supplies to miners. Geronimo killed a number of the Mexicans, stole
the mules, and carried off canned goods, flour, and other supplies. Afterward
Geronimo moved northward, attacking Mexicans as he found them.[45]

Lawton sent white scouts Billy Long and W. M. Edwaddy (*Edwardy*) out
to gather information, with Wood and twenty-five Indian scouts accompanying them. When Long and Edwaddy turned to the southwest, Wood continued northward. Martine and Kayitah, who were now under Lawton's
command, also went out to try and find the Chiricahuas' trail.

While Gatewood and Lawton waited for news, the rains continued to
cause problems. The Aros River neared flood stage and rafts had to be used
to cross it.

Martine and Kayitah returned within a couple of days. The rains had
made it impossible to find a trail over twelve hours old. After speaking with
them, Gatewood reported: "There is no information whatever as to the hostiles, nor are the two Indians able to form any reasonable judgment as to
their hiding place. It may require some time to find them."[46] Wood also
returned, having not accomplished anything.

Deep in the Sierra Madre, Gatewood was ill, with no chance of completing his mission in the near future. He also saw the writing on the wall: a long,
hard campaign was one thing, but dealing with men who did not want him
around was an entirely different matter. Gatewood's situation boiled down
to Lawton and the Fourth Cavalry wanting all the credit for the capture of
Geronimo and the hell with anyone who might overshadow their glory.[47]

Gatewood knew this and wanted out. He approached Wood and told him "that he want[ed] to go back to Bowie."[48] Wood understood Gatewood to say that he had "no faith in his work." Gatewood then got to the point: he wanted Wood to write him up on sick report. Wood refused, stating, "I do not think his case warrants it." Historian Jack C. Lane found an inconsistency in Wood's logic with regard to Gatewood's health:

> Yet earlier Wood concluded that Gatewood, bothered by an inflamed bladder, found riding difficult. One has the impression that Wood would have sent back any other officer in Gatewood's condition. But the sickly Lieutenant was their last hope, and nothing short of total disability would have led Wood to give him a medical relief from duty.[49]

Long and Edwaddy returned on August 8, and relayed reports of depredations 150 miles to the west, near Ures. Lawton did not bother to give chase. "This point [Geronimo's estimated location] was so far distant," Lawton reported, "that I could not reach it in time to get even a trail fresh enough to follow."[50] Another report placed an attack on a Mexican pack train one day's journey north of the Aros River. Ignoring this report, Long and Edwaddy's report, and the information Martine and Kayitah gave Gatewood the day before, Lawton reported that Martine and Kayitah "say the hostiles are *probably* southwest of us about six days march."[51] Lawton did not know which way to go. Seemingly confused, he then rafted his command across the Aros, marched northward to a canyon, and camped at a former bivouac, where that night it poured.

The next day everyone remained in camp. The heat was unbearable. Blowflies were everywhere: in the men's blankets; several animals suffered from the constant eating of their flesh by the pests. Wood wrote: "Bacon and flour in very bad condition and more fat in our clothing and blankets than in the bacon itself, which is so thin that it is nothing but hide and hair. The men are very thin, and about worn out."[52] That day Lawton sent Edwaddy and an unnamed courier out to Sahuaripa and Ures to learn the details of Geronimo's depredations. Torrential rains pounded the camp that night.

On August 10, Lawton did an about-face and marched south back to the Aros River. The next day was again spent in camp as Lawton waited for news from the south. The days passed slowly, not much progress was made, and when the command moved at all the mileage was quite low. On August 12, the command crossed the Aros again and marched up Nacori Creek. Distance traveled: five miles. That day Lawton suffered from what appeared to be ptomaine poisoning after eating Armour's corned beef. He was too weak to move the next day and the command waited while the captain struggled to regain his strength. On August 13 Wood wrote in his journal: "Weather frightfully hot, usual rains at night. A piece of fresh meat hung up for a couple of hours was simply filled with maggots from blow flies."[53]

The next day, the command marched up Nacori Creek and passed through Nacori. Turning almost due west, they marched another ten miles before stopping for the night. On August 15, the line of march continued toward the western leg of the Bavispe River. When the weary column reached Bacadéhuachi, Lawton halted for a couple of hours to buy supplies.

A number of the Indian scouts, including Martine and Kayitah, used the stopover as a chance to have a drink. One drink led to another, and soon they were all drunk, proposing to kill "some Mexicans. . . . Gatewood's two Indians were exceedingly drunk and dangerous."[54] With drunken scouts firing their weapons in all directions, sober compatriots waited for an opportune moment, and then belted the drunks with the butts of their rifles—eventually silencing the problem.

After regaining control, Lawton marched northward another fifteen miles. In bivouac that night he heard disturbing news that Miles considered replacing him. He did not want to lose his command and immediately addressed the problem.[55]

The march continued northward on August 16, across rolling country. Grass, oak trees, and plenty of water replaced the rugged terrain that had punished Gatewood and everyone else day after bone-weary day. But it did not last: the terrain quickly reverted to the norm southeast of Opoto, and a blazing sun once again baked the land, which was devoid of both water and vegetation.

Just when it was almost as if the mystic had prayed his people into departing from the face of the earth, Geronimo surfaced. On August 17, he was seen fifteen miles south of Fronteras on the main road to Nacosari. The old warrior made a *paraje,* an overnight camp, at the Quichula Ranchero.[56]

On August 18, unaware of Geronimo's reappearance, Lawton's column marched northeast from Opoto into a timber-filled canyon that had running water. Several miles into the canyon, it opened onto a rough trail that led to Nacosari. Plodding along on his mule, Gatewood must have wondered how long his tortured body would hold up.

That night a message arrived at the bivouac that would end the hesitant, endless marches to meaningless destinations.[57] Suddenly the old warrior's mystique beckoned. Gatewood's day of reckoning was not far off.

CHAPTER ELEVEN

Uncertain Trail to Destiny

Geronimo had been in many tight spots over the years. He had seen many die around him: all ages and races; loved ones and hated ones. Usually he emerged from the violence unscathed. His power had been strong, but he knew it could not last forever. Or, if it did, he would soon reach the day when he would have to carry on the fight alone, . . . for all his people would be dead.

Young or old, it made no difference. His family, and those of Naiche, were hungry and worn down. They needed food and rest—and maybe a good drunk to wash away the hardships of the last two moons. The ravages of war were plainly visible on everyone, even on Geronimo. His arm had been injured in a recent raid and he carried it bandaged in a sling.[1] Although he and Naiche had been fairly successful in keeping their people hidden from the pursuing armies, sooner or later they would be cornered. They would lose more food and supplies, and more people would die. The constant stealth, combined with long, hard marches—sometimes made at night—had taken its toll. Stress was evident everywhere. Geronimo needed to find a safe place to hide—if only temporarily.

Geronimo and Naiche talked over their situation with the others, and though they trusted the Mexicans less than the Americans, they decided to open negotiations with the Mexicans. They did not expect the talks to result in a peace; in fact, they viewed the talks as little more than a ruse that would allow them to secure their immediate needs—food, drink, and rest.

The small band moved northward up the western slope of the Sierra Madre Occidental, skirting mammoth canyons called *barrancas* that defied passage. They had moved past Campas and Nacosari, and into the Teres Mountains; and near Fronteras, a Sonoran pueblo thirty miles south of the American border, Geronimo sent two women, Lozen and Dahteste, to open negotiations with the Mexicans.[2]

Lawton's marches northward continued. The command came upon an old mine and halted. Here, Lawton and Gatewood, along with Martine and Kay-itah, spoke with some Mexicans who packed burros with acorns. The Mexicans said they knew where Geronimo could be found.[3] Near Fronteras, some seventy-five miles northwest of their present location, he was supposedly negotiating with the Mexicans.[4] This was the best information Gatewood had heard.

That afternoon, after making camp, Gatewood and Lawton agreed that Gatewood would leave that night and make a forced march to Fronteras. Gatewood packed for the trip; however, Wood recorded, "He was far from well."[5] Perhaps hoping his health would miraculously improve, Gatewood stalled his departure. Cloud bursts drenched the higher elevations during the day.

As minutes and then hours ticked by, Lawton became angry at Gatewood's inactivity. He considered arresting the lieutenant and replacing him with someone else; a totally absurd idea since everyone knew Gatewood was the only white man who had half a chance of getting close enough to Geronimo to talk to him.

Finally, Bay-chen-daysen was able to put his health problems aside and garner the strength required to accomplish his goal. At 2:00 A.M., on August 19, Gatewood and his party set out on mules.[6] Six of Lawton's men escorted him, along with a few packers (including Huston), Kayitah, Martine, and Wratten. Gatewood and his party rode and walked fifty-five miles. Worn out, they arrived at Cuchupa, a short distance from Fronteras, late that night.

Whether it was a power to foretell the future or just plain common sense based on the past, Geronimo had a clear picture of what he could expect from the *jefe político* of Fronteras. Still favoring his wounded arm, he waited just twelve miles from the pueblo. The women had to get what they actually had been sent to get—coffee, beans, and flour.

Lozen and Dahteste entered the pueblo of Fronteras somewhere around August 13 and met with Jesus Aguirre, the *prefect of Arispe,*[7] who happened to be at the pueblo. They told him that Geronimo was tired of war and wanted to talk about surrendering. The prefect told the women he did not have the power to set up the peace, but that he would look into it. The meeting ended.

Lozen and Dahteste waited. Days passed, and finally, on August 20, the prefect told the women that Geronimo should visit the pueblo to hear his answer. Before leaving the pueblo, the women wandered about buying supplies—the main objective of their mission.[8]

On the morning of August 20, Gatewood met with Forsyth (Troops D and E, Fourth U.S. Cavalry, four officers, one hundred men, and a pack train), who also camped at Cuchupa. A Mexican volunteer force of forty men was also present. The buzz around the pueblo was that Geronimo camped nearby. The old warrior supposedly wanted to form an alliance with the Mexicans against the Americans. Gatewood sent a messenger back to Lawton, informing him of the news.

That same August 20, Colonel Wade called for an assembly of the four hundred plus Chihenne, Chokonen, and Bedonkohe Apaches still at Fort Apache. When the Indians gathered, they were surrounded, searched for weapons, and made prisoners. Although Gatewood was not yet aware of this event, it would soon play a key role in his negotiations with Geronimo.

Bay-chen-daysen pushed on the remaining fifteen miles to Fronteras, where he presented himself to the prefect and stated his purpose. When Gatewood said that he had heard that the Chiricahua women were in the pueblo and he wanted to meet with them, he was told to keep away from the women. Surprisingly, he found the Mexican officials almost hostile toward him.[9]

While Lozen and Dahteste shopped for supplies in a *tienda* in Fronteras, Lieutenant Wilbur Wilder (Fourth U.S. Cavalry), who, with two troops happened to be in the pueblo, entered the store. Lozen and Dahteste noticed the white officer looking at them. When the lieutenant approached them, they ran but could not get away. Caught, they told Wilder:

> The entire party are pretty well broken down; Geronimo is in bad health, nearly blind and badly wounded in [his] right arm, and is nearly helpless. Entire band [has been] so harassed by U.S. forces that they see it is only a question of time [un]til they are exterminated unless they make terms.[10]

Playing both sides against the middle, the women offered to take Wilder and one interpreter to Geronimo's camp to talk of peace, but Wilder balked at the idea. He told the women to go back to their camp and get Geronimo's word of a safe conduct for himself and two other men. Lozen said they would do this and Wilder released them.

Instead of leaving the pueblo immediately, the women hung around and proceeded to have a drink of mescal. And then another. Soon they were rip-roaring drunk. The Mexicans left the women alone—allowing them to do whatever they pleased.

Around midnight, Lieutenant David McDonald (Fourth U.S. Cavalry), came across the women and wanted to arrest them, but the prefect, who had been keeping a close watch on the women, refused to allow the American to hinder them. Soon after this, two of Geronimo's warriors slipped into the pueblo and hustled the women and three ponies laden with food and mescal out of town. Again, the prefect saw to it that the Indians were not harassed.

After his interview with the prefect, Gatewood led his small command out of Fronteras. Three miles below the pueblo, he found Wilder's camp. Forsyth and his command were also present.

That night the prefect, made a point of visiting the American camp. In separate talks with Forsyth and Gatewood, he stated his intentions; intentions that varied with each officer. First, the prefect told Forsyth and Wilder to hide their troops as Geronimo would not appear with Americans present. When Wilder asked to attend the peace council, the prefect said no, he wanted to handle the terms himself. The Mexican official stated he wanted the American troops gone by morning.[11] Gatewood's meeting produced a completely different understanding. The prefect informed Bay-chen-daysen he hoped to get the Apaches drunk and then massacre them with two hundred Mexican soldiers who had assembled in Fronteras during the previous night. When he told Gatewood he wanted him to leave, the lieutenant refused, citing the treaty stipulations that gave him the right to remain. Realizing he could not get rid of Gatewood, the prefect "insisted that the Americans . . . not move in the direction the squaws had taken, because they would interfere with his well laid plans."[12]

The long night of negotiating and waiting finally ended.

Gatewood did not bother to send a messenger to Lawton on the twenty-first. Instead, he hung around camp, perhaps again tending to his health. But he did send Martine and Kayitah out to locate Geronimo's camp.[13]

Lozen and Dahteste and the two warriors did not head for Geronimo's camp that morning of August 21, for they knew it was deserted. Instead, they led their supply-laden ponies east to the Bavispe River before turning north, going farther into the Teres Mountains.

Geronimo and his people had moved during their absence. Instead of proceeding toward Fronteras and the proposed powwow, Geronimo led the band away from the pueblo—as planned. His intuition had served him well over the years, and it did not abandon him now. Figuring the Mexicans intended to kill him and his people, he put a safe distance between the Mexicans and himself.

Late that day, the two women and the two warriors reached the huge horseshoe bend of the Bavispe. Leaving the river, which flowed along the base of steep mountains, they scaled the cliffs. At the summit of a flat-topped monolith, they found Geronimo's bastion high above the river. The Apaches called the long peak they now held "Mountain Tall."

Lozen and Dahteste had succeeded. They had bought some time, but more importantly they had secured the much-needed supplies. Geronimo and his people settled down to feast on the food and mescal.[14]

Martine and Kayitah returned to Gatewood's camp late on August 21. They had found Geronimo's camp, but it was deserted. The scouts reported that the old warrior had struck out east, away from Fronteras.[15]

On August 21, Lawton heard a report that Gatewood had made no effort to meet with Geronimo. The next day, he, Wood, and Lieutenant Thomas Clay (Tenth U.S. Infantry) rode to Fronteras to find out first hand what was happening.

Just before reaching Fronteras, they met Wratten. The interpreter confirmed that Gatewood had indeed remained in camp. Lawton became livid and sent a messenger to tell Gatewood to report to him immediately. Lawton and his companions then entered Fronteras, where they found the pueblo swirling with action as Mexican soldiers hustled to hide themselves in strategic locations in the town, anticipating Geronimo's appearance.

The prefect met Lawton and invited him and the others to have a drink with him in a cantina, and Lawton readily accepted. Unfortunately he could not hold his liquor, got drunk, and began abusing Mexican soldiers. Fearing an international incident, Wood and Clay quickly hauled their inebriated commander into a back room to let him sleep off his stupor.

Gatewood appeared and asked to see Lawton. Wood did not want any American officers to see the captain in his present condition. He stepped up to Gatewood:

I assumed authority to tell [Gatewood] that Lawton was busy and [had] directed me to give him orders to take his Indians and immediately go out on the trail, and informed him that Lawton was extremely annoyed at his delay and the time which had been lost.[16]

After Gatewood left, Wood and Clay returned to Lawton's room. Wanting to return to their camp, they awoke Lawton. Still drunk, he leaped out of bed, grabbed a coffee cup, and threatened Clay with it. Clay was not about to take the abuse and drew his revolver. Lawton immediately placed his subordinate under arrest. Stepping between the two men, Wood prevented a bad situation from getting worse. Still, it was almost midnight before he and Clay got the captain safely back to camp. Here, Wood talked Lawton into dropping the charges against Clay.

Gatewood returned to the American camp just outside Fronteras. He knew what he intended to do and exactly how he would go about doing it.

Bay-chen-daysen's pidgin English-Spanish-Apache usually served him well enough. Besides, he had Wratten, probably the most fluent white man with the Apache language in the entire Southwest. Nevertheless, he decided to take no chances and picked up two other interpreters: Tom Horn and Jesus María Yestes. Horn, the former packer, served as chief of scouts with Lieutenant Robert Brown, who had replaced Leighton Finley as commander of Lawton's Indian scouts. Yestes lived in Fronteras, and had recently been seen with Geronimo. Horn would translate from English to Spanish and back, while Yestes would translate from Spanish to Apache and back.[17] Knowing how risky the next few days would be, Gatewood obtained between six and eight soldiers from Wilder.

As his command prepared to move out, Gatewood made a point to meet with the prefect, assuring the Mexican official that he intended to rejoin Lawton's command and had no intention of continuing his search for Geronimo. By the time Gatewood returned to his newly formed outfit, it was nearly dark. The timing could not have been better for his purposes. While Clay, Wilder, and the other officers frantically tried to control the free flow of mescal among their troops, Bay-chen-daysen led his men out of the bivouac and headed south. The march was nothing more than a ploy to convince whoever watched his movements of the truthfulness of his stated purpose to the prefect.

After traveling six miles, darkness sufficiently concealed his movements. Figuring that any Mexicans who trailed him had decided that he was heading toward where he had said he would go, Gatewood changed directions. Bay-chen-daysen ducked into an arroyo, then turned eastward into the mountains. Shortly after midnight, he changed his direction once again, heading north and marching in the general direction of Fronteras. He sent out Martine and Kayitah to pick up the trail the Apache women had made when they returned to Geronimo.

On August 23, Martine and Kayitah led Gatewood to Geronimo's abandoned camp at the top of a mountain not far from Fronteras. As it was early morning, Gatewood called a halt to give his men time for a much-needed rest. Later the same morning he sent a messenger back to Lawton with a note outlining his current situation and plans. He then resumed the hunt. With Martine and Kayitah leading the way, Gatewood's command moved down the mountain toward the Bavispe River, where the scouts found the trail of the two women and two men. Gatewood knew the four Chiricahuas would head for a set meeting point and decided to follow them.

When the small force reached the Bavispe, Gatewood halted his command while his scouts studied the sign. Martine and Kayitah told Gatewood that Geronimo headed north. More importantly, they informed Bay-chen-daysen that they were very close to the Chiricahuas, much closer than they anticipated.[18]

Geronimo's camp was safe. Sentinels commanded a good view of the surrounding terrain, watching the flow of the river curving far below while the rest of the people devoured the supplies. For the first time in many days, everyone ate until they were satisfied. Everyone drank and passed the mescal until it was gone, and most got drunk.[19]

Although Gatewood had not moved quickly before, he now marched very slowly as caution became essential. Every bend of the river offered high vantage points that could be used for an ambush. A flour sack served as a white flag. Carried at the point of Gatewood's command, it fluttered from a pole cut from the heart of a century plant.

Gatewood commented dryly on his courage: "as we approached dangerous looking places, Artemus Wards's magnanimity in sacrificing his relations in the war was nothing to my desire to give Ka[yitah] & Martine a chance to reap glory several hundred yards ahead."[20]

When Gatewood finally called a halt on August 23, it was almost dark. Everyone had been in the saddle close to twenty-four hours. His camp, next to the Bavispe, was about fifteen miles east of Fronteras. Knowing that the quarry had to be close, Gatewood ordered a cold camp. That night everyone ate cracked (or pounded) corn that was thickened into a mush with cane molasses.[21]

Early on the morning of August 24, Lawton sent Brown and thirty Indian scouts out to find Gatewood's trail, and if Gatewood needed help they were to get within supporting distance. Brown headed east, and a short while later Lawton led the rest of his command out, following Brown. Although Lawton had retained three scouts, they did not know the area and quickly lost Brown's trail, forcing Lawton and his command to haphazardly plod on in the general direction of the Bavispe.[22]

That morning (August 24), Gatewood's small force also moved out early, for everyone knew the trail they followed was hot. At the head of the canyon that led into the valley of the Bavispe, the women's tracks joined those left by Geronimo and the rest of his band. When Kayitah and Martine, who were in the lead, saw a pair of canvas pants fluttering in the breeze, they halted.

Gatewood called everyone together. Exercising the democracy that had served him well in the past, he gave everyone a chance to interpret what the pants meant. No one had any idea—other than the pants did not bode well for anyone who saw them. After listening to all comments, Gatewood announced that Martine and Kayitah would lead the advance, followed by Wratten, Huston and the pack mules, two soldiers, himself, and finally two more soldiers one hundred yards to the rear.

Martine and Kayitah refused to obey.

"I still think that was the best plan," Gatewood later remembered, "but the two Indians said that they were not greedy, but willing to divide the glory to be had equally among the whole party."[23]

The lieutenant opened the discussion a second time, and everyone agreed to go forward with the Indians. Gatewood accepted the group's decision, and everyone moved out together.

The canyon had a foreboding aura. Sheer cliffs towered over the small party, almost as if daring them to enter. They did, slowly—one step at a time, all eyes darting from crag to ragged crag as they moved forward. Finally, they reached the end of the confining canyon, where Gatewood's dry humor took center stage as he poked fun at his own heroic image: "That proved to be a very innocent cañon, & I was sorry after we got through that I had not gone ahead."

The march continued, with neither Gatewood nor his companions relaxing their vigilance. By now, the heat had become intense. Sweat rolled down their faces and burned their eyes as they made one mile and then another. Finally they reached the big bend of the Bavispe.

Just past noon, Gatewood made camp in a canebrake, the bivouac just below a peak that offered a good view of the surrounding country. He immediately stationed a picket on the summit, and a soldier planted the flag where it could be seen from a distance. Gatewood then told Kayitah and Martine that he wanted them to find Geronimo and talk with him. The Chokonen and Nednhi scouts knew the danger before them, but this time, instead of balking, they set out immediately.[24]

Kanseah, a Chokonen Apache and Geronimo's youngest warrior at fourteen years, stood guard atop the zigzag trail that led to the hideout. Looking through field glasses, he saw movement on the distant plain.[25] He yelled to Geronimo, and the old war leader crossed to him.

Geronimo knew it would take a long time for whatever moved in the distance to get close. He told Kanseah to call him again when he was certain they were men. Geronimo left and sent another guard to join Kanseah.

At 2:00 P.M. Kayitah and Martine found Geronimo's camp, and looking up at the precipice, they saw a few of the guards stationed in the rocks. All the warriors above them were armed and ready for an attack.

> We proceeded as carefully as we could but they saw us coming. We knew that they might shoot at us at any moment. In fact there was much danger of their doing this.[26]

They began to climb up to the stronghold.

Kanseah and his companion realized the small figures were Martine and Kayitah, but did not call Geronimo. The old warrior and some of his warriors, including the famous Chokonen warrior Yahnosha (*Yanosha, Yahnozha*), Fun, Eyelash, and Zhunne strode up to the overlook. Everyone sat: Yahnosha at Geronimo's right, and Eyelash, Fun, and Zhunne at his left. Seeing the white flag that Martine carried on a stick, Kanseah told Geronimo that Martine and Kayitah had arrived.

"It does not matter who they are," Geronimo said. "If they come closer they are to be shot."[27]

Yahnosha said: "They are our brothers. Let's find out why they come. They are very brave to risk this."

"They do not take the risk for us but for the money promised them by our enemies," Geronimo replied. "When they get close enough, shoot."

Yahnosha took a stand. "We will not shoot. If there is any shooting done it will be at you, not them. The first man who lifts a rifle I will kill."

Fun took Yahnosha's side. "I will help you . . . ," he stated.

Geronimo knew his brethren meant what they said. He grunted, "Let them live."

The afternoon dragged by with no word from Kayitah or Martine. Although the canebrake offered plenty of hiding places if the need arose, Gatewood remained uneasy: "this peace commission business was getting decidedly tiresome,"[28] he later commented. "The white flag was high up on a century plant pole all the time, but that don't make a man bullet proof."

Gatewood sent several messengers back to Lawton, advising him of the current situation. Anticipating a meeting with Geronimo the next day, he also requested tobacco and supplies. Minutes slowly turned into hours, as Gatewood continued to wait.

Late that afternoon Brown and thirty Indian scouts rode into Gatewood's camp at the canebrake. Brown announced that Lawton was following him and probably was not too far behind.[29] But Lawton was not close. A messenger rode into camp shortly after Brown's arrival, and delivered Lawton's note, which read:

My Dear Gatewood—

I have just arrived in Brown's camp, and have rec[eive]d your notes. My pack train got off the trail yesterday, and will not be in until . . . night. I have sent L[ieutenan]t [Abiel] Smith back on [a] fresh horse to bring up your tobacco and some rations and will send them over to you as soon as they arrive. I have ordered them to come forward if it kills the mules. It will be too late for me to go over tonight, and besides I do not wish to interfere with you, but will come over if you wish me. Send a man back to conduct pack mules over, and write me what you want. I hope and trust your efforts will meet with success.[30]

As requested, Gatewood immediately sent a messenger back to Lawton to guide the pack mules.

When Kayitah and Martine were within rifle range, a Chiricahua warrior leaped onto a rock towering above them. Kayitah recognized the warrior—it was his cousin, Yahnosha. That was good, for he knew his cousin did not want to see him killed.

Yahnosha asked them what they wanted.

Kayitah and Martine said: "we [a]re messengers from General Miles and Lieut[enant] Gatewood and . . . [wish] to discuss peace with Geronimo."[31]

"Come up! Nobody is going to hurt you,"[32] Yahnosha assured them.

The two peace emissaries finished the climb. After everyone filed back to the camp, Kayitah and Martine reminded Geronimo that it was useless to continue the fight: "every living thing—Mexicans, White Eyes, and even the beasts—[are your] enemies."[33]

"How do we know that Gatewood will keep his promise to take us to our families[?]"[34] Geronimo asked.

"He has given his word. He will take you first to Fort Bowie, and there he will put you on the train to go to your families in Florida. In three days, five at most, you will be with them."

"You know well how many Apaches have been taken under safe conduct and been murdered," Geronimo said. "And think what happened to Kaytennae!" Geronimo's eyes, red-lined from three days of drinking, blazed: "This is my home. Here I stay. Kill me if you wish, for every living thing has to die sometime. How can a man meet death better than in fighting for his own?"

"But your men do not have their families with them as you do. If you do not quit fighting soon there will be none of you left. The Chiricahua will be exterminated."

Geronimo refused to budge: "I prefer death to imprisonment."

"You will not be imprisoned. Lieutenant Gatewood has said so. He asks only that you meet him in council."

"Mangas Coloradas trusted to the white flag," Geronimo snapped. "What happened to him?"

"Gatewood will keep his word. Think of the women and children with you—your own wives and children among them."

Geronimo decided to meet Gatewood the next day—at a site of his choosing. He then cooked mescal. Taking enough to create a lump the size of a man's heart, he squeezed it, wrapped it, and told Martine to give it to Gatewood, saying that it "was a token of his surrender and that when the mescal had been sent there would be no reason for Gatewood to doubt his earnestness in planning to give up"[35]

Geronimo said: "tell [Gatewood] to eat it."[36]

Kayitah remained overnight with Geronimo, while Martine took the mescal and returned to Gatewood's camp.

Martine appeared at Gatewood's camp at sundown and told Bay-chen-day-sen that he and Kayitah had found Geronimo four miles from the white camp. He described the stronghold as "an exceedingly rocky position high up in the [Teres] Mountains in the bend of the Bavispe."[37] Gatewood reported that Martine said "that Geronimo and [Naiche] wanted to 'talk peace,' and that if I would meet them for that purpose there would be no harm done me; that I would be received in good faith, as they had known me for several years."[38] Martine told Gatewood that "[Geronimo] would talk with me only, & that he was rather offended at our not coming straight to his ranchería, where peaceably inclined people were welcome. [Naiche], . . . sent word that we would be perfectly safe so long as we behaved ourselves."[39]

Gatewood breathed easier.

Martine gave the mescal to Gatewood, who then sliced it into thin strips before distributing it to everyone in his party. Then Gatewood and his companions ate the mescal between pieces of bread. The prevailing mood turned jovial around the campfires that night, now that most everyone believed Geronimo truly wanted to end the war.[40]

As the camp prepared to bed down for the night, expectations were high, but emotions were mixed. Martine said: "The soldiers all lay down around the fire that night feeling that there was no danger of an attack."[41] Wratten painted a totally different picture: "We lay on our rifles all night, just to be ready in case of need, for we had not yet had our talk with them, and didn't know just what they would do."[42]

Lawton came through on his end. The supplies he had promised Gatewood arrived sometime during the night.[43]

CHAPTER TWELVE

Gatewood and Geronimo

Early the next morning (August 25), Gatewood packed his saddle with the fifteen pounds of tobacco, cigarette papers, and matches that Lawton had sent. After ensuring that everyone carried several days of rations, he called Martine to him. Bay-chen-daysen was anxious to meet with Geronimo. After a quick breakfast Martine led Gatewood and his small party, along with Brown and his command, out at sunrise. Their destination was Geronimo's camp perched high on the rocky crag. As Gatewood followed the trail to the stronghold, he felt somewhat safer knowing that Naiche would be at the meeting.

With the flag of truce leading the way, the group slowly moved forward. After traveling about two miles along the canyon floor, Gatewood saw some Chiricahuas coming down the mountain, and unsure exactly what to expect he left a soldier behind to show Lawton the trail when he arrived.

The lieutenant continued his advance and reached the base of the mountain that Geronimo held without incident. Martine estimated they were now about a mile from Geronimo's camp. Gatewood began the ascent, but before he had gone very far an unarmed Chiricahua warrior appeared on the trail before him. Gatewood halted and listened as the warrior delivered the same message Martine had relayed the night before: Geronimo wanted to *talk peace*. Three armed warriors appeared, one of whom was Geronimo's half-brother.[1]

Brown recalled that the unarmed Chiricahua "stated that the Scouts must go back, that they could not be permitted to come to Geronimo's camp for fear there would be some conflict."[2] Gatewood told Brown to return to their bivouac in the canebrake and wait, that any additional troops that might come up were to remain there with him. There was one more request. Naiche did not want to meet on top of the mountain; instead, he wanted to meet "down in the bend of the river where there was plenty of wood, water, grass & shade."[3] The new location was between two and three miles farther north. Gatewood agreed to the conditions.

Two shots high above the base of the mountain shattered the calm. Everyone looked up and saw smoke drifting skyward from the mountain top. Bay-chen-daysen interpreted the signal to represent Geronimo and Naiche's goodwill.[4]

After Brown and his command departed, Bay-chen-daysen, along with Martine, Wratten, Yestes, Horn, maybe one soldier, and the four Chiricahuas set out for the bend of the Bavispe. They reached the proposed location, a glade, at the river bottom. Gatewood was now between five and six miles from the canebrake. None of Geronimo's band were present or in sight. Gatewood gave the order for everyone to unsaddle the mules and put them out to graze. The time was between 8:00 and 9:00 A.M. Minutes ticked by. Nervously, everyone scanned the mountainside towering above them while they waited. They saw nothing. Then, armed warriors appeared, coming down the mountain toward them. Martine remembered: "We were very anxious for a few minutes[,] thinking that maybe Geronimo had changed his mind and meant trouble for us."[5] It was too late to run.

After reaching the mountain base, the Chiricahuas who had just appeared vanished. Suddenly, they began to reappear one by one; coming from the bush in different directions. "We did begin to feel a little creepy," Wratten admitted, "when we saw we were so badly outnumbered and surrounded."[6]

Kayitah appeared, but there was no sign of Geronimo.

The Chiricahuas unsaddled their ponies and put them out to graze. The rest of the band—women and children—began to appear. By now some twenty-one warriors, with a total Chiricahua count somewhere between thirty-five and forty, milled around them.

Greetings were exchanged. Gatewood took off his arms and attached them to his saddle. He then placed the saddle on a log. Some of the Chiricahuas did the same, using the saddles as seats. The Indians immediately asked for tobacco and alcohol. Gatewood did not have any alcohol, but he did have the makings for smokes. He broke out his supply of tobacco and paper, and passed it around. Bay-chen-daysen then directed that the rations (panoche, perrola, flour, bacon, and coffee), which he and his group had brought with them, be joined with the Chiricahuas' supplies (jerked horse meat and mescal cakes). One of the men from Gatewood's party served as cook, and with the Chiricahua women, began to prepare a meal.

As neither party had fresh meat, Wratten and several of Geronimo's warriors went hunting. However, Gatewood must have told Wratten to return quickly as his services were needed. The lieutenant had three interpreters with him for one reason: to ensure that the exchange of words between himself and Geronimo would not be muddled or misinterpreted.

Everyone rolled cigarettes and lighted up.

Satisfied that he had done everything he could to begin the peace council, Gatewood looked for a seat. A warrior had claimed his saddle, so he moved to an Indian's saddle and sat. The next few minutes passed easily, with Gatewood smoking and chatting with the Indians.[7]

Geronimo appeared. He set his Winchester down twenty feet from Gatewood, then crossed to Bay-chen-daysen. Gatewood stood and they shook hands. "Anzhoo,"[8] Geronimo said as he eyed the lieutenant. Before Gatewood could answer, Geronimo asked him about his "thinness & apparent bad health & asked what was the matter."[9] Gatewood answered him and they sat down together. Geronimo sat close to Gatewood, too close for the lieutenant's comfort.

To begin the conversation, Gatewood asked Geronimo why he had opened negotiations with the Mexicans.

Geronimo replied that "it was done to gain time to rest a little while."[10] He explained that he wanted to get supplies and mescal from the Mexicans and figured they would let him have what he wanted if they thought he would surrender to them.

Naiche walked in from the bush. He greeted Bay-chen-daysen in the same manner as Geronimo had, and, as Gatewood later commented: "the party was complete."[11]

The rest of the warriors pressed closer to Gatewood, sitting in a semicircle around him. Geronimo announced that he and his warriors were ready to listen to Miles's message. Gatewood did not feel very confident at that moment:

> gentle reader, turn back, take another look at [Geronimo's] face, imagine him looking me square in the eyes & watching my every movement, twenty-four bucks sitting around fully armed, my small party scattered in their various duties incident to a peace commissioner's camp, & say if you can blame me for feeling chilly twitching movements.[12]

Gatewood looked at the warriors as they puffed on their cigarettes: Naiche, Kanseah, Yahnosha, Fun, Eyelash, Perico, Chappo, Tissnolthos, Onodiah, Juan-si-got-si, Matzus (*Motzos, Molzos*), Sisnah, Hanloah (*Hanlonah*), and Kasegoneh, among others. Except for Naiche, Geronimo was related to everyone by blood or marriage.[13] Lozen was also present.

The moment of reckoning had arrived.[14]

Gatewood, seeing no reason to stall, said: "I am directed by Gen[eral] Miles to ask the surrender of yourself and followers to the United States government."[15]

"On what conditions?" Geronimo asked.

"An unconditional surrender."

Although Gatewood wrote Georgia that "[Geronimo] and I are grown to be great friends,"[16] this most likely was said only to ease her fears. The negotiation had just begun, and it would not be easy on anyone—especially

Gatewood. Feeling his way carefully through each passing minute, Bay-chen-daysen's position balanced precariously above treacherous waters.

"Surrender & you will be sent to join the rest of your people in Florida," Gatewood said, "there to await the decision of the President as to your final disposition. Accept these terms or fight it out to the bitter end."[17]

"The [talk] was broken off at times, then renewed, often tense."[18] As Gatewood remembered: "They all listened attentively, & a silence of several weeks fell on the party, at least so it seemed to me."[19]

Geronimo, who did all the talking, rubbed his hands over his face, his eyes. He then held his arms before Gatewood and made them tremble. Perhaps he did this to break the tension everyone felt. Geronimo said:

> We have been on a three days' drunk, on the mescal the Mexicans
> sent us by the squaws who went to Fronteras. The Mexicans expected
> to play their usual trick of getting us drunk & killing us, but we have
> had the fun; & now I feel a little shaky. You need not fear giving me
> a drink of whiskey, for our spree passed off without a single fight,
> . . . Now, in Fronteras there is plenty of wine & mescal, . . . We
> thought perhaps you had brought some with you.

Bay-chen-daysen said he had left Fronteras in a hurry and did not have any whiskey.

Replying to the question of surrender, Geronimo said, "we can't surrender."[20] Continuing, he said that he, Naiche, and their people "did not want to go to Florida."[21] Geronimo then stated: "[We want] to go back to the White M[oun]t[ain]s the same as before." Gatewood told Geronimo that this was out of the question; he had no authority to offer terms.[22] But this did not deter the old warrior. "[We will] leave the war path only on condition that [we] be allowed to return to the reservation, occupy the farms held by [us] when [we] left the last time, be furnished with the usual rations, clothing, farming implements[,] etc.[,] with guaranteed exemption from punishment for what [we have] done."[23]

Bay-chen-daysen wanted to agree to Geronimo's wish, but his instructions prevented him from doing so. As he put it: "If I was authorized to accede to these modest propositions, the war might be considered at an end right there."[24] He told Geronimo that he could not give him what he wanted, for he knew that whatever he said would eventually become a lie, and he did not want that.

"There are two sides to this question,"[25] Geronimo said. "We have had good cause for doing what we have done. I want you to listen to our side." He then narrated all the wrongs done to his people. He left nothing out as he told of the fraud and stealing by the Indian agents, along with the injustice perpetrated against Chiricahuas by the White Eyes. Gatewood sat and listened, taking no part in the discussion. One of Geronimo's grievances stood out: "Geronimo dislikes [Britton] Davis, Chatto[,] & Mick[e]y Free."[26]

Eventually the talk turned to what the Chiricahuas should do. At this point, tempers flared and the conversation got heated. Not wanting Gatewood and his companions to hear their words, Geronimo and his warriors moved to the other side of the canebrake. Although they had been negotiating with the Mexicans, it had been just a ruse to buy time and supplies. Until this time, neither Geronimo nor Naiche had considered surrendering. Back in March, Crook had "talked ugly to them,"[27] causing them to disbelieve his words; but now, Bay-chen-daysen's words sounded truthful. The argument over what to do continued.

Miles away from Gatewood, Lawton pressed forward with his command. When the terrain became too rugged for the pack train to safely navigate the trail, he sent Wood back to find a suitable camp site. Then with the soldier Gatewood had sent back with a message guiding them, he, Smith, and eight others continued on toward Gatewood's supposed location.[28]

Finally, after talking for over an hour, the meeting between Geronimo and his warriors ended. The time was somewhere between 11:00 A.M. and 12:00 noon when the old warrior returned to Gatewood. Before continuing the negotiation, lunch was served with coffee. Afterward, everyone returned to their original positions and the talk resumed.

Geronimo said the terms were unacceptable. His people "wanted the usual terms—to be returned to the reservation with wonted privileges and immunity from punishment for their crimes. They [a]re afraid to trust to a surrender without promises of safety."[29] Before Gatewood could respond, Geronimo asked Bay-chen-daysen to listen to the full story before making his decision. He then snapped: "to expect [us] to give up the whole Southwest to a race of intruders [i]s too much."[30] Gatewood listened through his interpreters while Geronimo continued: "[We] [a]re will[ing] to cede all of it except the reservation. [We] will move back on that land, or fight till the last one of [us] [i]s dead."

Geronimo refused to back down from his ultimatum. He looked Gatewood square in the eye. "Take us to the reservation or fight." Gatewood again felt the hopelessness of his situation—he could do neither; and surrounded as he was, he could not run either. The threat could not have been clearer. Gatewood definitely felt uncomfortable, not knowing what would happen next.

Just when matters might have become very dangerous for the lieutenant, Naiche, who until to this point had been sitting back and listening, spoke up. He said that Bay-chen-daysen had come in peace and would leave in peace, no matter what the outcome of the talks were, as long as he did not start any violence.

Gatewood breathed easier. Not ready to give up, he decided to gamble, to say something that was true and yet not true. He told Geronimo and Naiche "that the rest of their people who had remained on the reservation, between 400 & 500 in number, had been removed to Florida to join Chihuahua's band, & their going back to the reservation meant living among their enemies, the other Apaches." He concluded by telling Naiche that both his mother and daughter were among the prisoners now in Florida. These shocking words changed the tenor of the powwow.

Staring at Gatewood, Geronimo asked: "[Are you] telling the truth, or . . . [is this] a trick to get [us] in the white man's clutches[?]"[31] He wanted to know the source of the information, how the foul deed had been pulled off, and the reason none of his people had escaped to tell him. Gatewood did not have any answers.

The atmosphere became tense. Abruptly, Geronimo and Naiche pulled their warriors to the other side of the canebrake to talk among themselves. Another hour passed; by now the time approached late afternoon.

Geronimo returned to Gatewood, saying that their terms remained the same—a return to the reservation or continue the war. He then said he wanted to make a complete statement so that Gatewood understood everything and could explain it to Miles. This would take all night.

Bay-chen-daysen said no, he had talked all day. Geronimo would not take no for an answer. He sent warriors out to find a steer to kill so they could eat. More tobacco and paper were passed around, and everyone rolled cigarettes and smoked. The talk turned away from the question at hand. When the first round of cigarettes were gone, more were rolled and the smoking continued. Everyone relaxed a little.[32]

Geronimo knew Crook, knew what to expect. Miles was an unknown and he wanted to know everything about him from his age to the color of his hair to his experience with Indians to his honesty.[33] Everyone listened intently to Gatewood's answers. By the time he had satisfied their curiosity, it was almost sunset. "He must be a good man," Geronimo concluded, "since the Great Father sent him from Washington, & he sent you all this distance to us."[34]

When Lawton and the nine men with him reached Brown and the Indian scouts at Gatewood's camp just as night fell, he discovered Gatewood had not yet returned. After hearing that the lieutenant was negotiating with Geronimo, Lawton immediately sent a messenger back to Wood to follow the Indian trail and press on as he wanted all his troops together.[35]

Gatewood was worn out from the tension-filled, day-long negotiation. A messenger had brought word that Lawton had reached his camp, and he wanted to leave. Gatewood knew that Geronimo, Naiche, and the others intended to stay up that night to discuss their situation, and he did not want to be present for this meeting. Since the hunters had failed to return with a steer, he used that, along with being tired and sick, to excuse himself. He then suggested that their medicine men look into the future. Geronimo agreed.

But instead of ending, the talk continued. As Gatewood later recorded: "Thus passed several more hours in what appeared to be fruitless 'talk.' During this time, we ate, & smoked, & joked, & drank muddy warm water from the river."[36]

Finally, Gatewood found an opening and prepared to leave. But before he could, Geronimo had one final request. "We want your advice. Consider yourself one of us & not a white man. Remember all that has been said today, & as an Apache what would you advise us to do under the circumstances"[37]

Gatewood quickly replied: "I would trust Gen[eral] Miles & take him at his word."[38] Bay-chen-daysen's mind raced. He led a peace delegation and wanted the war to end. At the same time, he realized he was in their power—he had no intention of advising them to fight: "So, in the most earnest manner possible, I reminded them of the fact that I had always been a friend to them & if I tho[ugh]t it was best, I would advise them to fight it out (a small white fib), but my heart was drawn to them in brotherly yearning (another fib), & it was only for their good that I must council peace on the terms offered."[39]

Solemn Indian faces surrounded Gatewood, glared at him. He advised them "to lay down their arms and surrender as the best way to settle the war, and the quicker they did so the better the terms they might hope for; that another chance might not occur."[40]

The council over, Gatewood saddled his mule. Before he could mount, Geronimo stopped him. The old warrior begged him to see Miles in person and lay the case before him. His people were tired of fighting and wanted to be united with their families. Geronimo wanted Gatewood to leave the next morning for the nearest United States military post to send a message to Miles saying that he wanted to speak for the Apaches. Geronimo volunteered to send a few of his warriors with Gatewood to protect him against Mexicans or any other danger during the trip. Although Gatewood was touched that Geronimo and the others "believed that I would do my best in talking to [Miles] to get their families together,"[41] he told them it would be a wasted trip as Miles had made up his mind. Geronimo then said to Gatewood:

> You can come to our camp anywhere. You are no more responsible for this war than I. I know you. If Gen[eral] Miles won't make peace, you come & tell us. Never fear harm. If I want to talk, I will come to your camp anywhere and feel safe. I will go with you now, alone to Lawton's camp[,] if you desire it. That's the way I feel towards you.[42]

Bay-chen-daysen declined the offer.

"[I will] let [you] know the result of [our] council in the morning,"[43] Geronimo said. Gatewood shook hands all around, mounted, and with his small group left the meeting ground. Even though the departure was tempered by the seriousness of the immediate future, Gatewood wrote: "Every one of them showed great pleasure at meeting me."[44]

During the ride back to his bivouac, Chappo, Geronimo's teen-aged son, caught up to Gatewood. The lieutenant asked the boy where he was going. "With you. I'm going to sleep close to you tonight & tomorrow I'll return to camp. I have my father's permission to do so."[45] Gatewood could not allow this, for he knew of the Chiricahuas' hatred for the Apaches who served as scouts against them. As Daklugie said, referring to the time of Cibicue (1881): "Even then I knew how our people detested the scouts who were working for our enemies."[46] The scouts' hatred for the warring Chiricahuas was mutual. Gatewood told the boy that "the risk of getting a knife stuck in him during the night was too great to be taken."[47] Reluctantly, Chappo, who wanted to remain with Gatewood, returned to his father's camp.

It was dark by the time Gatewood reached his bivouac. He immediately reported to Lawton, telling the captain that Geronimo "declined to make an unconditional surrender."[48] After informing Lawton that he refused to ride to Miles to speak in the old warrior's behalf, and that Geronimo and Naiche would have an answer in the morning, Gatewood went to bed, dog-tired.

That night Geronimo had his last remaining wife, She-gha, by his side while he and Naiche discussed the band's future. Lozen, Dahteste, and all the warriors attended the council, as did Chappo, who had returned from Bay-chen-daysen.

The band was split on what to do. When one warrior proposed killing Gatewood, Naiche immediately spoke up: "No. [Bay-chen-daysen] ha[s] always been square, ha[s] always told the truth, ha[s] never deceived [us] and [I will] not . . . see him killed."[49] And there was no further talk of killing Bay-chen-daysen.

The Chiricahuas turned their attention to the matter at hand: surrender. Kaywaykla remembered one of the discussions during the day, and more likely than not, the night-long talk was similar:

> [Some] opposed the surrender. Naiche, warworn and discouraged, seemed indifferent. The warriors whose families were with them [wanted to remain free]. It was the lure of being reunited with their wives and children that turned the tide of opinion among the others.[50]

Undoubtedly, Geronimo led the talk. And most likely three things influenced him. First and foremost was his family—his family still with him (and that included almost everyone) and his family imprisoned in a far-away land called Florida. His first and last concerns were for his family: protecting them, caring for them, being with them.

This leads to the second influence. Charlie Smith, the Mescalero boy captured along with Ih-tedda the year before, was still with the band. Charlie summed up Geronimo's war quite well:

> When Geronimo crossed the border into New Mexico or Arizona, it was usually to get ammunition. I do not think that he wanted to kill, but there were cases when he had no choice. If he were seen by a civilian, it meant that he would be reported to the military and they'd be after us. So there was nothing to do but kill the civilian and his entire family. It was terrible to see little children killed. I do not like to talk of it. I do not like to think of it. But the soldiers killed our women and children, too. Don't forget that. There were times that I hated Geronimo for that, too; but when I got older, I knew that he had no choice. . . .
>
> But Geronimo was fighting not only to avenge his murdered mother, wife, and children, but for his people and his tribe. Later there were Apaches who were bitter against Geronimo, saying that it was his fault that they were sent to Florida and were prisoners of war for twenty-seven years. Well, if they'd had the fighting spirit of Geronimo, they need not have been sent. The big difference was that he had the courage to keep on and they were quitters. Some of them have 'gone white' and blame Geronimo for everything. I don't

respect them. They were cowards. I won't name them. I am ashamed
that they are Apaches.

And don't forget that Geronimo knew that it was hopeless. But
that did not stop him. I admire him for that. He was a great leader of
men, and it ill becomes the cowardly to find fault with the man who
was trying to keep them free.[51]

The old warrior had lived Charlie's words, but now he knew it was over.
Yes, he could continue the fight, . . . knowing everyone would die, but he did
not want this.

The third and final influence on Geronimo's decision would be Bay-chen-
daysen. Geronimo had been lied to, cheated, and betrayed so many times
that his opinion of the White Eyes was poor at best. Bay-chen-daysen represented both hope for the future and honesty, a trait Apaches valued over
all else. Geronimo had no choice. For his people to survive he had to entrust
their fate to Gatewood. Geronimo would sway his brothers to his view during the all-night talk.

The next morning when scouts on picket duty called "Bay-chen-daysen,"
Gatewood knew what the call meant. With Wratten in tow, he rushed to the
scouts who had called his name. They told him that Geronimo was near and
wanted to see him.

At the picket line, Gatewood saw Geronimo, Naiche, Perico and several
other warriors a few hundred yards away. Bay-chen-daysen, with Wratten,
Yestes, and Horn, began to walk toward the mounted Apaches.

When Geronimo saw Bay-chen-daysen, he and his men dismounted,
unsaddled their ponies, and laid their weapons on their saddles. They began
to walk toward Bay-chen-daysen and the interpreters.

Gatewood observed that all of the Indians were unarmed, . . . all except
Geronimo, who had a pistol that was partially covered by his coat. It was
stuffed in his belt on his left hip.

Gatewood and Geronimo shook hands.

Wratten and the other two translated for Gatewood and Geronimo. The
old warrior asked Bay-chen-daysen to repeat his message of the previous day.
He then asked in-depth questions about Miles. Satisfied, he said:

> We have talked the matter over, and if you will give your word that
> we can meet General Miles with safety, we will go to him and accept
> his terms. We will throw ourselves on his mercy, something we have
> never done before. Our experience leads us to be careful as to whom
> we trust. There are two sides to every question: and whoever is the
> cause of a war like this is a man with a bad heart.[52]

The talk turned to exactly what would happen and how it would happen. According to Gatewood, Geronimo then said words close to the following:

the whole party, 24 bucks & 14 women & children, w[ill] meet the General at some point in the United States, talk the matter over with him, & surrender to him in person, provided the American commander w[ill] accompany [us] with his soldiers & protect [us] from Mexican & other American troops that might be met on the way. [We will] retain [our] arms until [we have] surrendered formally, individuals of each party should have the freedom of the other's camp, & that [you/Gatewood] should march with [us] & when convenient sleep in [our] camp.[53]

Gatewood agreed to the terms.

"I want to meet the American Commander who has followed and fought me so long," Geronimo said, "and once surprised me in my camp."[54]

Bay-chen-daysen led everyone safely into the white bivouac and then to Lawton. Geronimo immediately hugged the captain. After greetings were exchanged all around, everyone sat down to talk. Gatewood sent for his supply of tobacco, and when it arrived he passed out the fixings. Since Lawton did not smoke, Gatewood rolled a cigarette for him.

Gatewood outlined Geronimo's terms while everyone smoked. As Lawton dutifully puffed away on his cigarette, he began to get sick. Luckily, his cigarette began to fall apart by the time Gatewood completed his narration and it had been translated to the Indians. Lawton agreed to the terms.

Skeleton Canyon, about sixty miles southeast of Fort Bowie, was selected as the location where Geronimo and Naiche would officially surrender to Miles. Lawton then invited Geronimo to move his camp near the white camp, while he sent a message to Miles to see if the proposed agenda was agreeable to the general. Geronimo agreed to this, then stated that his people were hungry. This brought up an embarrassing situation for the soldiers, but an amusing one to the Indians. Wood had still not arrived with the pack train. When Gatewood told Geronimo that Wood was lost and since he had the food, there would not be any to pass out until he arrived, Geronimo found the situation funny.

Geronimo and Naiche moved their camp close to the White Eyes. Everyone waited, for food, and for a reply from Miles.[55] Gatewood used the time to write a letter to Georgia. After apologizing for not writing in a while, and assuring her that he took no risks when meeting Geronimo, he described the events of the past thirty hours. He then broached the subject that both he and Geronimo held dear:

[Geronimo] is now loafing around the camp, having had his talk with Lawton. They really want to surrender, but they want their families with them. Can anyone blame a man for wanting to see his wife and children?[56]

Gatewood closed the letter with the comment that he was preparing his application for quartermaster. He planned to include Crook's, Miles's, and his reports; Crook's order relieving him from Indian duty; Miles making him an aide-de-camp; along with endorsements. He felt good, thinking that finally his career was about to go in the direction he wanted:

Seem to think of nothing but my promotion—would not give a cent for it except that you would be better off—little is the pleasure you have seen since you 'joined the Cavalry.' Keep on hoping for better times, they will come some day. Look at the future, are you not pleased with the prospect though delayed?

I must begin work on a memoir. My life has been more full of incident & adventure than that of any other l[ieutenan]t in the Army. I realize that more every day, . . . scenes and incidents . . . come back to my memory, . . . & soon I must begin to jot them down in a book, . . . when we are all together again.

That afternoon a torrential rain pummeled the earth.[57]

Word arrived from Miles that he would meet Geronimo near the Mexican border "if he sent an assurance that he was acting in good faith."[58] With the war seemingly over, it was time to move north.

CHAPTER THIRTEEN

Mexicans, Americans, and Apaches

"These people [a]re anxious to give themselves up,"[1] Gatewood wrote Miles. Although he never said it himself, the sudden halt to the war could plainly be attributed to him. He had been the key. James Cook would later write: "Geronimo knew that Gatewood's tongue was not forked, . . . Geronimo's faith in Gatewood's words must have been strong."[2] Nevertheless, the old warrior was wary; he had found himself in this position before. To protect his people, he and Naiche pitched their camp in a defensible position on the opposite side of the San Bernardino River, about one mile[3] from the soldier camp. Although both sides seemed to be in agreement, Geronimo and his people remained alert, ready for the first sign of treachery.

On August 26 Lawton remained in camp, which was near the junction of the San Bernardino and Bavispe rivers just north of the bend in the Bavispe. He waited for Wood and Smith to arrive with the now all-important supplies. Lawton realized just how critical his position was. He knew that Geronimo had run in the past, and could again, restarting the vicious cycle of hide-and-seek war in which Apaches excelled. He could see the Chiricahuas were suspicious. The stress began building for Lawton, and while waiting for supplies, he sent a dispatch to Forsyth at Fort Huachuca, updating him on the situation.[4] The waiting played on everyone's psyches; the lack of food did not help the situation.

During this time, the Apaches, who kept to themselves, remained vigilant. And as promised, Bay-chen-daysen moved to their camp.

The next day, August 27, Lawton's anxiety increased. "I am pretty tired and feel the strain of responsibility weighing on me,"[5] he wrote his wife. Finally, that morning, Wood and Smith reached the San Bernardino River, which was running near flood stage. By noon they camped directly across from Geronimo's camp, and supplies were ferried over the raging waters to the Indians.

A couple of hours later, Gatewood, Geronimo, Naiche, and most of the band visited Wood's camp. Both sides sat down for a smoke and talk, discussing the trip north to Skeleton Canyon. Located at the southern portion of the San Simon Mountains, some thirty-five miles north of Mexico on the

Arizona-New Mexico border, *Cajon Bonito,* as the Apaches called it, was reachable with short marches.[6]

During the talk, Geronimo stated: "We have not slept for six months and are worn out."[7] He also said "that he and his party were . . . anxious to join their relatives in Florida." The entire band feared what would happen to them if they were turned over to the civil authorities in Arizona.

His trepidation was not unwarranted. "There were no definite terms offered the Indians at this time,"[8] Wood recorded. "They were told that General Miles sent word that he would use every possible effort to send them promptly out of Arizona and to save their lives." Wratten's memory of the current situation came remarkably close to Wood's: "Yes, they were given certain promises in order to induce them to surrender; their lives were to be spared, and the Government would get them out of Arizona before the civil authorities could arrest them and try them for murder. They were to go east with their families to Florida, and maybe after awhile could come back to Arizona when things quieted down, say in two years or so."[9]

Geronimo must have been pleased with what he heard. He stayed for dinner. There were good feelings all around.

Early the next morning (August 28) the two groups moved out.[10] Geronimo, Naiche, and Gatewood kept to the foothills, maintaining a distance of one to two miles between themselves and the troops and Indian scouts. Lawton, Wood, and Smith marched along the valley floor, skirting the San Bernardino. The day's journey was uneventful and Gatewood and Geronimo halted early in the afternoon. After setting up camp, warriors saw Mexicans coming from the west several miles back on the trail, and the news spread quickly. Further observation showed that the white-clad infantry troops numbered about 180. Their presence meant but one thing—a pending attack—and everyone knew it.

About the same time, Lawton's command, which had just gone into bivouac, saw the advancing Mexicans. The American troops also believed the Mexicans were going to attack. Packs and stones were piled into breastworks. The soldiers actually welcomed a skirmish, hoping to even the score for Crawford's death.[11]

Ready, Lawton held his ground, hoping to speak with the Mexicans. Geronimo, on the other hand, had no intention of talking; nor did he intend to fight a pitched battle against heavy odds. Martine and Kayitah claimed: "Geronimo was frightened for he felt that he would be much safer with the American soldiers than in the hands of the Mexicans."[12]

Geronimo's suspicions were aroused. He told Gatewood he "began to believe that there was an understanding between the two commanders whereby his party were to be caught in a trap."[13] Gatewood talked quickly, trying to calm Geronimo and the rest of his wards, but the Indians refused to listen to reason, and it looked as though Gatewood would lose them to mass panic. Then Martine and Kayitah suggested that the Chiricahuas run for the border. Gatewood agreed. He told Geronimo that while the Americans stopped the Mexicans from coming any closer, he would run with him and his band. This eased Geronimo's fear that the Americans plotted against him.

Looking back, Bay-chen-daysen remembered that the sudden appearance of the Mexicans

> created quite a stampede among our new friends. While the command remained to parley with the Mexicans, our prospective prisoners & myself made a 'run for it' northward, thro' the bushes & over the rocks, at an eight or ten mile gait. Flankers & a small advance guard were thrown out, the rear guard being composed of the bucks under [Naiche].[14]

Lieutenant Robert Walsh (Fourth U.S. Cavalry) was in Geronimo's camp, and he fled with Gatewood and the Indians.

Gatewood and Geronimo held their pace for an hour, then pulled to a halt. The distance they had put between themselves and the Mexicans made the women and children momentarily safe. Geronimo would go no further; he wanted to remain within striking distance of Lawton's command. If there was a fight between Mexicans and Americans, he had every intention of fighting with the Americans.

Lawton sent orders to Wood and Smith to meet the Mexicans. Wood immediately set off on a mule, and Smith, with Horn by his side, was right behind him.

The Mexican army appeared in single file as they exited a canebrake. Jesus Aguirre, the prefect of Arispe, led his force up to the waiting Wood and Smith. As he approached, Wood sent Smith back to get Lawton. Then, perhaps letting off steam for the frustration of the last four months, he greeted the prefect aggressively. With Horn acting as interpreter, Wood told the prefect that the Americans and Apaches had joined forces and were ready to attack if he and his army proceeded.

The prefect looked Wood up and down, then questioned his authority. Wood wore an old blue shirt, flannel drawers, a pair of moccasins, and a hat with a crown. He looked more like a derelict than an officer in the United States Army. It was obvious the prefect was gunning for a fight, and it was also just as obvious that he did not want a fight with Americans. He halted the advance of his troops.

Lawton arrived and the talk resumed, with the captain telling the prefect that Geronimo had surrendered to the Americans. Like Wood, Lawton also took the offensive; and ignoring the fact that the Mexican army was armed with Remingtons and greatly outnumbered his force, he stated that he would not permit anything to happen to the Indians. The prefect demanded that Lawton hand over the Chiricahuas, whom he wanted to take to Sonora to be punished for their crimes. Although both sides recognized the other's point of view, the prefect was adamant: he wanted Geronimo.

Lawton avoided a crisis by saying he could set up a meeting with Geronimo. This was acceptable with the prefect, and Lawton sent Wood to get Geronimo. To the doctor's surprise, Gatewood and Geronimo were long gone from where he expected them to be. Riding bareback on a mule, he set out to find them.[15]

Suddenly Apache sentries surrounded Wood before he knew they were near. They accompanied him into Gatewood and Geronimo's makeshift camp, which was between four and six miles from Lawton's camp. Wood leaped off his mule and strode over to Geronimo, stating that the prefect wanted to hear directly from him that he intended to surrender to the Americans.

Fearing treachery, Geronimo refused to meet with the Mexican. Angry, Wood turned to Gatewood and told him to hold his position until he reported to Lawton; then he remounted and rode out. Wood's agitation and demands upset the Apache camp: only Bay-chen-daysen's influence stopped the band from fleeing.

Soon after Wood left, Lawton rode into Geronimo's camp. The captain told Geronimo that the prefect would not leave until he spoke with him. Geronimo again refused, but Lawton insisted upon the meeting. Before tempers flared, Gatewood stepped between the leaders and spoke quickly to the old warrior. Geronimo agreed to speak with the prefect, but only if certain conditions were met.

After listening to the war leader, Gatewood set the parameters for the meeting: 1) A new camp was to be established near Geronimo's current position; 2) the prefect and seven of his men would be allowed to enter the camp to talk with Geronimo and seven of his men; and 3) the Mexican army had to remain at least several miles away. Lawton left to arrange the new camp and to clear the terms with the prefect.[16]

Gatewood remained behind with Geronimo and a squad of warriors while the rest of the Indians moved yet farther to the north. It was not long before a courier rode up and told Gatewood what had been agreed upon. "It took not a little persuasion to induce the Indians to agree to this," Gatewood wrote, "they wanted nothing to do with [the Mexicans], fearing some treacherous plot against them."[17] Again, Gatewood's words prevailed; Geronimo agreed to meet the prefect.

The prefect and his escort, along with Lawton, Wood, Clay, and the other U.S. officers waited at the designated location. All were mounted. The Mexicans fidgeted nervously with their weapons.

Suddenly Geronimo appeared from the bush on foot. A revolver was at his left hip, and he held his Winchester by the muzzle, dragging it. An unarmed Gatewood stepped into the clearing behind him, and Naiche and the rest of Geronimo's escort followed. They too were armed with revolvers and with rifles cocked and ready to fire. Wratten and Walsh were the last to appear from cover. The group had left their animals in the bush, and after crossing half the distance to the Mexicans they halted.

The prefect and his escort hesitated. One or two of them pulled their revolvers around so that they were plainly visible. They dismounted and walked forward.[18]

Geronimo advanced with Gatewood behind him, and when they reached the Mexicans, they halted. Bay-chen-daysen made the introductions.[19] When the prefect extended his hand to Geronimo, the old warrior at first refused to shake, dropping his free hand to his revolver.[20] He then changed his mind and shook the prefect's hand. When his hand was free, the prefect yanked his revolver around to the front and did not let go of his weapon. Gatewood found himself a mite too close for comfort. He backed up to "get out of range of their guns."[21]

Geronimo drew his revolver halfway out of the holster. Gatewood saw "the whites of [Geronimo's] eyes turning red, & a most fiendish expression on his face."[22] Geronimo's pent-up hatred must have been a heartbeat or two from exploding. "For a minute it looked as though I had brought Geronimo there to get him entrapped and it didn't look healthy,"[23] Gatewood later said, understating the situation.

The prefect fidgeted, unnerving the officers with him.[24] Just when it looked like both sides would yank out their weapons and fire, the prefect let go of his gun and put his hands behind himself. Geronimo released his grip on his revolver, dropping his hand to his side. Gunplay had been averted.

The wary Gatewood had no intention of taking any chances. Even though the whites of Geronimo's eyes "resumed their normal yellowish color,"[25] he did not return to where he originally stood. Instead, he remained out of the line of fire—a few feet off to the side.

The prefect asked Geronimo why he had not surrendered at Fronteras.

Geronimo said that he did not want to be murdered.

"Are you going to surrender to the Americans?"[26] the prefect asked.

"Yes; you don't suppose that I would surrender to a lot of d—d greasers do you? I surrender to brave and honorable men who will keep their word, but to nobody whom I suspect of treachery. I cannot trust you or your people."[27] Geronimo also said: "Whatever happens, they will not murder me & my people."[28]

"Then I shall go along & see that you do surrender," the prefect said.

"No, you are going south & I am going north. I'll have nothing to do with you nor with any of your people."

Geronimo, Naiche, and their companions scowled, not making any attempt to hide their hatred of the Mexicans.[29] That was it. The conference ended.

Tragedy, not to mention an international disaster, had barely been averted. This, however, did not ease Geronimo's fear for the safety of his people. Nor did it ease Gatewood's burden of keeping his "new friends" from panicking and scattering to the four winds. And finally, it did not ease Lawton's unenviable position as lord-protector to these same "friends."

The prefect insisted that one of his soldiers accompany Geronimo north to witness the surrender. This was agreed upon, although Geronimo was adamant that the soldier could not travel with his band. The Mexican would remain with Lawton's command.

Geronimo and Naiche pitched their camp close to Lawton's that night,[30] for the old warrior did not trust the Mexicans. Although the Americans represented protection, Geronimo did not put it past the Mexicans to attack, and he did not think the U.S. force was strong enough to fend off the Mexicans if they resorted to treachery. As Gatewood listened to Geronimo and Naiche, he realized that he had a major problem: the Indians again felt that maybe the Mexicans and the Americans might join together to kill them.

Bay-chen-daysen found Kayitah, Martine, and Wratten, and discussed the situation with them. The two scouts suggested that he and Geronimo's band slip away while the Americans remained behind with the Mexicans.[31] This idea appealed to Gatewood. He knew they were close to the international border—about thirty miles—and knew his words could not curtail a panic that might erupt at any moment. Returning to Geronimo and Naiche, he again convinced them that the Americans did not plot to kill them. He then presented Kayitah and Martine's plan to them. Flight had been the major part of Geronimo's life for so long that it came naturally. He and Naiche immediately agreed: they would move northward that night. Next, Gatewood went to Lawton and told him about the plan, to which Lawton agreed. The captain would follow in the morning, using his command as a buffer between the Apaches and the Mexicans.

By the time Bay-chen-daysen returned to his wards' camp, the Indians were ready to move. Although Apaches disliked traveling in the dark, it had become a necessity to save their lives during the last few years. As Geronimo had shown Britton Davis when he returned to Arizona with the cattle herd in 1884, he now demonstrated to Gatewood just how quickly and silently an Apache could move. Gatewood mounted his mule, and along with Kayitah, Martine, and Wratten, headed north for the Arizona border with Geronimo and his band.[32]

Gatewood, Geronimo, and the others held a slow, steady pace all night until the comforting blanket of darkness gave way to the streaking rays of first light. Not knowing whether the Mexicans trailed behind them, Geronimo and Naiche refused to halt as the sun raced across Father Sky that August 29. They even discouraged their warriors from scouring the land for food or game. The refugees, with Gatewood encouraging them, plodded steadily northward. "It was a long, hot, dusty trail back to the U.S.,"[33] Wratten remembered.

That day, Lawton, Wood, Clay, Lawton's orderly (Huber), and Wood's orderly (George Williams) left Smith in command of the main column and pack train, and force-marched until they caught up to Gatewood and Geronimo. Finally, a halt was called. While everyone waited for Lawton's command to catch up, Geronimo and the band greeted the White Eyes. An hour passed, then two, and the command did not appear. When it became obvious that Smith had not seen Geronimo's trail veer away from the San Bernardino, Williams was sent back to look for Smith. Two more hours passed and still there was no sign of the missing command. Lawton became uncomfortable and set out with Wratten to find the missing troops and pack train.[34]

During the break Gatewood, Wood, and Clay decided their current position was precarious. Although they presumed the Mexican threat had ended, there were no American troops to offer a deterrent to a Mexican attack, and everyone realized that the prefect of Arispe and his troops might reappear. Gatewood repeated these views to Geronimo and Naiche and suggested they find a more suitable camp. They agreed.

Hunger supplanted the three officers' anxiety over the missing troops. Since they only had one can of condensed milk between them, Gatewood suggested they move among the Indians in the hope of securing a more nourishing meal. Wood and Clay's every step was watched by heavily armed warriors, making them nervous.[35] Bay-chen-daysen did not have this problem as he moved through the camp with the can of milk. He personally knew everyone, and his good word made him a welcomed and valued member of the band. He spoke easily as he walked, offering jokes or soothing words to all he encountered. Even among the tough-minded Apaches, his ragged, near-skeletal appearance must have incited sympathy.

Then, Gatewood saw Perico. The warrior held his son while his wife prepared the evening meal. Bay-chen-daysen smiled, offered the can of milk, and was invited to dinner. After accepting, he pointed out that his companions were also hungry. Perico immediately extended his hospitality to Clay and Wood.[36]

As the light in the sky began to fade, Bay-chen-daysen and Geronimo led the band northward. They hoped to increase the distance between themselves and the supposed location of the Mexican army and find a defensible position. Naiche and most of the warriors traveled at the rear of the advance, guarding against an attack, while Gatewood and Geronimo led the small, furtive procession. Clay, Wood, and Huber marched with the Indians. Night arrived, bringing with it both the security and danger of darkness.

Gatewood was well aware that his wards were suspicious and expected treachery. Keeping the advance moving and using every ounce of diplomacy to keep the Indians from bolting sapped his waning strength. His body had revolted at the rigors of campaigning at the beginning of the assignment, and ongoing hardships guaranteed his pain would not abate. The heat during the day, replaced by the nighttime dampness, intensified the pain in his aching joints, but he hung on with the conviction that completion of his mission was near at hand.

After marching another eight miles, Geronimo inspected the land to the east of the San Bernardino River and, finding it to his liking, called a halt for the night. Even though it was too late to erect shelters, the people set up a makeshift camp, spreading out over a large, defensible area. Sentries positioned themselves among the rocks, with their weapons cocked and at the ready, and everyone who could sleep now slept in the wet grass.

That night, Naiche approached Wood. "You are in our camp," the chieftain said, "but our camp is your camp, and you can be here just as at home."[37] The words somewhat reassured the white man who, unlike Gatewood, remained uneasy while with the Indians.

Early next morning, the Indians again demonstrated their generosity when they shared their breakfast with the White Eyes. Afterward they told Gatewood: "Grub's getting short."[38]

Miles had sent word that he wanted assurance that Geronimo would surrender. Gatewood and Geronimo knew that Miles was the key: the general had to appear at Skeleton Canyon, or all their efforts to end the war would be for naught. To assure Miles of Geronimo's intentions and impress upon him the importance of meeting Geronimo at Skeleton Canyon, Gatewood and Geronimo sent four messengers ahead with assurance that the desire for peace was real. Bay-chen-daysen chose Kayitah and an unnamed white man to carry his message, and Geronimo selected Perico and another warrior. The four left immediately for Fort Bowie.[39]

Reaching the American border before something happened to negate the chance for peace remained Gatewood's main concern. Although everyone wanted Lawton's troops as an escort, Gatewood and Geronimo knew it would be foolhardy to wait for the troops because they might never arrive. Breakfast over, Gatewood and Geronimo got the refugees on the move northward at first light. "[Naiche] with the main band started out first," Clay later recalled, "with his men deployed in a skirmish line about a mile in length. After he had been gone about half an hour, Geronimo, with the old men, women, children and pack horses, followed in the rear of the center of the line."[40]

After traveling eight miles they reached Alias Creek, which offered good water. Although it was still only mid-morning, everyone was hungry, worn out, and Gatewood and Geronimo decided to halt for the day. Around 10:00 A.M., Wood left the camp, setting out on his mule to find the missing troops.[41]

In the meantime, Lawton, who had found his errant command, was now some five miles south of John Slaughter's San Bernardino Ranch. It was already August 30—a day after he had predicted he would arrive at the ranch with the Indians.[42] Lawton had to be wondering if he would ever cross the international border with the Chiricahuas. Smith's failure to follow the trail had cost time. Anxious to report to Miles and to receive further orders, Lawton—whose nerves were on edge—confided in Smith his concern over his promise to deliver the Indians safely.

"I haven't promised them anything," Smith said to Lawton. "You . . . communicate with Miles and I'll take command."[43]

Not reading anything ominous in Smith's offer, Lawton set out for the closest heliographic station, which was at Slaughter's ranch. A heliograph was a device that used mirrors to reflect beams of sunlight to send messages in Morse code. By covering and uncovering the mirror, short and long flashes of light representing dots and dashes could be transmitted over long distances of open land.[44]

A disturbing message must have awaited Lawton at the station, for the captain immediately sent a reply to Miles:

> Indians are camped 15 miles below here waiting to hear from the General. I have no idea [if the] hostiles will surrender to me or anyone but the General, and then only upon a distinct understanding as to what is to be done with them. To deliver up their arms and surrender unconditionally, they, it appears, believe means that some of them will be killed. They prefer to die with arms in their hands and fighting. It is a difficult task to make them fight when they do not wish, and more so to surprise and surround them when they are watching your every movement.
>
> . . . I earnestly wish the General would himself come and conduct affairs in person. If they do not surrender[,] I feel they will raid again in the States, and it will be again as terrible as they can make it, as they will be desperate.[45]

Shortly after Lawton left his command, Wood rode in on his mule. The doctor found Smith in command of the troop. Wood's return did not usurp Smith's position; he remained in control. However, Wood's arrival set in motion a series of events that would lead to a confrontation that should never have happened.

Lack of time seemed to be foremost in everyone's mind that hot August 30. Wood and Smith decided not to wait for Lawton to return. Taking the command, they set out for Geronimo's camp. Knowing that Lawton would return to the same location he had decamped, they left word of their intended destination.

Vulnerable in a land that once harbored them from all their enemies, the Apaches remained vigilant. The slightest sound, every change in the breeze, jerked them into readiness. If they were to die, they would do so as Apaches—fighting to the end. Gatewood saw the fear, the torment of the unknown that haunted his Indian friends. He constantly moved among them, soothing them, assuring them that everything would be all right. His influence over Geronimo and the rest of the band remained powerful.[46] It was almost as if he inherited the at-times mystical hold that Geronimo himself wielded.

As one, these people hated the White Eyes. Only a few had ever earned their respect: Crook, Crawford, Britton Davis, Gatewood. But they were all gone now, all banished, dead, or quit—all except for Gatewood. He too had gone away, but he had come back. He had risked death to find their camp, and now he would lead them back to the road of peace.

Geronimo stayed with Gatewood. When he had said "I am your friend, and I'll go with you anywhere,"[47] back at the Bavispe, his words were iron-clad. The old warrior had great faith in Gatewood, knew the slender nantan had never deceived him. He had taken Bay-chen-daysen as a friend, trust-ing and confiding in him.[48]

Two men, so different, and now inseparable. One squat, short, broad, old, mystical, a warrior now and forever. The other tall, slender to the point of emaciation, sickly, honorable, a southern gentleman now and forever.

All they had was time, but there was precious little of it. They had to reach their destination—Skeleton Canyon—before it ran out.

Gatewood and Geronimo remained in camp the rest of August 30. They waited for Lawton to come up with the soldiers, but Lawton never came: he had remained at San Bernardino. Smith and Wood, however, came up with the troopers, camping a quarter of a mile away from the Apaches.

The next morning, both outfits set out at 7:00 A.M., with Gatewood rid-ing with Geronimo near the rear of the native procession and the soldiers fol-lowing the Indians at a discreet distance. Three miles after breaking camp a messenger overtook Smith and Wood.[49] Perhaps he brought copies of Miles's most recent dispatches to Lawton, two of which read:

> Whenever you have a good opportunity to secure the persons of Geronimo and [Naiche,] do so by any means, and don't fail to hold them beyond the possibility of escape.[50]

> If you think best when you receive this[,] you can send for [Geron-imo and Naiche] saying you have a message from the President, and when it is read to them you can tell them to lay down their arms and remain in your camp, or you can do whatever you think best.[51]

Even if Wood and Smith never saw these messages, they received some com-munication that changed their outlook toward the Indians.

The day's march progressed uneventfully. Then as the Apaches closed on Guadalupe Canyon, they began to get agitated, nervous. The canyon, which marked the entrance into the United States, should have calmed them as they would soon be beyond the long reach of the hated Mexicans; instead, the canyon posed an even greater threat—the Americans. For it was at Guadalupe Canyon that they had killed some of Lawton's men several months earlier.[52]

Their history had been filled with treachery, and certainly looming in their minds now was the possibility that foul play could again strike. Gatewood did what he could to soothe the Indians' frazzled nerves. He could not alter their destination, however. Guadalupe Canyon held, albeit precious little, much-needed water.

When Gatewood and Geronimo reached the canyon, and as soon as the White Eyes marching behind them halted for the day, warriors rode to the soldier camp. They watched the soldiers and studied the back trail to see whether Mexicans secretly followed.

Smith had had most of the day to mull over the situation and the messages he and Wood received. He apparently wanted to disarm the Indians and make them true prisoners, and was not discreet when he discussed the matter with his officers. Undoubtedly believing that the Indians could not understand English, he openly stated his plans. "We had quite a discussion about the matter," Wood wrote, "and it was arranged that in case of any ugly spirit breaking out during the conference or the Indians refusing to be reasonable that each man should kill the Indian next to him."[53]

Warriors heard Smith's words. Perhaps they did not understand all of them, but they understood enough to get the gist of what he proposed. They raced back to Gatewood and Geronimo and spit out what they had heard—Smith "expressed a desire to pitch in with the troop & have it out right there."[54]

The word spread among the Indians with the speed and ferocity of a prairie fire. Women, children, and warriors mounted, and with the women leading the way, the Apaches hurried to get out of the canyon. At about the same time, the soldiers, who were a short distance south, "started for Geronimo's camp."[55] Wratten, who was in the soldier camp, hurried forward to be with Gatewood, telling Bay-chen-daysen that Smith and Wood were coming at a leisurely pace.

Watching the Indians run, Gatewood knew he had to act quickly. He leaped on his mule and rode after the fleeing Geronimo. The warrior rode fast, and Gatewood had to gallop to overtake the old man, to whom he repeated what he had just heard of the soldiers' advance. Geronimo slowed his pony to a walk.

Geronimo asked, "what . . . should [you] do in case [we are] fired on by the troops[?]"[56]

"I [will] proceed toward the troops & endeavor to have the firing stopped," Gatewood replied; "otherwise I [will] run away with [you]."

Naiche, who had ridden up and had heard the conversation, said: "You must go with us, for fear some of our men might believe you [are] treacherous & try to kill you."

Gatewood did not reply to Naiche's comment. Instead, he cautioned Geronimo and Naiche to keep a good lookout, in all directions, as American patrols scoured the area. He reminded them that earlier the Mexicans had gotten close because security had grown lax, and warned them to be sure that it did not happen again. Finding a defensible location, the band halted and set up camp.

Bay-chen-daysen told Geronimo and Naiche that he intended to meet with the American officers and talk matters over with them. Then, with Geronimo and Wratten as escort, Gatewood rode back to confront the soldiers. When they saw the American column in the distance, Gatewood and his companions halted and waited as the Americans came forward in single file—first Wood, then Smith.[57]

Gatewood approached Smith and asked what he wanted. Smith said he intended to meet with Geronimo and the Indians. Gatewood told Smith that there would be no meeting. An argument started. Smith outranked Gatewood and intended to take control, but Gatewood replied that the Indians knew and trusted him; Smith's name meant nothing to them. When a satisfactory solution could not be agreed upon, Gatewood broached the real reason for the confrontation: the proposed murder of Geronimo. When Smith continued to insist upon a meeting with the Indians, Gatewood made a stand. Wratten stated that Bay-chen-daysen "threatened to blow the head off the first man if he didn't stop."[58]

At that moment, Wood happened to be in the unenviable position of being first in line, first to receive a bullet. The good doctor, sensing the danger of the situation, pulled back and sent an orderly to San Bernardino to fetch Lawton. Smith, now in the primary position, must have sensed that Gatewood was at the end of his rope and would carry out the threat, and he too backed down. The argument over who was the superior officer, and the thought of surrounding the Indians and killing any who did not surrender their weapons, went by the wayside.

Gatewood, the Sixth Cavalry interloper who had dared to butt in on the Fourth's glory, became a marked man, a hated man. Gatewood's firm hand had averted tragedy, but Smith, Wood, and the Fourth U.S. Cavalry, Miles's chosen regiment to end the war, would never forget the man who dared to take the Chiricahuas' side.

CHAPTER FOURTEEN

Skeleton Canyon

Geronimo, Naiche, and Gatewood hastily moved their camp farther from the Americans. Everyone was alert, ready for an attack. By this time, Geronimo and Naiche were fed up with the trip back to the United States. When the prefect of Arispe and his army had appeared, they feared that the Americans might be capable of treachery. Now, they knew in their hearts that the White Eyes' words were no better than the hated Mexicans. At the same time, their faith in Bay-chen-daysen's word did not waver, and if anything, they now trusted and depended upon him more than ever.

Despite the recent treachery of the Americans, the Apaches still wanted to surrender to them. Bay-chen-daysen represented salvation from the dark night that closed on them and threatened to smother them with doom. One thought obsessed them during their waking hours: get to Miles and surrender before they were murdered.

Geronimo and Naiche approached Gatewood and proposed that they, with him, make a run for the Chiricahua Mountains, where they would hide their people until he met with Miles at Fort Bowie and convinced the general that they wished to surrender.

Gatewood did not know if Miles would be at Bowie. Realizing that it might take time to find the general, and fearing the Apaches would run in the meantime, he refused to take part in such a plan. He had no intention of being the scapegoat for yet another breakout. At the same time, he knew that his position was precarious at best. Already an outsider from the Fourth and the officers leading it, he now found himself in a sort of no-man's-land. The realization that the Americans were capable of murder increased the burden that had been firmly placed on his shoulders. An outcast entangled in what seemed to be a doomed mission, with his only friends the enemy, Gatewood undoubtedly wondered if one of the bullets intended for Geronimo now bore his name. He must have considered everything—Miles's silence regarding Geronimo, the despicable plot by U.S. officers, and the skittishness of the Indians—and questioned just what the hell he was doing.

Although a number of the soldiers present would later claim that Gatewood had complete control of the Apaches, and that they never would have returned to the United States to surrender without his soothing influence,[1] his faith in his own ability failed him. Quite possibly, his deteriorating health played a role in his lack of confidence. Most likely, the American army, which he had to have viewed skeptically, frightened him. Did disaster hover just beyond the next bend in the trail? He saw himself center stage in a budding tragedy.

Lawton had hurried to reclaim control of his command. After meeting with his officers, he feared the Apaches had once again run. Upset, he, along with Wood and several orderlies, hastened to the Chiricahuas' camp, arriving about 8:00 P.M. Lawton immediately sought out Geronimo, Naiche, and the other warriors, telling them that everything was all right.[2] But it was not all right: anyone could see that trouble could erupt at any moment. Geronimo and his warriors were ready, their hands never far from their weapons.

Lawton and Wood stayed for dinner.

Tension rose to near fever pitch as both sides warily watched for the first sign of treachery. Gatewood, fearing the worst, made a decision. He wanted out, he had to get away now. "I wanted to take my baggage and join some other column."[3] He approached Lawton. "I ha[ve] been ordered simply to see that the two Indians went to the hostiles & delivered their message," he said, then stated that he wanted to leave.

Lawton wanted Gatewood to remain. He told the lieutenant why it was necessary that he stay with the Indians, then reminded him that they would both be in a lot of trouble if Geronimo ran. Gatewood refused to accept the captain's answer. Lawton needed Gatewood more than ever to keep Geronimo and his people from stampeding once again and he was not about to risk failure because a subordinate was unhappy with the situation. When Gatewood persisted, Lawton threatened him. If Gatewood attempted to leave, Lawton stated he would use force to stop him. Gatewood, realizing the futility of further argument, ended the confrontation and remained.

Everyone passed an uneasy night.

The next day, September 1, the two groups moved two miles up Guadalupe Canyon, halting at an old ranch that had cottonwood trees and good water.[4] Although the strain from the previous day's events remained on everyone's mind, Geronimo camped near the soldiers.

Warriors and soldiers alike waited for news from Miles. Would the general appear at Skeleton Canyon, or not? If Miles did not show, what would happen? That day a continual stream of couriers rode into and out of Lawton's camp. Also, there was a steady movement of troops coming and going from Lawton's camp. As more and then more soldiers joined Lawton's command, the Bedonkohe warrior became more and more alarmed. In fact, everyone in the Indian camp was restless, uneasy.[5] Gatewood did what he could to keep the old man focused on surrender.

After resting for a day, both groups moved out the afternoon of September 2. Covering the final twelve miles just before nightfall, they finally reached their destination: the entry to Skeleton Canyon. Gatewood and Geronimo found regulars from several commands already there when they arrived, and this immediately played on the old warrior's fears. Before anyone could settle down, more troops arrived. The drastic difference in fighting strength between the two sides made the Indians even more aware that they could still be annihilated.[6]

Geronimo talked with Gatewood. He did not like the situation and proposed again that they leave the soldiers and move on to Fort Bowie. He told Bay-chen-daysen that his people wanted to see Miles and would do whatever he told them to do. Gatewood believed Geronimo, but he would not consider deviating from the original plan. They must remain where they were: Miles would come to them.

When it became evident that Geronimo was very nervous staying where he was, Gatewood sent his interpreters to Lawton with the message that the Indians intended to move their camp. Gatewood made it clear that this in no way meant the Apaches had lost interest in surrendering.[7] He then rode with Geronimo when he moved his camp into the foothills east of the soldiers' camp. The old warrior did not stop until he found a position in the low mountains that could be defended, and there he set up camp, roughly two miles from the White Eyes. Naiche moved even further up into the mountains.[8]

That same September 2, Miles made it known that within a day or two he intended to begin moving the rest of the Chiricahuas from the reservation to their banishment in Florida.[9] It did not matter that these Indians had remained at peace on the reservation, or had served the United States loyally as scouts. President Cleveland, Sheridan, as well as Arizona, and the rest of the West, wanted them gone.

Five days earlier, Miles had written Acting Secretary of War R. C. Drum: "My purpose was, if the Government approved, to move [the Chiricahuas] at least 1,200 miles east, completely disarm them, . . . scatter the grown children through the identical schools of the country, . . ."[10] He went on to say that "Geronimo has been notified that he can surrender, but subject to the disposition of the Government." The question arises: Did Miles mean what he said about Geronimo? Perhaps not.

Although the general had written Lawton, "[The Indians] need have no fear of being killed,"[11] on August 31, he also sent a string of other dispatches to Lawton that same day that belied his first message. In two of the communications, Miles made it clear that he wanted Geronimo disarmed and made a hostage. In yet another, he wrote: "If the Indians give you any guarantee or hostages that they will surrender to me, I will go down, or you can use any other means you think advisable. You will be justified in using any measures."[12] The implication was obvious.

Lawton, like Gatewood, did not enjoy his current situation. Miles's veiled suggestions that he wanted Geronimo surrounded and killed if he did not throw down his arms immediately did not help the matter. Although the captain's standing order had been to destroy Geronimo, he was now on the brink of ending the war without further bloodshed. His commander's lack of haste, combined with an overt hint of treachery, bothered Lawton, and on September 2 he wrote Miles:

> [The Indians] are unusually alert and watchful, and to surprise
> them is simply impossible. I could by treachery perhaps kill one or
> two of them, but it would only make everything much worse than
> before. . . .
> Their coming up so far has been the result of circumstances, first
> the Mexican troops, then our own. They are suspicious and timid,
> and the gathering of troops has made them suspicious of me. . . . [13]

Feeling trapped by the entire situation, Lawton wanted release from the responsibility entrusted in him. He closed with a very telling comment, especially when set in the context of his refusal to let Gatewood leave: "I would be glad to have an officer directly from yourself come out and take command."

"A perfect epidemic of couriers,"[14] Wood recorded in his journal on September 3. "No news. Everybody trying to do something and doing nothing."

The day brought a swirl of activity on the flat land at the entrance to the canyon. It had to have been disconcerting to Geronimo as he studied the White Eyes from his mountain perch. The stress had to have been no less for Bay-chen-daysen. Together, both waited, . . . and watched—alert for anything.

Under a burning September sun, the day slowly dragged on, and by noon nothing had changed. A miasma of soldiers milled about, their growing numbers swarming like maggots. Still no news of Miles arrived.

As the day began to wane, Lawton sent a message to Acting Assistant Adjutant General of the Department of Arizona William A. Thompson. He, in turn, heliographed Miles: "Lawton says the hostiles will surrender to you, but if he does not see you today he is afraid they will leave."[15]

Miles, who was only eighteen miles from Skeleton Canyon, must have realized that if he continued to vacillate, he would lose Geronimo. With his entourage he traveled to the meeting point, arriving at 3:00 P.M.[16]

Kayitah and Martine rode to Geronimo's camp to tell the old warrior that Miles had arrived and wanted to meet with him.[17] "[This] created quite a stir in the camp,"[18] Gatewood remembered. "The Indians naturally were very curious to see him & you may imagine were extremely interested in finding out what he had to say."

Geronimo immediately sent word to Naiche that the general had finally come to see them. Naiche refused to meet the White-eye leader, but this did not matter to Geronimo. He quickly mounted and rode to the soldier camp, with Bay-chen-daysen accompanying him. They dismounted when they reached the camp. Geronimo left his weapons on his horse, guards announced their arrival, and Miles and his aides appeared from the general's tent.

Responding to the call for interpreters, a man named Nelson and another named José María Yaskes arrived. Nelson would translate from English into Spanish and back, and Yaskes would perform a similar task between Spanish and Apache. Along with interpreter José María Montoya (who just listened), Wood and Clay were also present.[19]

"I have come to have a talk with you,"[20] Miles said.

For Geronimo the wait had ended. He had no intention of wasting time.

I . . . told him how I had been wronged, and that I wanted to return to the United States with my people, as we wished to see our families, who had been captured and taken away from us.[21]

Miles listened as Geronimo continued. The general wrote:

[Geronimo] stated that he had been abused and assailed by the officials, and that a plot had been laid to take his life by Chatto and Mick[e]y Free, encouraged by one of the officials; that it was a question whether to die on the war-path or be assassinated; that at that time he was cultivating a crop, and if he had not been driven away he would by this time have been in good circumstances.[22]

"A part of this story I know to be true," Miles commented.

Then, according to Geronimo, Miles said:

The President of the United States has sent me to speak to you. He
has heard of your trouble with the white men, and says that if you
will agree to a few words of treaty we need have no more trouble.
Geronimo, if you will agree to a few words of treaty all will be satis-
factorily arranged.[23]

Miles continued:

I informed him that Captain Lawton and Lieutenant Gatewood were
honorable men, and that I was there to confirm what they had said
to [him]; that though Captain Lawton, with other troops, had followed and fought them incessantly, yet should they throw down
their arms and place themselves entirely at our mercy we should certainly not kill them, but that they must surrender absolutely as prisoners of war to the Federal authorities and rely upon the Government to treat them fairly and justly.[24]

Miles then spoke at length regarding Geronimo and his people's future.
According to Geronimo, Miles said:

I will take you under Government protection; I will build you a
house; I will fence you much land; I will give you cattle, horses,
mules, and farming implements. You will be furnished with men to
work the farm, for you yourself will not have to work. In the fall I
will send you blankets and clothing so that you will not suffer from
cold in the winter time.
    There is plenty of timber, water, and grass in the land to which I
will send you. You will live with your tribe and with your family. If
you agree to this treaty you shall see your family within five days.[25]

Much has been said about Geronimo's interpretation of this meeting. The
main gist is that his words were recorded long after the fact and that they
were self-serving at best. Perhaps they were, but less than a month after the
surrender, Geronimo told Colonel David S. Stanley, then stationed in San
Antonio, Texas, that Miles said to him: "Lay down your arms and come with
me to Fort Bowie, and in five days you will see your families, now in Florida
with Chihuahua, and no harm will be done you."[26]
    "All the officers that have been in charge of the Indians have talked that
way, and it sounds like a story to me,"[27] Geronimo said, "I hardly believe
you."
    "This time it is the truth," Miles replied.

"General Miles," Geronimo said, "I do not know the laws of the white man, nor of this new country where you are to send me, and I might break the laws."

"While I live," Miles said, "you will not be arrested."

Miles then drew a line on the ground. "This represents the ocean,"[28] Miles said. He then placed a rock by the line. "This represents the place where Chihuahua is with his band." Miles picked up a second stone and placed it near the first. "This represents you, Geronimo." Miles picked up a third stone. "This represents the Indians at Camp Apache," he said as he placed the stone a short distance from the other two. "The President wants to take you and put you with Chihuahua." Miles picked up the stone that represented Geronimo and placed it next to the stone that represented Chihuahua. He then picked up the third stone a second time and set it down next to the first two. "That is what the President wants to do, get all of you together."

Miles's view of the essence of the negotiation differed: "I informed [Geronimo] that I was moving all [the] Chiricahua[s] from Arizona, and that they would be removed from this country at once and for all time. Geronimo replied that he would do whatever I said, obey any order, and bring in his camp early next morning, . . ."[29]

Two sides, one talk, two versions of what the final result would be. Either one side lied or the translation from English to Spanish to Apache and back was poor.

Gatewood, who saw and heard everything, did not help in clarifying the matter. "Gen[eral] Miles told them what he would [do], the gist of which was that they would be sent to Florida & there await the final action of the President of the United States."[30]

Geronimo turned to Gatewood and smiled. "Good, you told the truth."

The old warrior seemed pleased with the surrender. No more Chiricahuas would die, his people would be reunited with their families, and at some unnamed date they would have good land. "I agreed to make the treaty,"[31] Geronimo said.

Finished, Miles turned to the interpreter. "Tell them I have no more to say. I would like to talk generally with them, but we do not understand each other's language."[32]

The war had not ended—not yet. Naiche, the last chieftain of the Chiricahuas, remained in the hills, refusing to come in to talk. Between twelve and fifteen of the warriors from the band were with him.[33] Add their families to the count, and most of the Chiricahuas returning from Mexico had still not surrendered. For the war to end, Naiche also had to submit to Miles's terms. Naiche sent word that he desired twelve days; he wanted to go to the White Mountains to think over the situation. Miles surmised: "[Naiche] was wild and suspicious and evidently feared treachery."[34] Miles denied the request.

Geronimo knew that the last hope of resistance had passed. He sent word to Naiche to come in and surrender. Naiche replied that he would, but only if Geronimo would come out and get him. The next day, September 4, Geronimo brought his camp into the soldiers' bivouac. He then asked Gatewood to ride out to find Naiche with him. Gatewood agreed, calling for a couple of interpreters to accompany them. When they neared Naiche's camp, they dismounted and walked in on foot. Gatewood and Geronimo found Naiche on a ridge looking toward Mexico. Bay-chen-daysen asked the chieftain why he had not come in to talk with Miles.

"I am looking for one of my relatives who I sent back to Mexico after some cached horses which we left there," Naiche said, "and as he has not returned, I fear something wrong has happened to him."[35]

Gatewood told him, "the big White Chief ha[s] arrived, & [your] presence [is] necessary to complete the formalities of surrender." Continuing, he said, "Among the whites such delay for the reason stated [i]s never made, & it would appear better . . . to control [your] grief . . . & conform to the usual custom of such occasions as the present."[36]

Naiche replied that this was a hard request since he did not know "the fate of his brother."

"[Naiche]," Gatewood said, "you promised me that when we got to the line you would talk to General Miles about surrendering."[37]

Naiche considered Bay-chen-daysen's words. Finally he said: "That's so."

Gatewood continued to talk. His words, perhaps for the last time, soothed and persuaded. Naiche listened to Gatewood and believed him. He said "he did not wish to show disrespect to the big chief[:] he would go immediately."[38] Naiche spoke and the people began to pack. As soon as they were ready, the band moved down from the mountain and toward the white encampment at Skeleton Canyon.

Geronimo and Naiche rode into Miles's bivouac together, and Gatewood accompanied them, for the last time. They dismounted and met Miles. The general basically repeated what he had said to Geronimo and Naiche heard the words as Geronimo did. The surrender final, Geronimo and Naiche placed themselves and their people under the control of the United States military.

A short while later a violent thunderstorm pounded the land. While Geronimo and Naiche stood under a shelter, Miles took the opportunity to explain "that I hoped it was a good omen, that there was evidently a silver lining to that war cloud, and that the sunshine of peace would bless [the] land after the turmoil of relentless war."[39]

Perhaps Miles's omen held true for Arizona and New Mexico, but not for Gatewood and Geronimo. The dark cloud that pummeled Mother Earth violently that fateful day in September 1886 never gave birth to the new life that both Gatewood and Geronimo hoped the future held. Fate had thrust them together to reach the turning point in both their lives as one. It did not matter if this so-called pinnacle they had fought so hard to attain was called a high point or a low one, it was now over. Gone. A memory, cherished or hated, but no more than a string of events that would be partially remembered, . . . then stolen, reworked, and finally forgotten. They had reached across the wide chasm of racial hatred and struggled side by side to bring about a peaceful end to the final Apache war.

They would now walk the uncertain trail of the future on separate paths.

CHAPTER FIFTEEN

Campaign's End

Despite the overwhelming odds that he would not complete his assignment, Gatewood had come through. He had found Geronimo and convinced him that he had to surrender or die. And finally, he had protected the old warrior from everything that would have caused him to bolt during his return trek to the United States.

In the army, Bay-chen-daysen's years of service had been unique. He had led many scouting parties in pursuit of recalcitrant Apaches. During those years he had also worked side by side with Apaches who had tried to make a go of it on the reservation. He had seen both sides of the conflict, and now, by getting Geronimo to surrender, he knew he had accomplished an extraordinary feat.

Gatewood's bone-weary body had been on the verge of quitting at every pain-induced step during the long venture into Mexico. Now, it must have felt revitalized, invigorated by the realization that his entire future suddenly looked brighter. Miles had dangled the aide-de-camp position tantalizingly before him back in July, and now it was his for the taking. Not only would it mark a major turning point in his military career, but it would mean the end of the fieldwork his body was no longer capable of handling. He was sure that promotions would follow, along with better living conditions for his young family. Gatewood's future looked promising indeed.

Geronimo, too, had hopes for a better future. Along with Naiche and the others, he looked forward to being reunited with his loved ones, as well as with Chihuahua and his band. Miles had promised that they would go to another land. An era of peace seemed to have arrived.

On the morning of September 5, Geronimo, Naiche, Perico, and two other Chiricahuas traveled with Miles and his escort to Fort Bowie.[1] The Indians rode in the back of an ambulance, while Miles sat next to the driver. That same day Wade, who still held the four-hundred-plus Chihenne, Chokonen, and Bedonkohe Apaches at Fort Apache, told them why they were being held and where they would be shipped.[2]

Clay joined the detail that protected the general and his cargo, riding behind the ambulance during the eleven-hour trip. His instructions were simple: "kill any one who attempted to escape."[3]

Looking at the Chiricahua Mountains as they neared Bowie, Geronimo said to Miles: "This is the fourth time I have surrendered."[4]

"And I think it is the last time you will ever have occasion to surrender," the general replied.

Lawton, Wood, and Gatewood followed at a more leisurely pace with the rest of the band, taking three days to complete the sixty-mile journey.[5]

Geronimo and Miles reached Fort Bowie the night of September 5. Wratten remembered the scene: "we were so dusty [the soldiers at Bowie] hardly knew us."[6]

Miles took no chances. Soldiers were everywhere. He had ordered extra men to protect Geronimo and Naiche. Arizona's populace, as well as the civil authorities, wanted the two leaders to stand trial in Tucson.[7] Miles had no intention of allowing a U.S. Marshal to enter the compound and claim them, for a trial would amount to little more than mob law with the verdict a foregone conclusion. To Miles, the Apaches were military prisoners and would remain so.

Geronimo and Naiche surrendered their arms. "There was no place [at Bowie] to put [Geronimo] in except an old calaboose or crib of some kind," Wratten later said, "and we put him in that. He was now a prisoner of war."[8] Although Geronimo was not aware of it, the fight for his head had begun and his fate depended upon who won.

Miles met with Geronimo and Naiche on the parade ground. During the meeting Miles bent down and cleared a piece of the ground with his hand, then said: "everything you have done up to this time will be wiped out like th[is] and forgotten, and you will begin a new life."[9]

Miles had been ordered to ship the reservation Chiricahuas to Fort Marion, Florida.[10] As far as he was concerned, this meant all of the two groups. On September 6, he issued Field Orders Number 89:

In obedience to telegraphic instructions from the Acting Secretary of War, dated Washington, September 4, 1886, Capt[ain] H. W. Lawton, Fourth Cavalry, accompanied by First Lieut[enant] A. L. Smith, Fourth Cavalry; First Lieut[enant] T. J. Clay, Tenth Infantry; Ass[istant] Surg[eon Leonard] Wood, U.S. Army, Interpreters George Wratt[e]n, Edwa[d]dy, J. M. Montoy[a], and twenty men of Troop B, Fourth Cavalry, *will take charge of the surrendered Chiricahua Indian prisoners of war, and proceed with them to Fort Marion, Fl[orida].*[11]

Miles, to his credit, stood by his statement that he would get Geronimo and his people safely out of Arizona. "There was quite a demand at the time for the immediate trial and execution of the principal Indians," Miles would later write, "but it would have been impossible to have obtained an unprejudiced jury and difficult to obtain the evidence of actual participation of individual Indians in the atrocities."[12] The order to move Geronimo's band to Florida set off a controversy that ranged all the way to the White House and put Miles on the defensive for his actions.

Lawton, Wood, and Gatewood marched northward with the rest of the prisoners. During the day's trek on September 6, the command halted for an hour while a young girl gave birth. The next night, they camped a short distance from Fort Bowie. The Indians still had their arms and would not surrender them until they reached the fort.[13]

That day President Cleveland sent a telegram to Acting Secretary of War R. C. Drum which did not bode well for Geronimo and Naiche: "All the hostiles should be very safely kept as prisoners until they can be tried for their crimes or otherwise disposed of, and those to be sent to Florida should be started immediately."[14]

Gatewood knew he would soon be an aide to Miles, as this possibility had been suggested before he went to Mexico in search of Geronimo; however, he considered this position a second choice. His first choice was a detail in the staff corps, and because the timing would never be better he applied for the position. Right after talking Geronimo into traveling north to meet Miles, Gatewood began a letter to Georgia, which he did not complete on August 26, probably because there was no way to have it delivered. At an undetermined future date, he wrote, "Later," and continued: "I am getting my application for Q. M. [quartermaster] into shape." After describing the attachment and endorsements that he intended to submit, he closed with: "Seem to think of nothing but my promotion."[15]

Yes, the lieutenant was feeling good, his mission accomplished. The accolades would soon follow, as would hopefully, the first of many promotions. Back in Arizona, he began his quest in earnest for the quartermaster position.

Although Miles had wanted Wade to begin moving the reservation Apaches to Florida on September 3 or 4, the colonel met with transportation delays. On September 7, he finally began the removal of the Indians. It was anticipated that he would reach Holbrook, Arizona, by the thirteenth, and from there the prisoners would be shipped to Albuquerque, St. Louis, and Atlanta on their journey to Florida, the land of their future exile.

Miles acted quickly, knowing that he could not stall if he hoped to move Geronimo. On September 7 he telegrammed Sheridan: *"To-morrow I hope to start the prisoners with Geronimo and [Naiche] east via New Orleans."*[16]

Sheridan immediately replied: "As the disposition of Geronimo and his hostile band is yet to be decided by the President, and as they are prisoners without conditions, *you are hereby directed to hold them in close confinement at Fort Bowie until the decision of the President is communicated to you."*[17]

Miles hurriedly answered: "There is not accommodation here for holding these Indians, and should one escape in these mountains he would cause trouble and the labor of the troops be lost. Everything is arranged for moving them and I earnestly request permission to move them out of this mountain country, . . ."[18] Miles was justly concerned, for shortly before dawn on September 8, three male and three female Apaches escaped from the Lawton/Wood/Chiricahua camp.[19]

That day at Bowie, Geronimo and his people were allowed to obtain some much-needed clothing. While Geronimo and Naiche waited for what would happen next, an enterprising photographer took several photographs of them. Finally, orders were given to move the Indians to the railhead. At 11:00 A.M. the prisoners boarded wagons, and Lawton and Wood led the Fourth Cavalry escort as the wagons filed out of the fort and down the dusty, winding trail toward Apache Pass.

During the trip, Wood rode with Acting Assistant Adjutant General Thompson, who had had a few drinks, perhaps celebrating the victory or, more likely, bolstering his courage for what could be interpreted as a criminal act. He patted his pocket, indicating he carried a recent communiqué. "I have got something here which would stop this movement," he said in a confidential tone, "but I am not going to let the old man [Miles] see it until you are gone, then I will repeat it to him."[20] He went on to explain that he carried orders from Washington prohibiting Geronimo and his band's removal from Arizona.

Lawton's escort made good time and the procession reached Bowie Station by 1:30 P.M., where the train was ready and waiting. Miles and his staff also made the journey, for events were too important for the general to be absent. Gatewood was the only notable participant not present; this was the Fourth's victory. Final photos were taken, then the Indians and troops boarded the train. Martine and Kayitah also got on board. There had been no pretense with the two scouts: there would be no awards, no show of gratitude, for they too were now on their way to Florida, to begin their confinement.[21] Miles would accompany the prisoners to the New Mexico bor-

der, and only then, with the Indians safely out of his department, would he
be able to breathe easily.

While the White Eyes were jubilant, every warrior, woman, and child on
the train tensely awaited the inevitable. "When they put us on that train at
Bowie," Kanseah said, "nobody thought that we'd get far before they'd stop
it and kill us."[22] Their fear grew as the train crossed New Mexico, entered
Texas, and came to an unceremonious halt before it could cross the state. On
September 10, Drum telegraphed Texas departmental commander D. S.
Stanley to remove the Indians from the train in San Antonio and hold them
until he received further orders.[23] Stanley confined the prisoners at Fort Sam
Houston.

Interpreter Wratten had made the journey with Geronimo. Living with
the Apaches, he tried to reassure everyone that everything would be fine,
even though he himself began to think otherwise. One day passed, and then
another, and another. Soldiers were everywhere: their weapons at the ready.
The Indians wondered what was happening. Why had the journey to the
land called Florida stopped? Geronimo met with Wratten. "They are going
to kill me,"[24] the old warrior announced. He then said:

> Ussen . . . promised that I should live to be an old man and have a
> natural death. But he made no stipulations regarding the braves. It is
> for them that I fear. They are unarmed. If we had weapons we would
> fight it out as we have in the past.

Wratten had become an exile voluntarily. He thought about Geronimo's
words, then reached within himself to find a truth he could live with. Not
about to watch unarmed men die, Wratten told Geronimo that he had guns
and ammunition hidden in his tent. "Tell your warriors [that] if the attack
comes, they are to get them. I can't let unarmed men be murdered even if I
have to join them." Time would prove Wratten one of the best friends the
Apaches ever had.

Kanseah, although young at the time, remembered the turmoil that
enveloped his people, smothering them with a feeling of doom:

> The word was passed, but the odds were too great for the Apaches
> to have any hope of surviving an attack. We all expected it, and my
> mother told me that if it came I was to show these White Eyes how
> an Apache can die.

Meanwhile, New Mexico prepared to celebrate the banishment of the
dreaded Apaches. That September, the city of Albuquerque hosted a sixteen-

day festival that included dances, dinners, and receptions.[25] Fittingly, late at night, the ten-car train carrying the reservation Chiricahuas and their guards sped through Albuquerque without disrupting the celebration. Miles and Wood became inseparable during the fete, carrying the party to Las Vegas, New Mexico, for an additional two days and then back to Albuquerque. The bond that joined the general and doctor that September may have played a part in Gatewood's future.[26] Wood could never forget, nor could he forgive, the lieutenant's audacity in confronting the plot to murder Geronimo. And now he had the general's ear.

Chatto and the Apaches who had visited Washington were not forgotten. On September 12, Acting Secretary of War Drum ordered Alfred Terry, who commanded the Division of the Missouri, to ship them to St. Augustine, Florida.[27]

This was Chatto's bitter reward for loyal service to the United States military: he would now join his brethren in exile; the same brethren who hated his guts and considered him little more than a traitor. Carrying the silver medal bearing ex-president Arthur's image that Interior Secretary L. Q. C. Lamar had awarded him when he visited Washington, he had to be a totally confused and angry man. No wonder the *San Francisco Chronicle* called Chatto "a rather quiet, deep-thinking Indian. He has a sullen look always."[28] Surprisingly, the pride the medal initially gave Chatto never faded.

American treachery was not reserved for Chatto alone. The Chiricahuas who had served loyally as scouts, and had refused to ride the war trail with Geronimo, had been rounded up with the rest of their people at Fort Apache and now journeyed eastward with Wade.

Geronimo had come in, surrendered, and the war had ended. One sickly white man with two Chiricahua scouts and one interpreter had pulled off what approximately five thousand U.S. troops and three thousand Mexican regulars had not been able to do. Forget the impossible odds! No gambler in his right mind would have bet money on Gatewood succeeding. Bay-chen-daysen had marched into Mexico the previous July on a fool's errand, a dead man still walking. By all rights, Gatewood and his party should have perished in the wilds of the Sierra Madre, as a recent news clipping had surmised,[29] but he did not. Instead, he accomplished a nearly impossible task.

Few of the men who had chased Geronimo after Miles took command knew Gatewood, as none were from his regiment. But now they certainly knew his name. Charles Riepert (Troop B, Fourth U.S. Cavalry) later wrote:

I was only a private soldier at that time, so I did not know [Gatewood] personally, but everybody [knew] that if it was not for L[ieutenan]t Gatewood the campaign would [have] lasted much longer. . . . he was very popular amongst the men [as] we were sick and tired of the chase.[30]

Charles Maurer, another soldier with the Fourth, wrote: "All the [m]en, right after the campaign and since I have spoken to, were all of the same mind that Lieut[enant] Gatewood was the [m]an who persuaded Geronimo to surrender[.]"[31]

Riding the crest of his achievement, Gatewood anticipated that his career would flourish. Never one to brag, Bay-chen-daysen mistakenly *assumed* that his deeds would speak for themselves—and in so doing, he made a fatal mistake, a mistake that essentially ended his military career.

Although Gatewood was a Crook outcast, he was ironically still known as a Crook man. And the fact that he messed with the Sixth, and not the Fourth, confirmed his status as outsider. The Fourth, and not the Sixth, had braved the hardships of the Mexican wilds during the final months of the campaign, and they believed that the glory belonged to them. Worse, Gatewood had constantly clashed with officers of the Fourth during his expedition into the Sierra Madre, and these officers, who understood the unwritten rules for climbing to the top of the military ladder, hated him not only for his success but for his audacity in crossing them.

From Miles on down, everyone scrambled to take credit for the final surrender—everyone but Gatewood. Lawton's report of September 9 singled out, for exceptional service, Wood;[32] lieutenants Walsh, Finley, Brown, Smith, H. C. Benson (who kept Lawton's command supplied); along with chief packer William Brown; and scouts Edwaddy, Long, and Jack Wilson. By ignoring Gatewood in this section of his report, Lawton had begun the onslaught. Although Miles's book, *Personal Recollections and Observations of General Nelson A. Miles*, would not be published until the year of Gatewood's death, the general, without actually saying so, delivered the final thrust that displayed his total contempt for Gatewood's contribution when he gave all the credit for the surrender to Lawton.[33]

The anti-Gatewood attitude did not go unnoticed. On September 13, the *Arizona Citizen* printed:

Lieut[enant] Gatewood performed his hard duty with a faithful adroitness and after its completion he has unostentatio[us]ly resumed his routine duties at one of the posts in this department, asking noth-

ing of the praise or glory of his contributions to the grand achieve-
ments of the past few weeks, and expressing no discontent that his
services have been scarcely noticed.[34]

Gatewood observed the war that raged around him. But, as the *Citizen*
stated, he refused to fight for what he had earned. As the controversy—*who
was responsible for bringing about the end to the war?*—swept through military circles and across the Southwest, Gatewood's detachment increased.
On the surface, his refusal to seek allies for his cause gave the appearance
that he did not care who got the credit for Geronimo's surrender. But that
was not the case. What began as a snub, and would grow into an attempt
to rewrite his part in the final surrender, wounded Gatewood more deeply
than any bullet or arrow ever could. He would never recover from its effects.

On September 10, Thompson wrote Miles, who had gone to Albuquerque
after seeing Geronimo safely out of his department: "Can I order Gatewood
to report to you at Albuquerque en route to F[or]t Stanton[?]"[35] The answer
must have been in the affirmative. On September 14, Miles issued General
Orders No. 21:

> 1st Lieutenant C. B. Gatewood, 6th Cavalry, is hereby appointed
> aide-de-camp to the Brigadier General commanding, and will be
> obeyed and respected accordingly.[36]

Although this was not the position Gatewood wanted, he was well suited for
it. The ravages of rheumatism had once again shown that he was no longer
capable of extended field duty. Sheer will, fortified by Lawton and Wood's
refusal to dismiss him, had pulled him through in Mexico. With several years
of reservation administrative duty behind him, he was well prepared for the
next phase of his professional life.

For the second time in his career, Gatewood found himself working hand
in hand with his commanding general. For many, this was an enviable position. Reporting as ordered, he immediately assumed his responsibilities, issu-
ing reports that kept Miles updated on current affairs in the Department of
Arizona.[37]

As Gatewood settled into his new position, the controversy over what to
do with Geronimo and Naiche swirled. An angry Sheridan wrote the secretary of war: "It was my understanding that Geronimo and the hostiles surrendered unconditionally, and it was on that account I recommended that
they should be turned over to the civil authorities of Arizona and New Mexico for trial and such punishment as might be awarded them."[38]

Miles found himself defending his actions and requested permission to see President Cleveland.[39] His request was denied.[40] On September 29, he wrote Drum that the militant Chiricahuas' "status is the same as that of Chief Joseph, Sitting Bull, and hundreds of others; they are strictly prisoners of war, . . . They could not have been legally held as prisoners of war by the military twenty-four hours in [Arizona], and had they not been removed, the result would undoubtedly have been escape or massacre; and turning them over to the local authorities at that time or now would be simply a mockery of justice." Miles concluded with: "it was an imperative necessity to remove the entire tribe to a place of safe custody."[41]

As the Miles/Cleveland/Sheridan battle for Geronimo's head wore on, Gatewood found himself in Santa Fe, New Mexico, where the favorable reception he received pleased him. He liked being hailed as a returning hero. After voicing all the proper comments regarding the end of the Apache war, Gatewood turned his back on the controversy and came to his commander's defense:

> I didn't come here to talk about the Indian question. It has been
> worn thread-bare. However, I do feel like saying one word in behalf
> of Gen[eral] Miles. For this officer's splendid services in accomplish-
> ing what others had failed to do, never was a man more basely mis-
> represented and maligned . . . [42]

Gatewood closed his comments by damning "the petty official jealousies and venality of the Eastern press, . . . which have attempted to besmirch [Miles's] fair record."

On October 20, O. O. Howard reported that the last holdout in Mexico, Mangus, had been captured the day before after being pursued "through Chihuahua and Southern New Mexico, since September 7."[43] Mangus had two warriors, three women, and five children with him.

Contrary to this and subsequent military reports, Mangus was not captured. As Daklugie, who was with Mangus, remembered: "Mangus attacked nobody unless forced to do so in self-defense. We could have killed many had we wished."[44] By keeping a low profile, he had avoided contact with the White Eyes.

Until Mangus appeared near Fort Apache that October, no one had any idea what had become of him.[45] Like Geronimo, Mangus wanted to be reunited with his people; and when he heard that Geronimo and Naiche had turned their backs on war, he decided it was useless to continue the fight. Daklugie remembered that one of the scouts with the soldiers "advised me to arrange for a meeting . . . under a flag of truce. . . . And that is what was done. *Mangus went in voluntarily and surrendered.*"[46]

Many have damned Miles, claiming duplicity in the surrender terms he made with Geronimo and Naiche. Maybe this was so, or perhaps it was simply confusion. The Indians believed they would return to their homeland within a few years. Miles held that he had banished them forever. This was, and would forever be, a chasm as wide and deep as the Grand Canyon, a rift that would never be bridged. Still, one very important thing must be remembered: Miles put his career on the line when he hustled Geronimo out of Arizona Territory.

And the risk was worth the hellish aftermath. Miles won the fight for Geronimo's life. On October 29 Sheridan ordered Terry to send Geronimo, Naiche, Perico, Fun, Ahnandia (*Abnandria, Ahnondia, An-nan-dia*), Nahi, Yahnosha, Fishnolth, Touzee, Kitldigai, Sephanne, Bishi, Chappo, Lazaiyah, Matzus, Lonat, and the interpreters with them to Fort Pickens. And again, another discrepancy surfaced. Geronimo and Naiche understood that they would be reunited with their families when they surrendered, but this was not to be. They would not be shipped to the place where Chihuahua was held. Nor would they be reunited with their loved ones who had remained on the reservation. And worse, they would now be separated from their wives and children who had survived the war trail with them. The eleven women and six children who had surrendered with them, along with Martine and Kayitah, were sent to Fort Marion, Florida.[47] But this was not Miles's doing.

The report announcing Geronimo's arrival at his destination in Florida on October 25 was succinct: "Geronimo and fourteen bucks with interpreter [Wratten] are in Fort Pickens."[48] The report also stated: "Geronimo says they are well satisfied." Nothing could have been further from the truth.

Geronimo and Naiche had escaped the hangman's noose. They must have been relieved when they were finally loaded aboard a train at San Antonio and found themselves heading east toward Florida. But the elation did not last long. At Fort Pickens, Pensacola, Florida, they realized that they had been lied to—their families were elsewhere; maybe even dead.

Geronimo's comments are mild. "Here they put me to sawing up large logs. There were several other Apache warriors with me, and all of us had to work every day." After commenting on the separation from their families, he said: "This treatment was in direct violation of our treaty made at Skeleton Cañon."[49] And he was right. Maybe he was lucky to be alive, but this was not what he understood his future to hold.

One needs to return to the basis of Apache culture to understand the tragedy of Geronimo's situation. Although a major part of Apache culture was based upon warfare, the main ingredient of their lifeway was family structure. For Geronimo and Naiche, there was no family. Cast adrift in a living hell, they had no life. Daklugie's words summed up the situation:

> [Geronimo] was the embodiment of the Apache spirit, of the fighting Chiricahua. Where were they now? Never would he have quit had it not been that the enemy had the wives and children of some of his warriors, including one of Naiche's. As long as Geronimo lived, he regretted having surrendered. He often said that he wished he had died fighting in Mexico.[50]

While Gatewood performed the duties of his new position, controversy continued to swirl around him. Some of the articles stretched the truth so much they hovered on the verge of legend. The *San Francisco Chronicle* and the *Kalamazoo Telegraph* fell into this category when they reported that Gatewood walked into Geronimo's camp with only one Chiricahua guide and stayed twelve days until he talked the old warrior into surrendering. After complaining about Lawton getting all the credit, they proclaimed that Gatewood alone deserved the credit.[51] Heady stuff, even if the facts were distorted.

But there was another force working the publicity junket that fall and winter. For every article that commented favorably on his feat, another surfaced relegating him to the part of bit player.

On November 15, Gatewood assumed a new responsibility. He took charge of, and conducted the business of, the judge advocate's office of the Department of Arizona.[52] At the same time, he continued his quest for the assignment he really wanted. He applied for the rank of captain in either the Quartermaster or the Subsistence departments. Gatewood enlisted, among others, Thomas McCulloh, his father-in-law, to aid in this effort.

One day, while stationed at Whipple Barracks, outside Prescott, Arizona, Gatewood went to town, where he bumped into his old packmaster, Henry Daly, that evening. They decided to get a drink, went into a saloon, and soon their conversation turned to the recent campaign. Daly entered forbidden territory when he told Gatewood that Miles would never give him the credit due him.

"I [don't] owe my commission to General Crook,"[53] Gatewood snapped.

Daly surmised that Gatewood's anger still smoldered over the Zuck affair. "Well, Lieut[enant,] just wait and see. You do not know Gen[eral] Miles as well as I do."

Having had a few drinks, Gatewood began speaking loud enough that others heard him. "Daly, what is the matter with you?" he asked.

"Well, Lieutenant, if you know me, as I know you, you would never make the proposition to Miles to bring about the surrender of Geronimo, and mark my words, you will live to regret it." Daly then added that "as a Crook man, [Miles] has no use for you."

"The hell you say," Gatewood said.

"Yes, Lieutenant[,] I regret it, because I value your experience and have always felt a sincere attachment for you, and you know that I do."

The tension between them grew. They stood and moved outside to the sidewalk. To ease the heated air, they changed the subject to how Gatewood met Geronimo and the terms of surrender.

Suddenly, an ambulance pulled up at the curb beside them. Miles leaned out of the ambulance and said: "Mr. Gatewood[,] get into this ambulance with me."

"[I will] return [to the post] when [I get] good and ready," Gatewood replied—not the correct answer to give a general, and not the correct answer for a man physically larger and stronger than himself.

The general climbed down from the ambulance, grabbed Gatewood by the shoulder and pushed him into the ambulance. Climbing back aboard, Miles drove off.

Gatewood felt no loyalty toward Crook, and up to this point in time, felt his connection to Miles secured his future.

Whatever was said during the ride back to Whipple Barracks remains unknown, but it did not sour one officer against the other. Gatewood's performance in his new position had to have supported his request to become captain. Miles may have attempted to deny Gatewood credit for his part in ending the war, but he would not shortchange the lieutenant in his *Efficiency Report*:

> Is aide-de-camp to the Com[manding] Gen[eral] of the Dep[artment]. Is efficient in all that pertains to the duties of his office. Attention to duty, conduct and habits, Excellent; is qualified to fill any detail to which his rank makes him available. Is well qualified for the management of Indians. 'A brave officer and a gentleman of integrity and good character.'[54]

A glowing recommendation!

On December 28, Miles seconded Gatewood's application, stating, "His zeal and courage are of the highest order, . . ."[55] But there were no openings. A letter dated December 4, 1886, to McCulloh, stated: "Senator Gorman himself called on the Secretary [of War] and personally urged the appointment of Lieutenant Gatewood as Captain and Assistant Quartermaster or Commissary of Subsistence, but that there is now no vacancy in either of the departments named, and until one occurs no appointment therein can be made. The Secretary suggests that Lieutenant Gatewood place his application for the appointment on file in this office, . . ."[56]

A trend had begun, one that would continue to haunt Gatewood for the remainder of his career.

Gatewood, Geronimo, and the USA

Gatewood and Geronimo, two men, different in race and culture—one had found acceptance in the other's world through his honesty and fairness; the second, propelled by a burning hatred that could never be quelled, carved a name for himself that struck terror throughout the Southwest. While the lanky White Eye walked begrudgingly among the Apache, the stocky Bedonkohe medicine man returned to the war trail again and again as he fought to keep the life to which he was born. During these years their lives became intertwined without either of them knowing it. They only met a few times, and yet those seemingly random encounters made it possible for them to meet one final time in August 1886. Somehow their lives had prepared them to bridge the deep chasm of racial and cultural prejudice that separated them and allowed them for the brief span of a few days to join hands and work as one to reach the location where a final peace could be agreed upon.

The war had ended for all time. Never again would Geronimo stalk human prey. Never again would he strike with lightning swiftness, only to disappear into the vastness of the American Southwest or the Mexican Sierra Madre. And never again would Gatewood give chase over trails so faint that only his Apache scouts could follow them. Never again would he push himself to the brink of collapse in an effort to accomplish his task.

Yes, the Apache war had finally ended. And with it—although as yet unknown to both of them—so had the future they had both envisioned.

Chihuahua and those who had surrendered to Crook in March had reached Florida first, on April 13. They were already crammed together at Fort Marion, St. Augustine, in an area not much larger than a football field, when the Chokonen and Chihenne who had kept the peace arrived from Fort Apache in September.

"They were almost dead," Eugene Chihuahua recalled about the new arrivals: "they were almost naked; they were hungry; and they were pitifully dirty."[1] There were two bathrooms (one for the men and one for the women), and two bathtubs; and the people had to stand in line for hours to use the facilities.

For Geronimo, conditions were not nearly so bad. Segregated with the warriors and boys who had ridden the war trail with him, they had their new home, Fort Pickens, Pensacola, to themselves. The dilapidated old stone fortress, located on a small island off the southern coast of western Florida, immediately eliminated any thoughts of escape.

What happened to Geronimo's wives and children? Had they been killed? The seeds of deceit propagated. Being separated from his family became the first lie. Blame it on treachery, blame it on the translation of words from one language to another; it did not matter where the blame was placed, for this new life was not the life Geronimo thought he had agreed upon. This perfidy marked the beginning of a change that saw perhaps the most feared and hated man in two countries transformed from a legendary guerrilla fighter into a bitter old man.

A culture stood on the brink of extinction.

There were now 381 Apaches in Florida: 278 adults and 103 children. While unsanitary, overcrowded conditions at St. Augustine began to exact a toll in lives, Geronimo and the few with him adjusted to their life of solitude.

For Daklugie, who at fourteen had not quite reached manhood, the bitterness, as with his uncle Geronimo, grew with each passing day. He would later say: "No Apache was ever cruel enough to imprison anyone. Only a White Eye was capable of that."[2]

As the year ended, Gatewood's health once again began to fail, for he had never recovered from the hardships suffered while in Mexico. On December 8 he was granted a leave of absence, and taking Georgia and his small family, he traveled to Frostburg, Maryland, to visit Georgia's family. Two months later, his health had still not recovered enough for him to return to active duty. He requested a two-month extension of his leave, which was granted.[3]

The U.S. government quickly initiated the next and most important step, in destroying the Chiricahua Apache culture. Beginning in 1887, Bedonkohe and Chokonen children were taken from their parents and shipped to an "Indian" school at Carlisle, Pennsylvania. Here, their clothing and scant possessions were taken from them, their hair was cut in the White-eye way, they were dressed in White-eye clothing, and they were given new, "American-ized" names. Daklugie became Asa Daklugie and Batsinas became Jason Bet-zinez. They were forbidden to speak their own language or to practice any of the *old ways*. Against their will, they were forced to learn the language and customs of the White Eyes.[4]

Many of the children—including Geronimo's son, Chappo[5]—would die from diseases contracted in the land so foreign to them.

Justifying the cruelty, the U.S. government claimed the schooling, com-bined with the destruction of a culture, was absolutely necessary if the Apaches had any chance of assimilating into white society.

Children longed for the love and comfort of their mothers and fathers, and their parents yearned to know if their children were dead or alive. This did not matter, however, because the Chiricahuas were prisoners of war. As such, their rights as human beings no longer existed.

On April 27, 1887, the Apaches at Fort Marion boarded a westbound train, which stopped that night at Pensacola. There, twenty women and eleven chil-dren were boated out to Fort Pickens to rejoin their husbands and fathers. Two or three women did not reunite with Geronimo and Naiche's band, but continued on with the rest of the tribe, arriving the next day at their new home, the Mount Vernon Barracks in Alabama. Geronimo and Naiche, with their warriors and families, arrived in Alabama on May 13, 1888. Sandy pine forests and swamps surrounded the 2,160 acres of land that was not suitable for farming. "We . . . thought Fort Marion a terrible place with the mosquitoes and rain," Eugene Chihuahua said, "but this was worse."[6]

"We had no property," Geronimo later said, "and I looked in vain for General Miles to send me to that land of which he had spoken; I longed in vain for the implements, house, and stock that General Miles had prom-ised me."[7]

During the 1880s, the residents of Los Angeles, California, "wept over *Ramona,* rode the new cable cars, watched the orange groves at Fifth and Charity (Grand) give way to the State Normal School, spoke for the first time on a telephone, [and] thrilled to the introduction of electric lights . . ."[8] The City of Angels was also the new home of the Department of Arizona, which moved its headquarters to the coastal suburb of Santa Monica.[9]

Gatewood finally saw an improvement in his physical condition, and on May 22, 1887, he reported for duty at his new station, Miles's headquar-ters.[10] Undoubtedly, the sea air helped his rheumatic condition. There is even documentation hinting that he took advantage of the abundance of available land for sale.[11]

Gatewood found himself in a new world. Suddenly, the arid, vacant hostility of the Southwest seemed far, far away. The lieutenant must have welcomed the change, but if he did, his private celebration did not last long.

During Gatewood's absence the controversy over who did what to end the Apache war gained momentum. With Lawton and Wood leading the way, advancements were bestowed upon the deserving: Wood eventually received the Medal of Honor.[12] It seemed as if almost every officer who served in Mexico the previous summer was honored in one way or another—every one, that is, except Gatewood.

Summer arrived, with the lieutenant performing his duties as aide to Miles. But a change had begun to take place in him. The reduction of his part in Geronimo's final surrender—and in some cases, the total elimination of it—took a toll on his self-esteem. Although he got along adequately with his comrades, he became increasingly aloof. Refusing to take an active part in the debate about the surrender, he now held himself with a stoicism that belied the pain that he tried to hide from the world.

Then word arrived that Arizona Territory intended to celebrate the victory over Geronimo in November. Gatewood looked forward to the coming event, and it appeared as though he would the be the guest of honor at the festivities. He did not have anything to wear and had clothes made. But it would not be.

Gatewood, despite the fact that he served as Miles's aide, remained an outsider. Perhaps if he had been a member of the Fourth's mess, Miles would have welcomed his feat with open arms. Unfortunately, for Gatewood, he was not a member, and never would be. Miles had commanded the victorious force; it was his victory and would remain so. Miles did not host the upcoming celebration, but he did control who attended. Georgia claimed Miles was jealous of her husband and had no intention of being upstaged by him. To keep Gatewood in his place, he ordered him to remain in Los Angeles "to do," as Georgia later wrote, "some unnecessary writing."[13]

On November 8, Tucson welcomed the victorious soldiers "with triumphal arches, parades, and prodigious banquets, and told them sober and told them drunk how much obliged [the] citizens [of Arizona Territory] were for giving them back their business and their sleep."[14] That evening Miles was presented with an ornamental sword at a grand reception and ball at the San Xavier Hotel.[15] All of Miles's officers were praised for their efforts in bringing Geronimo to bay; all except Gatewood.[16]

At the celebration, when Miles was asked about Gatewood's participation in the surrender, the general stated that he "was sick of this adulation of L[ieutenan]t Gatewood, who only did his duty."[17] The packer Daly later surmised that Gatewood had been kept from the fete as he "may have told the Committee a thing or two, not to the liking of Gen[eral] Miles."[18]

Although he must have felt some pangs of jealousy while his contemporaries celebrated, Gatewood performed what amounted to little more than clerical work without complaint. He completed his tasks by-the-book, never deviating from military protocol. The lieutenant's *integrity,* as Miles noted in Gatewood's "Efficiency Report," would once again come to the fore. As with Crook and the Zuck debacle, Miles now broached that area to which Gatewood could not venture. For Gatewood, black was black and white was white; right was right and wrong was wrong. Papers arrived that required Gatewood's signature. Miles employed a number of servants in his household, and not wanting to pay them out of his pocket, he decided to list them as packers and make the government responsible for covering their wages. When Gatewood saw that he was required to sign a document that certified the servants as packers, he refused and the servants did not get paid.

When Miles heard of Gatewood's refusal to pay his servants, he became livid. Keeping Gatewood quiet was one thing, having him do as expected as aide-de-camp was a totally different matter. Miles ordered Gatewood to sign the paperwork. Gatewood remained adamant: he would not break the law.

As he had severed his relationship with Crook by adhering to what he considered to be morally right, Gatewood now saw lightning strike in the same place a second time. After the war ended, he had found himself an outsider trapped within Miles's inner circle. Now, he had become an outcast within that same circle.

Miles had no further use for Gatewood. In fact, if we can believe Georgia Gatewood, Miles now searched for ways to have Gatewood court-martialled and done away with, "but failed to find a reason which would not show up some of his own practises."[19] Miles even tried to get Gatewood to contradict one of Lawton's reports during the campaign, so he could court-marital him for contradicting a superior officer. Gatewood realized what Miles was up to and refused to make the statement.[20]

It had not been that long ago when Geronimo had proudly shown Britton Davis his blistered hands—the hard-won badge of his attempt to fit into the world of the White Eyes. So close and yet now it could have been two centuries ago. Life for him would never again be as it had been.

Although Geronimo hated his new life, he realized that his name was known by White Eyes everywhere. He had not asked for this fame, but he took advantage of his celebrity. He began making bows and arrows to sell, and business became so good that he could not make enough artifacts to supply the demand. When his brethren offered to give him what they made to sell as though he had made it, he saw nothing wrong with the proposal of sharing in the profits. The old warrior even learned how to sign his name, adding yet another item to his business inventory—autographed photos.[21]

The move of the Chokonen, Chihenne, and Bedonkohes from Florida to Alabama did not improve their living conditions. On January 2, 1890, Crook visited the exiles at Mount Vernon Barracks. When he asked about their condition, Noche said:

> I thought we were coming to a place that was healthy, but you can see for yourself that we are not so many as when you saw us last. A great many have died. We lost more than a hundred. More than fifty have died since leaving St. Augustine. About thirty children have died at Carlisle. Between fifty and a hundred have died here.[22]

Official government death figures differed from Noche's. The United States listed the deaths through November 30, 1889, as:

1886	(St. Augustine, Florida)	18
1887	(St. Augustine and Fort Pickens, Florida, and Mount Vernon Barracks, Alabama)	31
1888	(Mount Vernon Barracks, Alabama)	14
1889	(Mount Vernon Barracks, Alabama)	26
	Deaths at Carlisle, Pennsylvania, over same period	30
	Total	119

The same document listed the Chokonen, Bedonkohes, and Chihenne prisoners still living as:

At Mount Vernon Barracks (79 men, 167 women, and 142 children)	388
At Governor's Island, New York (undergoing punishment)	2
At Carlisle School	70
Total	460[23]

Regardless of which figures—Noche's or the government's—were closer to the truth, an alarming number of people had died.

❖❖❖

On June 2, 1890, Lieutenant Charles Gatewood, two days before he would begin a two-month leave of absence, requested a two-month extension. "My reason for requesting an extension," Gatewood wrote, "is the necessity of attending to private business in the [E]ast, which will very probably require the four months [originally] asked for."[24] His request was granted that same day.[25]

Gatewood's request may have been straightforward. But then again, he may have needed the time to bolster his fading health. Gatewood spent the summer months in Frostburg, Maryland, with Georgia's family. Most likely Georgia's father, Thomas McCulloh, once again used his influence in an attempt to help his son-in-law secure his future, either in or out of the army. However, nothing seems to have come from his efforts.

On September 13, while still on leave in Maryland, Gatewood's tenure as aide-de-camp to Miles ended. Official notes circulated about the adjutant general's office in Washington, D.C., questioning why Gatewood had not put in for his next assignment as per Army Regulation 37 (amended in General Orders No. 52, 1890). That day, Gatewood was officially relieved from duty as aide-de-camp on Miles's staff, effective September 14. Orders were sent to Gatewood on September 15, requesting him to rejoin his old Troop H (Sixth U.S. Cavalry), now stationed at Fort Wingate, New Mexico, at the conclusion of his leave on October 4. He was also required to explain why he had failed to adhere to the regulation. Three days later, Gatewood answered that he was not aware of the new regulation.[26]

Four years had passed since the end of the last Apache war, and Gatewood had seen no change in his life—other than the continual deterioration of his health. By now he must have begun to seriously wonder if he would ever make the rank of captain. Most of his contemporaries during the Apache wars had begun to climb the military ladder, an ascension that would see almost every one of them end their army career as either a colonel or a general.[27]

In 1890, the Ghost Dance religion began to sweep across the frontier, promising to bring back not only the buffalo but previous generations of Indians. "All would dwell blissfully and eternally without want, sickness, or discomfort."[28] Wovoka, a Paiute shaman from Nevada whose vision initiated the Indians' hope for the future, preached: "You must not fight. . . . Do no harm to anyone. Do right always." Most of the tribes complied with the request to practice the new religion peacefully. However, in the north, the Sioux Nation turned the peaceful intentions into one final call for warfare in a last-ditch effort to save their heritage. In Dakota Territory, a ghost shirt was created that would protect the wearers while they swept the hated white man from the face of Mother Earth.

Alarmed, Major General Nelson Miles, who had assumed command of the Division of the Missouri upon George Crook's unexpected death earlier in the year, acted quickly, reinforcing the troops already stationed in the area. This included Gatewood's Troop H (Sixth U.S. Cavalry), which was reassigned to Dakota Territory at the beginning of December 1890. Gatewood served "in the field in South Dakota, in operations against hostile Sioux Indians at Pine Ridge Agency and vicinity, to January 10, 1891."[29]

Two events happened in quick succession and led to the end of the Indian wars: the murder of Hunkpapa Sioux medicine man and chieftain Sitting Bull on December 15 and the massacre of Big Foot's Miniconjou Sioux at Wounded Knee Creek, South Dakota, on December 29.[30]

Gatewood, who was not present at either tragedy, could not physically endure the severity of the harsh winter that the Northern Plains experienced in 1890–1891. An attack of rheumatism struck him at the beginning of January, and apparently he waited, postponing the request for sick leave in the hope that his condition would improve, but it continued to deteriorate. Finally it reached the point where the rheumatism had rendered both of his shoulders so stiff that he could not move his arms, and Gatewood could not report for duty. On February 16, 1891, he wrote the post adjutant at Fort Meade, South Dakota, requesting a "leave of absence on account of sickness for the period of one month. As soon as able to travel, I desire to go to Hot Springs, S[outh] D[akota], in the hope of being benefited by the use of the waters there."[31] The leave was granted seven days later, with the medical certificate accompanying the application recommending that Gatewood visit the Hot Springs.

For Gatewood, the end of his military career had begun. It had become apparent to everyone who came in contact with him that he was no longer fit for military service. The army had been his life, and he did not want it to end. This was not a selfish desire on his part, for he had a much greater concern than the agony that he endured—the support of his family. Gatewood found himself in a race against time. He had to find a duty he could perform before the army declared him totally unfit and forced him into retirement. Although his ongoing efficiency report, detailing his service record, stated that Gatewood "[h]as given attention and study to the history and character of Indians, especially the Apaches, the duties of a cavalry officer and aid-de-camp,"[32] and claimed that he was fit for college or recruiting duty, nothing ever materialized.

Gatewood remained on duty on the frontier. Troops C, H, and D, Sixth

U.S. Cavalry, were assigned to Fort McKinney, Wyoming, to maintain the peace between warring factions of cattlemen, and Gatewood reached his new post in June 1891. That winter (1891–1892) everyone suffered through a succession of violent storms. "The blizzards [were so bad that they concentrated] many years of misery . . . in a few days."[33] The harshness and extreme temperature differences played havoc with Gatewood's physical condition, but he held on, fighting his personal war to remain in the army.

The increasing local tension came to a head when the large ranchers created their own army of gunmen to go after rustlers. Small ranchers, fearing for their lives, joined forces with the rustlers, and when the illegal army of gunmen moved out to attack, the combined force of small ranchers and rustlers struck first, pinning down the invading gunmen. Hearing of the battle, the Sixth Cavalry rode to the rescue, and after saving the raiders from probable annihilation, they escorted the illegal army of gunmen back to Fort McKinney. On May 18, 1892, the small ranchers and rustlers, enraged at being kept from wiping out the gunmen, set fire to the buildings where the army had confined the cattle barons' hired killers.

The fire spread, threatening to destroy the entire post. Gatewood joined a small group of volunteers hurriedly placing cans of powder in the burning buildings. The plan was to blow up the buildings already engulfed in flames and save the remaining buildings. W. H. Carter described what happened next: "Some burning rafters parted, fell and prematurely exploded a can of powder. Lieutenant Gatewood was blown violently against the side of the building[,] and . . . badly crippled . . ."[34]

Gatewood knew his career was now in great jeopardy. Realizing that he and his family faced an uncertain future, he again applied for promotion to the rank of captain. Ordered to take a physical examination in August, Gatewood reported for the physical at Fort Custer, Montana, on October 3, 1892.

The examination disclosed: "Lieutenant Gatewood has suffered intermittently with articular rheumatism during the past twelve years. At present it exists in a subacute form, and affects chiefly the right shoulder and hip."[35] Although his shoulder and hip were not overly enlarged, the slightest motion caused him a considerable amount of pain. Consequently, he had lost a lot of functionality on his right side. When combined with his injury from the explosion, which rendered his left arm "almost completely disabled," the result was a foregone conclusion: "Permanently disqualified physically to perform the duties of a captain of cavalry, and that his disability occurred in the line of duty."[36]

One month later the army issued Special Orders No. 258: "By direction of the acting Secretary of War [First] Lieutenant Charles B. Gatewood, [Six]th Cavalry, having been found by an examining board physically unfit for service, will proceed to his home and report by letter to the Adjutant General."[37]

On November 22, 1892,[38] Gatewood arrived at his home in Denver, Colorado, to await his muster out of the service. Surprisingly, the next year and a half passed without result. By June 1894, Gatewood found himself still a member of the Sixth Cavalry. This did not alter his situation, which was still desperate. Refusing to quit, refusing to accept the inevitable, on June 4 he requested permission to act as military advisor to the sheriff of El Paso County, who had his hands full trying to deal with brewing trouble at Cripple Creek, Colorado. The secretary of war responded quickly, denying Gatewood permission to act as advisor.[39]

The downhill spiral continued. By September of 1894, Gatewood admitted that he was in debt. The money situation had become so bad that he resorted to juggling bills; but this did not solve the problem, only prolong it.

Although his bills were in arrears, Gatewood had no intention of stiffing anyone to whom he owed money and he took offense at any accusations that besmirched his character. On October 10, 1894, he wrote the adjutant general regarding a seventy-five-dollar check he had sent to C. W. Hine. "Mr. Hine is an ex-post trader at Fort McKinney, Wyo[ming], & understands how easily an officer may be humiliated by a letter such as he wrote that leaves out all reference to previous dealings & correspondence, & that leaves the impression that a [contractor] has been defrauded by a man [who] attained credit on account of the uniform he wore."[40]

Gatewood moved with his family to Fort Myer, Virginia, which would be his last home. With all hope for the future gone, and barely holding onto his military commission, Gatewood reached back to that one shining moment when he had walked into Geronimo's stronghold and told the old warrior what he had to do if he wanted his people to survive. With his career basically over, Gatewood wanted to hang on to the one accomplishment that had made his military career worthwhile. In May 1895, he put in for the Medal of Honor.

Miles endorsed the request—as did others.

The acting secretary of war made his decision on June 24: Request denied.[41] The reason: Gatewood did not distinguish himself *in action*. Putting oneself in jeopardy and walking into Geronimo's camp did not count. This rejection—the total denial of his most outstanding accomplishment—marked Gatewood's last attempt to save his career.

By this time Gatewood had become the senior lieutenant of his regiment. The army kept him on leave, refusing to issue his final discharge until he made captain. He must have been very appreciative of still being on the military payroll: his family had a roof over its head and food on the table.

Gatewood never attained the rank of captain. His physical condition continued to deteriorate. On May 11, 1896, he was admitted to the post hospital at Fort Monroe, Virginia. He died nine days later, on May 20, of a malignant tumor of the liver.

Georgia Gatewood had no money to bury her husband and requested that the army be responsible for the arrangements. For once, the U.S. government did right by Gatewood. He was buried in the military cemetery in Arlington, Virginia.[42]

Geronimo lived to see yet another change of address. On August 6, 1894, Congress agreed to move the Chiricahuas to Fort Sill, Oklahoma. The old Bedonkohe warrior held on to the faint hope that he would see his homeland once again before he died.

During his final years, Geronimo agreed to tell his life story to S. M. Barrett, the superintendent of schools at Lawton, Oklahoma. With Daklugie acting as translator, Geronimo, who was still officially a prisoner of war, was cautious and did not tell everything. Although he was careful of what he said about Chatto and Noche, he did take the opportunity to lash out at both Crook and Miles.

Geronimo met Miles one final time: at the Trans-Mississippi and International Exposition of 1898. He called Miles a liar. Smiling, the general agreed, then said: "You lied to Mexicans, Americans, and to your own Apaches, for thirty years. White men only lied to you once, and I did it."[43] Geronimo made a plea to return to his homeland. Miles denied it.

After being cheered as a hero in Theodore Roosevelt's inaugural parade on March 4, 1905, Geronimo repeated his appeal to the president:

> Great Father, other Indians have homes where they can live and be happy. I and my people have no homes. The place where we are kept is bad for us. . . . We are sick there and we die. White men are in the country that was my home. I pray you to tell them to go away and let my people go there and be happy.
>
> Great Father, my hands are tied as with a rope. My heart is no longer bad. I will tell my people to obey no chief but the Great White Chief. I pray you to cut the ropes and make me free. Let me die in my own country as an old man who has been punished enough and is free.[44]

His request was again denied.

Although liquor was taboo for Indians, Geronimo and others had little trouble getting it when they wanted it. Drinking too much had always been a problem for Geronimo, and it would kill him. In February 1909, he shared his last drunk with Eugene Chihuahua. Riding to the timber at Cache Creek, they knocked off a bottle of whiskey, and inebriated, they decided to sleep off their stupor on the ground. A drizzling rain awoke them. Burning up, the old warrior had pneumonia. Both Eugene Chihuahua and Daklugie *made medicine* for Geronimo, who took the White Eyes' medication without complaint as he drifted in and out of consciousness. Geronimo never saw his beloved homeland again, he died on February 17.[45]

Four years later, the Apache incarceration as prisoners of war ended. They were free to either remain at Fort Sill or join other Apaches on the Mescalero Reservation in New Mexico.

Although he may not have been aware of it at the end of his life, a transformation had begun. Geronimo had been the most feared and hated man in the Southwest. Today, Geronimo's image is split between two extremes: a patriot who fought for freedom and a bloody killer with few redeeming qualities.

Historian C. L. Sonnichsen wrote: "So this is what we have done with Geronimo. We have adopted him and transformed him, made him a priest and a prophet of his people, deeply spiritual and in touch with the Great Mystery, a symbol of our most heroic and unselfish impulses, an epitome of humanity at its best."[46]

Sonnichsen was being sarcastic. Why? Geronimo was merely a man who loved and cared for his wives and children. His life focused on the survival of his family circle, the survival of his small band. He had been born into a time of change, a time when life as the Apache knew it was brutally being brought to an end. His people had always survived by their wits and warrior skills. As he was exceptional in these skills, and because he had suffered tremendous personal losses over the years, it is not surprising that his ferocity would eventually make him an object of hatred by his foes.

In war, one side wins and the other loses. The winning side records the history, and the losing side is relegated to the role of villains. There are exceptions—such as the South during the American Civil War—but they are rare. Had Geronimo and the Apaches won the war, who would have gone down in history as the murderous villains? Sheridan? Crook? Miles? Certainly not Geronimo.

Sonnichsen also wrote: "Unfortunately Geronimo lived too long. He should have perished in Mexico, fighting valiantly beside his men."[47] No, that would not have made him an heroic martyr. He would have remained the bloody villain, albeit a dead bloody villain.

Everything must be put aside when evaluating Geronimo. Since that can never be, everything must be considered when looking at him. This includes his children, his wives, his family group, his bitter fight to keep the life he had been born into.

Who can damn Geronimo for saying "I am a Bedonkohe Apache"?

And what about Gatewood? Certainly he is not hated. Actually, his fate is worse: he has been relegated to the circular file. He has become a sort of *Everyman*. Like all of us, he had hopes and dreams and ambitions. And like many of us, he struggled his entire life against heavy odds. He had a family, whom he loved dearly. And he had a job that he tried to perform to the best of his ability. Like most people, sometimes he did a good job, sometimes he even excelled. At other times his performance was only average.

His reward: obscurity.

But there is more here. Gatewood had a fortitude that gave him the courage to go on when the frailties of his body demanded that he call it quits. In a day and age when acute racial prejudice defined frontier society, he had drawn the assignment of dealing with a race totally foreign to his upbringing. Gatewood's background stemmed from his southern-bred feelings of superiority to other races and the newfound hatreds created by the tyranny of the aftermath of America's civil conflict. He reached across the boundaries of race and culture, and though he could never totally subscribe to that which was foreign to him, he could accept it. Gatewood could even join it to the extent that the Apache looked upon him as one of only a handful of white men who dealt with them fairly.

This was not a small accomplishment.

Daklugie knew his uncle Geronimo better than anyone at the end of the old warrior's life. He told historian Eve Ball:

> Geronimo died regretting that he had trusted Miles. He did not
> blame Gatewood in the least; he knew that that young man was just
> obeying orders, and that if the general was treacherous it was not the
> fault of Gatewood. The Apaches admired and respected [Gatewood]
> for his courage in going to Geronimo, and they had contempt for
> Miles and his officers who played safe by remaining at a distance—
> with Miles the furthest away.[48]

From all the heated arguments that have ensued since the end of the Apache wars, one thing remains a constant—Gatewood met Geronimo in Mexico. Together, they did what was necessary to get the Apaches back to the United States where the war ended for all time.

Notes

Chapter One

1. Charles Gatewood had a large nose, to which most of his nicknames referred. He preferred the name the Apaches gave him—*Bay-chen-daysen*, claiming that it meant "long nose." Lieutenant Charles B. Gatewood, "The Surrender of Geronimo" (1895), Gatewood Collection, Arizona Historical Society, Tucson, Box 4, Folder 5, 36 (hereafter cited as Gatewood, "Surrender"). It has also been translated to mean "beak." John Upton Terrell, *Apache Chronicle* (New York: World Publishing, 1972), 384. Another translation of *Bay-chen-daysen* is the "chief with the crooked nose." *Prescott Courier,* Nov. 23, 1886. Gatewood has also been called the *Nantan Bse-che,* which means "big nose captain." Odie B. Faulk, *The Geronimo Campaign* (New York: Oxford University Press, 1969), 38 (hereafter cited as Faulk, *Campaign*). Gatewood had a third name, *Shonbrun,* which also means "long nose." "Geronimo: Details of His Submission to the Inevitable," *Mississippi Republican,* Nov. 22, 1886 (hereafter cited as "Inevitable").

2. Charles Baehr Gatewood (Apr. 5, 1853—May 20, 1896) was born at Woodstock, Virginia. "Gatewood Biography;" and Headquarters Sixth Cavalry, General Orders No. 19 (May 23, 1896), Letter 54, Gatewood Collection; Thomas Cruse, *Apache Days and After* (1941; repr., Lincoln and London: University of Nebraska Press, 1987) 35 (hereafter cited as Cruse, *Days*); "Inevitable," *Mississippi Republican*; Faulk, *Campaign,* 38. Gatewood accepted his appointment as second lieutenant, Sixth U.S. Cavalry, in a letter dated June 30, 1977. National Archives Microfiche Publication M1395 (five fiche relating to Gatewood's career), Letters Received by the Appointment, Commission, and Personal Branch of the Adjutant General's Office, 1871–1894 (hereafter cited as NA M1395). He was five feet, eleven inches tall.

3. Britton Davis, *The Truth about Geronimo,* ed. M. M. Quaife (1929; repr., New Haven and London: Yale University Press, 1963), 223 (hereafter cited as Davis, *Geronimo*).

4. "A Gallant Young Officer," *The Mining Journal* (1885), *Gatewood Scrapbook,* Gatewood Collection.

5. Headquarters Sixth Cavalry, General Orders No. 19 (May 23, 1896), op. cit. This document claims that Gatewood remained in charge of Indian scouts until January 13, 1886; however, this claim is in error. See Crook to John Pope (Oct. 2, 1885), NA M1395. Gatewood was officially removed from duty in Arizona and ordered to rejoin his regiment in New Mexico in October 1885.

6. Thomas Cruse to Charles Gatewood, Jr. (Mar. 3, 1926), Gatewood Collection, Letter 181. Also, see "A Thrice-told Tale," *St. Louis Republican*, Nov. 10, 1886 (hereafter cited as "Thrice-told").

7. Cruse, *Days*, 48-49.

8. *Prescott Courier*, Nov. 23, 1886.

9. J. A. Dapray to Gatewood, Jr. (Apr. 5, 1909), Gatewood Collection, Letter 80.

10. Charles Gatewood, "Gatewood on the Control and Management of the Indians (including the Outbreak of May 1885)," Gatewood Collection, Box 3, Folder 50, 1 (hereafter cited as Gatewood, "Management"). Listed as 8 unnumbered pp., this manuscript actually ends on the top of p. 9. Written in 1885, this is perhaps the first of what would be a series of reminiscences composed by Gatewood. As the years passed, he hoped to write a book describing his experiences with the Apaches. Unfortunately, he never completed the project.

11. Charles Gatewood, "Gatewood on the Apache Indians, Government Relations, Reservations, Courts, and Scouts," Gatewood Collection, Box 3, Folder 39, 19 (hereafter cited as Gatewood, "Indians"). Listed as 62 numbered pp., the manuscript begins on p. 9.

12. Charles Gatewood, "Gatewood on Experiences among the Apaches," Gatewood Collection, Box 3, Folder 49, 18 (hereafter cited as Gatewood, "Experiences"). This manuscript is numbered pp. 1-23 for chaps. 1-3, and pp. 1-6 for chap. 4.

13. Cruse, *Days*, 55-56.

14. Davis, *Geronimo*, 74.

15. Charles Gatewood, "Gatewood on Experiences among the Apaches," Gatewood Collection, Box 3, Folder 48, 3-4 (hereafter cited as Gatewood, "Apaches"). This manuscript has 34 numbered pp., with additional ones inserted. Although this manuscript carries the same title as the manuscript in Box 3, Folder 49, it is different and should not be confused with the document in Folder 49.

16. Geronimo, *Geronimo: His Own Story*, ed. S. M. Barrett; newly ed. Frederick W. Turner III (New York: E. P. Dutton & Co., 1970), 27 (hereafter cited as Geronimo, *Geronimo*). The editors point out the inconsistencies in the old warrior's narrative, such as hunting buffalo in the Southwest. Also, see Gatewood, "Experiences," 18.

17. Gatewood, "Indians," 10.

18. Morris Edward Opler, *An Apache Life-way: The Economic, Social, and Religious Institutions of the Chiricahua Indians* (1941; repr., New York: Cooper

Square Publishers, 1965), 1–3 (hereafter cited as Opler, *Life-way*). Also, see Geronimo, *Geronimo*, 67–68. Thomas E. Mails, *The People Called Apache* (1974; repr., New York: BDD Illustrated Books, 1993), 251 (hereafter cited as Mails, *People*). Mails agrees with Opler for the first three bands. His breakdown, into four bands, includes: the *Chiricahua*; the *Warm Springs* (the *Chihinne* or *Red People*); the *Nednhi*; and the *Bedonkohes*. Also, see Jason Betzinez, with Wilbur Sturtevant Nye, *I Fought with Geronimo* (1959; repr., Lincoln and London: University of Nebraska Press, 1987), 56 (hereafter cited as Betzinez, *Geronimo*); Eve Ball, with Nora Henn and Lynda Sanchez, *Indeh: An Apache Odyssey* (Provo, Utah: Brigham Young University Press, 1980), 11, 19, 22, 43, 47 (hereafter cited as Ball, *Indeh*).

19. Mails, *People*, 254; also, see 253.

20. Geronimo (c. 1823—Feb. 17, 1909) was born in a canyon on the middle fork of the Gila River roughly two hundred miles north of present-day Clifton, Arizona. His wife, Alope; mother; and three children were murdered in Janos, Mexico, in 1850, setting him off on a campaign of vengeance against Mexicans. He received the name *Geronimo* soon after the loss of his family during an attack against Mexicans, and as the years passed his stature as a war leader grew. Geronimo surrendered on a number of occasions, but reservation life did not suit him and he ran a number of times, including 1878 and 1881, basing his operations from the Sierra Madre in Mexico. Ball, *Indeh*, 11, 177; Dan L. Thrapp, *Encyclopedia of Frontier Biography*, 3 vols. (Glendale, Calif.: The Arthur H. Clark Company, 1988), 2:547–549 (hereafter cited as *Biography*); Colonel H. B. Wharfield, *Apache Indian Scouts*. (El Cajon, Calif.: privately printed, 1964), 6 n. 4.

21. Ball, *Indeh*, 13–14; also, see 4, 11, 13 n. 1, 22.

22. Cruse, *Days*, 83. His extended leave for health reasons was confirmed on Nov. 24, 1880 (Special Orders No. 152, Headquarters Department of Arizona): "Leave of absence for the month is granted Second Lieutenant C. B. Gatewood, Sixth Cavalry, with permission to apply to the proper authority for an extension of five months." NA M1395.

23. NA M1395.

24. Ibid. Also, see the Gatewood Collection: "1896 Report of the Association of Graduates of the United States Military Academy," by A. P. Blocksom, Letter 467; Gatewood to Georgia Gatewood (June 25, 1886), Letter 12; and Cruse to Gatewood, Jr. (Jan. 19, 1926), Letter 179. However, in "Lieut. Gatewood's Bravery," a Washington, D.C., paper, May 1886, *Gatewood Scrapbook*, reports: "He was on leave of absence and absent sick to August 13, 1881." One thing is certain: after going on medical leave on June 30, 1880, Gatewood did not again command a company of Indian Scouts until Nov. 12, 1881. Headquarters Sixth Cavalry, General Orders No. 19 (May 23, 1896), op. cit. Gatewood's father-in-law was the Honorable Thomas G. McCulloh, of Frostburg, Md. "A Gallant Young Officer," op. cit.

25. Betzinez, *Geronimo*, 56–60; Angie Debo, *Geronimo*. (Norman: University

of Oklahoma Press, 1976), 142–45. The very opinionated Thrapp, in *Biography*, 2:548 (Geronimo), cites a few references that lead him to believe Juh led the raid. He discards the Indian testimony, which fails to mention Juh's presence. However, on 753 (Juh), he merely mentions the event. Thrapp did not like Geronimo, and one wonders how much his prejudice influenced how he molded events to fit his view.

26. Betzinez, *Geronimo*, 63; Debo, *Geronimo*, 144–45; General George A. Forsyth, *Thrilling Days in Army Life* (1900; repr., Lincoln and London: University of Nebraska Press, 1994), 115 (hereafter cited as Forsyth, *Days*). Forsyth attacked Geronimo, but he did not press the assault. On April 28, a wounded Chiricahua woman told Forsyth that the Indians lost thirteen dead in the fight, a far cry from one dead. The woman was given water and bread and left.

27. Opler, *Life-way*, 216. Most likely, this quote, from an unnamed informant, did not occur at this instance. However, Debo, *Geronimo*, 145, suggests that a similar event could have taken place.

28. Forsyth, *Days*, 113–14; Alexander B. Adams, *Geronimo* (New York: G. P. Putnam's Sons, 1971), 231.

29. John G. Bourke, *An Apache Campaign in the Sierra Madre* (1886; repr., Lincoln and London: University of Nebraska Press, 1987), 22; also, see 23 (hereafter cited as Bourke, *Campaign*).

30. Forsyth, *Days*, 108–14. Forsyth has some problems with his dating. He lists the date of April 23 as the day before Gatewood joined him. The next day he names in the text is April 27, when he crossed into Mexico. However, he describes too many days between the two dates. If you count backward from April 27, Gatewood met him on April 23. If you count forward from April 23, he entered Mexico on April 28. Also, see Dan L. Thrapp, *The Conquest of Apacheria* (Norman: University of Oklahoma Press, 1967), 247–48 (hereafter cited as Thrapp, *Conquest*); Adams, *Geronimo*, 233.

31. Geronimo, *Geronimo*, 113. Geronimo called Juh *Whoa*.

32. Betzinez, *Geronimo*, 68–69. Thrapp, *Conquest*, 245–47, 249 n. 39. Sierra Enmedio is near present-day Los Huerigos. Rafferty and Tupper attacked, but pulled back when they were almost out of ammunition. Seventeen Apache men and seven women died, and many more were wounded. Fifteen Indian ponies were killed and others captured. One soldier died and another was wounded badly. Scout Al Sieber claimed the Apaches lost their cool during the fight. There has been some confusion concerning the identity of the first Apache male killed, or even if he was killed. Thrapp says he was Loco's son. However, Debo, *Geronimo*, 147, states that he was Loco's grandson, later known as Talbot Gooday, and that he was not killed. Also, see Adams, *Geronimo*, 231. Forsyth, in *Days*, 115, claimed six warriors died.

33. Forsyth, *Days*, 113–14; Thrapp, *Conquest*, 247–48; Ball, *Indeh*, 85; Adams, *Geronimo*, 233.

34. Betzinez, *Geronimo*, 72; also, 70–71. Debo, *Geronimo*, 150–53; Thrapp, *Conquest*, 249; Adams, *Geronimo*, 233–36.

35. Debo, *Geronimo,* 151.

36. See Eve Ball and James Kaywaykla, *In the Days of Victorio: Recollections of a Warm Springs Apache* (Tucson: University of Arizona Press, 1970), 144 (hereafter cited as Ball, *Days*), for the entire exchange between Geronimo and Fun. Also, see Debo, *Geronimo,* 151–52. Debo cites this incident, but could not explain Geronimo's behavior. However, she brings up a good point: during his lifetime Geronimo lost wives and children in battle three times while he escaped. She wonders if this was coincidence or "a significant revelation of his practice in extremity?"

37. Forsyth, *Days,* 116–21; Adams, *Geronimo,* 236; Debo, *Geronimo,* 153. García commanded 250 soldiers; 3 officers and 19 men were killed during the fight.

Chapter Two

1. Paul Andrew Hutton, *Phil Sheridan and His Army* (Lincoln and London: University of Nebraska Press, 1985), 185.

2. Robert M. Utley and Wilcomb E. Washburn, *The American Heritage History of the Indian Wars* (New York: American Heritage Publishing Co., 1977), 170, 301 (hereafter cited as Utley, *History*). Lieutenant Colonel Eugene A. Carr called Crook a *fool* in 1876, but he was not the only officer to speak out against Crook. For an anonymous petition (March 29, 1882) to the President of the United States, see Brigadier Gen'l. George Crook, *Resumé of Operations against Apache Indians, 1882 to 1886* (1886; repr., London: The Johnson-Taunton Military Press, 1971), 27–28 (hereafter cited as Crook, *Resumé*). In an effort to block Crook's promotion to brigadier general, a group of officers wrote: "It is disgraceful that he should belong to the Army at all! But it would be insulting, should his imbecility and dishonesty be rewarded by promotion." Also, see David Nevin, *The Soldiers* (Alexandria, Va.: Time-Life Books, 1974, 110–13, 173, 176.

3. Donald Dale Jackson and Peter Wood, *The Sierra Madre.* (Alexandria, Va.: Time-Life Books, 1975), 21–22 (hereafter cited as Jackson, *Madre*). The camp was located on the eastern side of the Sierra Madre Occidental.

4. Betzinez, *Geronimo,* 76–80; Debo, *Geronimo,* 157; Adams, *Geronimo,* 238–40; Thrapp, *Conquest,* 263–64. Bourke, *Campaign,* 7, put the warrior death count at ten or twelve and the women captured at between twenty-five and thirty.

5. Davis, *Geronimo,* 29–30; Thrapp, *Conquest,* 250 n. 43, 256. Thrapp names the date of return as September 3, 1882.

6. Crook report (Sept. 22, 1882), George Crook Collection, No. 27, Rutherford B. Hayes Memorial Library, Fremont, Ohio (hereafter cited as Crook Collection). Also, see Davis, *Geronimo,* 30, 32; George Crook, *General George Crook: His Autobiography,* ed. Martin F. Schmitt (Norman: University of Oklahoma Press, 1946, 243–44 (hereafter cited as Crook, *Autobiography*); Thrapp,

Conquest, 256–58, 261 (Indian agent J. C. Tiffany was accused of Indian fraud, but never convicted of any crime); Mails, *People,* 36, 39, 117; Betzinez, *Geronimo,* 122–23. Gatewood, in "Indians," 12, placed the number of Indians on the White Mountain Indian Reservation at sixteen hundred. However, it may have been as low as one thousand at this time. Also, see 13.

7. Gatewood, "Experiences," chap. 4, 3–4.

8. Davis, *Geronimo,* 42–43.

9. Gatewood, "Indians," 12.

10. Crook, *Resumé,* 9.

11. Davis, *Geronimo,* 31; also, see 30.

12. Ibid., 33.

13. Gatewood, "Apaches," 23. Also, see Crook, *Annual Report,* (Sept. 27, 1883), Crook Collection, 2 (hereafter cited as Crook, *1883 Annual Report*); Crook, *Autobiography,* 245; Davis, *Geronimo,* 39.

14. Crook, *1883 Annual Report,* 3; Davis, *Geronimo,* 34.

15. Gatewood, "Apaches," 26; also, see 23–25. Gatewood mistakenly names the month as September, instead of October.

16. Crook, *Resumé,* 11.

17. Gatewood, "Experiences," 14.

18. Davis, *Geronimo,* 93.

19. Thomas Cruse to Gatewood, Jr. (Jan. 19, 1926), Gatewood Collection, Letter 179. Also, see Leonard Wood, *Chasing Geronimo: The Journal of Leonard Wood; May-September, 1886,* ed. Jack C. Lane (Albuquerque: University of New Mexico Press, 1970), 117 (hereafter cited as Wood, *Chasing*).

20. Betzinez, *Geronimo,* 90. Also, see 83–92, 98.

21. Crook, *1883 Annual Report,* 7. Also, see Crook, *Autobiography,* 244; Davis, *Geronimo,* x; Thrapp, *Conquest,* 261; Opler, *Life-way,* 369. Tizwin (tiswin), also known as *grey water,* was a weak corn beer. It had many functions, other than making the drinkers of it inebriated. A nourishing beverage, the Apaches also considered it food, as it helped many endure long and difficult travel. It was also the beverage Apaches served during social occasions.

22. Cruse to Gatewood, Jr. (Jan. 11, 1928), Gatewood Collection, Letter 187. An article, "Lieut. Gatewood's Bravery" (May 1886), in *Gatewood Scrapbook,* erroneously put the date of Gatewood taking control of the reservation as July 24, 1883. Also, see Davis, *Geronimo,* ix–x, 30, 71; Crook, *Autobiography,* 244.

23. Gatewood, "Apaches," 27. Also, see 28.

24. Gatewood, "Indians," 16–18; Gatewood, "Experiences," 8.

25. Gatewood, "Apaches," 28.

26. Crook, *1883 Annual Report,* 3. Also, see Davis, *Geronimo,* 38, 55; Bourke, *Campaign,* 10.

27. Crook, *Autobiography,* 245; Davis, *Geronimo,* 40; Gatewood, "Indians," 19.

28. Davis, *Geronimo,* 43; also, see 38, 124. Crook, *Resumé,* 10.

29. Cruse to Gatewood, Jr. (Jan. 19, 1926), op. cit.

30. Gatewood, "Apaches," 30.

31. Davis to Gatewood, Jr. (Sept. 3, 1925), Gatewood Collection, Letter 282.

32. Davis, *Geronimo,* 145. The Apaches also had a less-than-flattering name for Davis, the *Fat Boy.* Ball, *Indeh,* 49, 128.

33. Cruse, *Days,* 131–133. Lori Davisson, "Fort Apache, Arizona Territory: 1870–1922," *The Smoke Signal* 33 (Spring 1977), 68–69. See 71 for a map of the post.

34. Gatewood Statement of Service, NA M1395. Also, see Crook, *Resumé,* 10.

35. Cruse to Gatewood, Jr. (Feb. 9, 1926), Gatewood Collection, Letter 180. This happened after Troops D and E left Fort Apache. Also, see Cruse, *Days,* 118 and photograph facing 112. In an interesting side note, Gatewood later told Georgia that he considered Sanchez a friend. Gatewood to Georgia Gatewood (Mar. 1, 1893), Gatewood Collection, Letter 50.

36. Gatewood to Miles (Oct. 15, 1886), Gatewood Collection.

37. S. M. Huddleson, "An Interview with Geronimo and His Guardian, Mr. G. M. Wratten," Gatewood Collection, 6 (hereafter cited as Wratten Interview).

38. Thomas W. Dunlay, *Wolves for the Blue Soldiers: Indian Scouts and Auxiliaries with the United States Army, 1860–1890* (Lincoln and London: University of Nebraska Press, 1982), 101–2.

39. Gatewood, "Apaches," 31. Also, see Gatewood, Jr., Memorandum for *Collier's* (Mar. 10, 1933), Gatewood Collection.

40. Betzinez, *Geronimo,* 97–102; Thrapp, *Conquest,* 272.

41. There has been a lot of confusion over which raid Chihuahua took part in. Betzinez, *Geronimo,* 102, wrote: "Our party under Geronimo and Chihuahua again planned to go toward Ures and even further south while Chatto and Benito proposed a raid north into Arizona and southwestern New Mexico." This would seem to place Chihuahua with Geronimo. However, conflicting statements claim that he or Benito (both of whom held more power than Chatto) led the raid into the United States. Thrapp, *Conquest,* 271 n. 10, 268, claimed Eve Ball insisted that Chihuahua led the raid. Daklugie, in Ball, *Indeh,* 50, stated that even though Chatto convinced Britton Davis that he had led the raid, Chihuahua was the actual leader. "Chihuahua was chief of this band, and it was Chihuahua's raid." The verbal testimony points to Chihuahua leading Chatto's raid. I concur for two reasons: 1) Betzinez's memory may have failed him regarding this incident, and 2) Ball's research has been the best I have seen regarding the Chiricahua Apaches.

42. Gatewood to Indian Agent, San Carlos (Feb. 8, 1883), Letters Received by the Commissioner of Indian Affairs (1881–1886), Bureau of Indian Affairs, National Archives, Washington, D.C., Letter No. 4140.

43. Bourke, *Campaign,* 8–9.

44. Crook, *Autobiography,* 245; Davis, *Geronimo,* ix. Also, see Shelley Bowen

Hatfield, *Chasing Shadows* (Albuquerque: University of New Mexico Press, 1998), 53 (hereafter cited as Hatfield, *Shadows*). The agreement was signed July 29, 1882. "Neither a treaty nor a law," Hatfield summarizes, "the accord did not require confirmation by the Senate of either country. The agreement, to be in effect for two years, could be terminated by either country with four months' notice."

45. Betzinez, *Geronimo,* 102–7.

46. Ball, *Days,* 147. Also, see Crook report (Mar. 26, 1883), Crook Collection, No. 34; William Hafford, "Chat[t]o the Betrayed," *Arizona Highways* 69, no. 2 (February 1993), 16 (hereafter cited as Hafford, "Chat[t]o"); Thrapp, *Conquest,* 267, 270. See Crook, *1883 Annual Report,* 5, for a lower fatality count of eleven. Crook also states that the Indians did not secure much ammunition. The raid's most infamous depredation took place south of Silver City. Judge Hamilton C. McComas, his wife, Juniatta, and six-year old son, Charlie, were attacked on March 28. Judge and Mrs. McComas's naked bodies were found later that day. The boy was never seen again. Marc Simmons, "The McComas Massacre," *New Mexico* 74, no. 1 (January 1996), 60–65 (hereafter cited as Simmons, "McComas").

47. Crook, *1883 Annual Report,* 5.

Chapter Three

1. Crook, *1883 Annual Report,* 5–6; Crook, *Autobiography,* 246; John G. Bourke, *On the Border With Crook* (1891; repr., Lincoln: University of Nebraska Press, 1971), 453 (hereafter cited as Bourke, *Border*). Bourke also mentions a General Bernardo Reyes. He spelled Zubrian, *Zubiran.*

2. Bourke, *Campaign,* 18–19; Sherman to Crook (Apr. 28, 1883), Crook Collection, No. 40.

3. Crook, *Autobiography,* 246.

4. Crook to AG, U.S.A. (Sept. 30, 1883), Crook Collection, No. 50. Allowing the Indian scouts to keep what they captured came back to haunt Crook when Mexican authorities later claimed that the Chiricahuas' possessions originally had belonged to Mexican citizens and rightfully should be returned to Mexico. Crook fought for his scouts' rights. Crook to AAG, Division of the Pacific (July 23, 1883), Crook Collection, No. 45; Anton Mazzanovich, *Trailing Geronimo* (Los Angeles: Gem Publishing Company, 1926), 221 (hereafter cited as Mazzanovich, *Trailing*); James H. Cook, *Fifty Years on the Old Frontier as Cowboy, Hunter, Guide, Scout, and Ranchman* (1923; repr., Norman and London: University of Oklahoma Press, 1980), 144–46 (hereafter cited as Cook, *Years*); Crook, *Autobiography,* 246. Also, see Thrapp, *Conquest,* 267. Mazzanovich claims James Cook served Gatewood as a scout during this campaign. He is wrong. Cook did not meet Gatewood until shortly after Geronimo broke out from the reservation in 1885.

5. G. J. Fiebeger, "General Crook's Campaign in Old Mexico in 1883; Events Leading up to it and Personal Experiences in the Campaign," in *The Papers of the Order of Indian Wars* (Fort Collins, Colo.: The Old Army Press, 1975), 198 (hereafter cited as Fiebeger, "Campaign").

6. Bourke, *Campaign,* 22; also, see 21, 27.

7. Thomas Cruse to Gatewood, Jr. (Mar. 3, 1926), Gatewood Collection, Letter 181.

8. Betzinez, *Geronimo,* 111. Also, see 110. Debo, *Geronimo,* 169–70, states that the Mexicans killed eleven. Betzinez claimed the Mexicans suffered heavy casualties.

9. Crook, *Autobiography,* 246–47; Bourke, *Campaign,* 38–39.

10. Bourke, *Campaign,* 39.

11. Crook to Acting AG, Division of the Pacific (July 23, 1883), Crook Collection, No. 45; Bourke, *Border,* 453; Betzinez, *Geronimo,* 107; Bourke, *Campaign,* 39–41; Crook, *Autobiography,* 247; Davis, *Geronimo,* 67. Davis erroneously claimed the U.S. forces crossed the border and entered Mexico in early April. He put the number of Indian scouts at two hundred. Bourke, in *Border,* placed West with the Indian scouts. However, in *Campaign,* he put West with the detachment of Sixth Cavalry.

12. Bourke, *Campaign,* 44; also, see 45–46, 48. See also Cruse, *Days,* 47, 56.

13. Bourke, *Campaign,* 49–50; also, see 56.

14. Ibid., 61–62; also, see 57–60. Crook to Acting AG (July 23, 1883), op. cit. Crook dates the entry into the Sierra Madre as the night of May 8.

15. Bourke, *Campaign,* 66; also, see 62–64.

16. Betzinez, *Geronimo,* 113. Betzinez (Batsinas), who, as Geronimo's assistant, had cooked the meat the old warrior ate, said: "This was a startling example of Geronimo's mysterious ability to tell what was happening at a distance. I cannot explain it to this day. But I was there and saw it. No, he didn't get the word by some messenger. And no smoke signal had been made." This event took place on May 10. Also, see 114. Debo, in *Geronimo,* 170 n. 29, says that Betzinez must have been mistaken when he said the women were from Casas Grandes. Logically, this follows, as the women were a long way from that town. Crook to Acting AG (July 23, 1883), op. cit.

17. Bourke, *Campaign,* 69. Also, see 23, 67–68.

18. Ibid., 70. Also, see Crook to Acting AG (July 23, 1883), op. cit. Crook states that scouts only carried three days of rations, but were expected to make the rations last four days.

19. Bourke, *Campaign,* 72–73, 75. In Crook to Acting AG (July 23, 1883), op. cit., the general's numbers differ from Bourke's. Crook reported that scouts discovered the camp, but then "scouts incautiously fired upon a buck and squaw" before the village could be surrounded.

20. Crook to Acting AG (July 23, 1883), op. cit.

21. Bourke, *Campaign,* 77; also, see 76. See also Debo, *Geronimo,* 180.

22. Betzinez, *Geronimo*, 118, 120. Betzinez's source was Chihuahua's daughter, Ramona, who was in the village and saw Charlie killed. Although the Chiricahuas did not condone murder, they remained quiet to protect Speedy. Also, see Simmons, "McComas," 65. Little Charlie's murder has basically remained unconfirmed. Chiricahua silence, combined with reports that he wandered off during the attack and died of exposure, have added to the confusion.

23. Bourke, *Campaign*, 78; also, see 76–77, 80. See also Crook to Acting AG (July 23, 1883), op. cit; Thrapp, *Conquest*, 287. Crook, *Autobiography*, 247, says nine warriors died. However, as stated, at least one of the deaths was of a woman. Most likely, other deaths were also women or children. One of the children was Naiche's daughter.

24. Betzinez, *Geronimo*, 115–16.

25. Bourke, *Campaign*, 82–84; Crook to Acting AG (July 23, 1883), op. cit.

26. Crook to Acting AG (July 23, 1883), op. cit.

27. Betzinez, *Geronimo*, 116. Bourke, *Campaign*, 84, claims the old men were old women. Also, see Debo, *Geronimo*, 182.

28. Bourke, *Campaign*, 86; also, see 85. Thrapp, *Conquest*, 288.

29. Bourke, *Campaign*, 85.

30. Ibid., 86, for quotation. Crook to Acting AG (July 23, 1883), op. cit. Crook calls Geronimo, Hieron[y]mo. He states that Chatto, Benito, Loco, Naiche, and Kaytennae also took part in the surrender talks.

31. Bourke, *Campaign*, 87.

32. Thrapp, *Conquest*, 290, citing the *Star*, June 21, 1883. Also see Crook to Acting AG (July 23, 1883), op. cit. Here, Crook wrote: "The chiefs said that they wanted to make peace and return to the San Carlos reservation. I replied that they had committed atrocities and depredations upon our people and the Mexicans and that we had become tired of this condition and intended to wipe them out; that I had not taken all this trouble for the purpose of making them prisoners; that they had been bad Indians, and that I was unwilling to return without punishing them as they deserved; that if they wanted a fight they could have one any time they pleased; I told them that the Mexican troops were moving in from both sides, and it was only a matter of a few days until the last of them should be under the ground." For the meaning of Nantan Lupan, see Ball, *Indeh*, 125–26 n. 2. "You White Eyes think that Lupan means Gray Wolf," Eugene Chihuahua said, "but it does not. [The Chiricahuas] named the general [Nantan Lupan] because of the color of the clothes he wore most of the time, and they were not gray; they were tan."

33. Thrapp, *Conquest*, 291. Also, see Crook to Acting AG (July 23, 1883), op. cit. At this time, Crook put the number of Chiricahuas at 384. He also makes a very telling comment: "The chief is no more guilty than every member of his band, since he has often less influence than individual members, being merely their mouthpiece or spokesman. To punish individuals guilty of particular crimes

could be done, were it possible to get evidence, but from the nature of things this is impossible."

34. Bourke, *Campaign,* 89–90.

35. Daly to Gatewood, Jr. (Apr. 25, 1924), Gatewood Collection, Letter 581.

36. Crook to Acting AG (July 23, 1883), op. cit.; Thrapp, *Conquest,* 292; Bourke, *Campaign,* 87.

37. Daly to Gatewood, Jr. (Feb. 6, 1924), Gatewood Collection, Letter 580; and Daly to Gatewood, Jr. (Apr. 25, 1924), op. cit.

Chapter Four

1. Thrapp, *Conquest,* 295.

2. Bourke, *Border,* 454. Also, see Crook, *1883 Annual Report,* 15.

3. Davis, *Geronimo,* 34. Also, see Crook *Annual Report* (Sept. 9, 1885), Crook Collection, 4 (hereafter cited as Crook, *1885 Annual Report*); Crook, *Autobiography,* 248–49, citing the Secretary of War, *Annual Report* (1885), 171, 179–80.

4. Crook to J. M. Schofield (June 19, 1883), Crook Collection, No. 44.

5. Bourke, Border, 458, citing Emmet Crawford. This total also includes the crops raised at San Carlos. Also, see Crook, *1883 Annual Report,* 7–8. Davis, *Geronimo,* 40, lists the types of Apaches under Gatewood's control: "The Coyotero were a small band, twelve or fifteen families, a connecting link between the White Mountain bands and the hostile Chiricahua." E. Lisle Reedstrom, *Apache Wars: An Illustrated Battle History* (1990; repr., New York: Barnes and Noble Books, 1995), 36, calls the White Mountain Apaches Coyoteros. He claims Coyotero means "wolfmen" in Spanish.

6. Charles Gatewood, "The Judge's Trial," Gatewood Collection, Box 3, Folder 40, 2; also, see 1 (hereafter cited as Gatewood, "Judge"). This manuscript, which is nine pp., is one of three documents that Gatewood wrote regarding his arrest of Thomas Zuck and his cohorts.

7. Memorandum signed by Lincoln and Teller (July 7, 1883), National Archives Microcopy 689 (1066 AGO 1883), Roll 174 (hereafter cited as NA M689, Roll 174; other rolls will be referred to by their roll number). Also, see Robert M. Utley, *A Clash of Cultures: Fort Bowie and the Chiricahua Apaches* (Washington, D.C.: National Park Service, 1977), 56 (hereafter cited as Utley, *Clash*); Crook, *1883 Annual Report,* 6–7; Crook, *Autobiography,* 249–50.

8. NA M689, Roll 174.

9. Crook, *1884 Annual Report,* undated, Crook Collection, 3. Also, see Crook, *1883 Annual Report.*

10. Crook, *1885 Annual Report,* 7. Also, see Crook, *Autobiography,* 251, 173; Utley, *Clash,* 56; Gatewood, Jr. to E. A. Brininstool (June 4, 1925), Gatewood Collection, Letter 99.

11. Davis, *Geronimo,* 77; Utley, *Clash,* 56.

12. Davis, *Geronimo,* 79-80, 84; Thrapp, *Conquest,* 293. Thrapp cites Davis's book as his source, but his numbers differ from Davis's numbers. The first group (he does not name Naiche) only contains thirteen—eight warriors and five women and children. He puts Chatto's entire party at twenty.

13. Crook report (Nov. 3, 1883), Crook Collection, No. 51.

14. Davis, *Geronimo,* 84; see 84-101 for the rest of the quotes concerning Geronimo's return to San Carlos. Also, see Crook to AG of the Army, Washington, D.C. (Mar. 19, 1884), John E. Clark to Britton Davis (Mar. 8, 1884), and Britton Davis to John E. Clark (Mar. 8, 1884), all three in NA M689, Roll 175. Davis, in *Geronimo,* claimed Geronimo had 350 cattle. This seems to be in error, as Crook, writing at the time, put the number of beeves at 135. Only 88 cattle reached the reservation: the unaccounted animals died, were killed for food, or gave out during the journey north.

15. Betzinez, *Geronimo,* 122. Also, see Davis, *Geronimo,* 101; Thrapp, *Conquest,* 294.

16. Davis, *Geronimo,* 102. Crook report (Mar. 19, 1884), Crook Collection, No. 56.

17. Britton Davis, "A Short Account of the Chiricahua Tribe of Apache Indians and the Causes Leading to the Outbreak of May, 1885," Gatewood Collection, 3-4 (hereafter cited as Davis, "Tribe"); Davis, *Geronimo,* 106-7. Davis's number of Chiricahuas ranged as high as 550.

18. Acknowledgment of Sheridan's May 24, 1884, endorsement of Crook's request to retain Gatewood received by General John Pope's office (Division of the Pacific) May 26, 1884, NA M689, Roll 175; Cruse to Gatewood, Jr. (Jan. 19, 1926), Gatewood Collection, Letter 179.

19. See Crook to AG of the Army (May 25, 1884), No. 61, for this and the next quote. Also, see Crook to AG of the Army (Nov. 24, 1884), No. 78, and Crook to Z. L. Tidball (Nov. 25, 1884), No. 77, all in Crook Collection.

20. Georgia to Gatewood (Aug. 25, 1884), Gatewood Collection, Letter 1.

21. Thomas McCulloh to Gatewood (Oct. 13, 1884), Gatewood Collection, Letter 2. McCulloh secured a loan of 825 dollars for Gatewood in September, payable six months later on March 18, 1885. At that time, Gatewood could extend the loan by paying the accumulated interest on it.

22. M. Barber, AAG, to Gatewood (Aug. 22, 1884), T. M. Zuck, T. F. Jones, and J. C. Kay Trial; Record Group 21, Records of the District Court of the United States for the Territory of Arizona, Third Judicial District, 1869-1910, Criminal Cases A-83-5 to A-85-19, Box No. 4, #52, National Archives—Pacific Southwest Region, Laguna Niguel, Calif. (hereafter cited as Zuck Trial).

23. Charles Gatewood, "How the Judge was Arrested & Tried," 3 (of 23 pp.) (hereafter cited as Gatewood, "Arrested"); and Charles Gatewood, "The Trial Chapt[er]," 8-9 (of 13 pages) (hereafter cited as Gatewood, "Trial"). Both in

Gatewood Collection, Box 3, Folder 40. These are the other two of the three manuscripts Gatewood wrote regarding his troubles with Zuck.

24. Gatewood to Zuck (Aug. 28, 1884), Zuck Trial.

25. Gatewood to AAG, Department of Arizona (Aug. 28, 1884), Zuck Trial.

26. Gatewood testimony (Oct. 27, 1884), Zuck Trial.

27. Gatewood, "Trial," 4.

28. Gatewood testimony (Oct. 27–28, 1884), Zuck Trial. Indictments for False Imprisonment of Thomas M. Zuck (No. 49), Thomas F. Jones (No. 50), and Joseph C. Kay (No. 51) by Charles B. Gatewood; all filed in the District Court of the United States for the Territory of Arizona, Third Judicial District on Feb. 10, 1885. RG1, Apache County, SG8, Superior Court. Phoenix, Ariz., Arizona State Archives, Department of Library, Archives, and Public Records (hereafter cited as Gatewood Trial). The meeting took place fifteen to twenty days before the arrest, which was on October 15. As the warrants for the arrests of Zuck, Kay, and Jones were signed on October 1, and time was necessary for the meeting, the cutting, the delivery of the ox, and Pedro's complaint, it appears likely that the meeting did occur some twenty days prior to the arrest—probably around September 25. In Gatewood, "Trial," 4, Gatewood stated that Kay agreed "to pay therefore so much money per ton, when [the grass was] gathered & stacked."

29. Gatewood, "Judge," 4–5.

30. Henry Daly to Gatewood, Jr. (May 28, 1924), Letter 584. Also, see Daly to Gatewood, Jr. (Feb. 6, 1924), Letter 580. Both in Gatewood Collection. Daly mistakenly placed the mail contractor incident between June 1883 and March 1884. Daly thought it was the mail contractor (Zuck) who Gatewood saw in Holbrook. This too seems to be an error, as Gatewood stated at the trial that he did not see Zuck again, after their initial meetings in August, until the day of the arrest on October 15. Daly called Gatewood's companion an *old scout* and an *old timer/officer*. As Gatewood had Conley with him during the investigation, it seems more than likely that the old timer Daly mentions was also Conley.

31. Three separate arrest warrants for Zuck, Kay, and Jones issued on Oct. 1, 1884. Zuck Trial.

32. See Gatewood, "Trial," 8, for this and Zuck's next quotation. Also, see 4.

33. False Arrest Indictments No. 49, No. 50, and No. 51, Gatewood Trial. See Daly to Gatewood, Jr. (Feb. 6, 1924), op. cit. Daly mistakenly implied that the arrests happened at the time of the saloon incident, but the false arrest indictments disprove this.

34. Daly to Gatewood, Jr. (Apr. 25, 1924), Letter 581; Daly to Gatewood, Jr. (Feb. 6, 1924), Letter 580; and Thomas Cruse to Gatewood, Jr. (Jan. 19, 1926), Letter 179, Gatewood Collection.

35. Gatewood testimony (Oct. 28, 1884), Zuck Trial.

36. Single summons delivered on Oct. 21, 1884. Zuck Trial.

37. Three separate arrest warrants for Zuck, Kay, and Jones issued on Oct. 1, 1884. Zuck Trial.

38. Gatewood, "Trial," 9–10. See Gatewood testimony (Oct. 28, 1884), Zuck Trial, for the date of the trial and the judge's name.

39. See Gatewood testimony (Oct. 28, 1884), Zuck Trial, for this quotation and the rest of the quotations from the trial until recess was taken at 7:00 P.M. on October 28.

40. See Gatewood, "Trial," 10–12, for this quotation and quotations related to Gatewood not having the right to ask questions.

41. Zuck Trial (Oct. 28, 1884).

Chapter Five

1. See Gatewood, "Arrested," 6–10, for this quote and the rest of the quotes from Gatewood paying Kay's legal fees through the Grand Jury deciding to indict Gatewood. Both Kay and Jones were Mormons. Gatewood does not name Kay specifically, but since Kay had the most dealings with Gatewood, it logically follows that he would be the one to go after Gatewood. Gatewood also did not name Show Low as Zuck's home town, but it too is the most logical choice.

2. Crook to Gatewood (Feb. 10, 1885), Gatewood Collection, Letter 5.

3. Crook, *Autobiography*, 251. Also, see Davis, *Geronimo*, 40–41, 138, 141; Crook, *1885 Annual Report*, 8. Crook places the change of agents in December 1884. He also mentions that Wilcox was "relieved." Crawford to AAG, Department of Arizona (Mar. 27, 1885) and Crawford to Crook (Jan. 18, 1885, two letters with this date), attachments to Crook, *1885 Annual Report*.

4. Ford to the Commissioner of Indian Affairs (Dec. 2, 1884), Letters Received by the Commissioner of Indian Affairs (1881–1886), Bureau of Indian Affairs, National Archives, Washington, D.C., Letter No. 23038.

5. Crook to AG, Division of the Pacific (Dec. 16, 1884), Crook Collection, No. 83.

6. Edward E. Hill, comp., *Guide to Records in the National Archives of the United States Relating to American Indians* (Washington, D.C.: National Archives and Records Service, 1981), 291.

7. Crook to AG, U.S. Army, Washington, D.C. (Dec. 27, 1884), No. 86, and (Jan. 13, 1885), No. 90. Both in Crook Collection.

8. Davis, "Tribe," 4; Davis, *Geronimo*, 114, 133, 223.

9. Carter statement on Gatewood, Gatewood Collection.

10. Daly to Gatewood, Jr. (Apr. 25, 1924), Gatewood Collection, Letter 581.

11. Wratten Interview, 6.

12. Statement of Service, and Adjutant General's Office (June 5, 1896), NA M1395; Gatewood Biography, and Headquarters Sixth U.S. Cavalry, General Orders No. 19 (May 23, 1896), Letter 54, Gatewood Collection.

13. Crook to Gatewood (Jan. 22, 1885), Gatewood Collection, Letter 4.

14. Crook to AG, U.S. Army, Washington, D.C. (Jan. 18, 1885), Crook Collection, No. 91.

15. False Arrest Indictments No. 49, No. 50, and No. 51, Gatewood Trial.

16. Warrant for Gatewood's arrest (Feb. 18, 1885), Gatewood Trial.

17. Gatewood, "Arrested," 11; also, see 10–13 for the attempted serving of the warrant on Gatewood, and the rest of the court proceedings. Gatewood's main attorney was either E. M. Sanford or J. T. Bostwick, as stated in the Zuck Trial. See Gatewood Trial for the bond fees.

18. Pierce to C. S. Roberts (Sept. 11, 1885) attachment to Crook, *1885 Annual Report*, 33.

19. Crook to Chanler (Mar. 2, 1885), Crook Collection, No. 99.

20. Davis, "Tribe," 5.

21. Gatewood, "Management," 2.

22. Georgia to Gatewood, Jr. (Jan. 15, 1928), Gatewood Collection, Letter 176.

23. Good-en-na-ha statement regarding Gar's escape (Nov. 17, 1885), Gatewood Collection (hereafter cited as Good-en-na-ha statement).

24. See Ta-gar-Kloé, statement regarding Gar's escape (Jan. 30, 1886), Gatewood Collection, for this and the next two quotations. Betzinez, *Geronimo*, 128, states that Gar shot Eshe-jar with a revolver that his mother had hidden in the brush, but the guards' testimony discounts this story. See Pi-cosh-cou-ge, statement regarding his sleeping through Gar's escape (Nov. 17, 1885), Gatewood Collection.

25. Good-en-na-ha statement.

26. Cruse to Gatewood, Jr. (Jan. 19, 1926), Gatewood Collection, Letter 179.

27. Davis, *Geronimo*, 132; also, 133. Davis mistakenly set the date as the fall of 1884. He correctly places the event after Gar's escape from the guardhouse.

28. Davis, *Geronimo*, 133.

29. Cruse to Gatewood, Jr. (Jan. 19, 1926), Letter 179. Betzinez, *Geronimo*, 128, describes Gar's end in a slightly different way: "One night while some of the Apaches had gotten together for a session of story telling, [Gar] came into the camp. A middle-aged woman recognized him, seized and held him while her husband got his gun and shot [him]."

30. Davis, "Tribe," 5.

31. Ball, *Indeh*, 49.

32. Ball, *Days*, 168.

33. Betzinez, *Geronimo*, 129.

34. Davis, *Geronimo*, 136–137, 142. Debo, *Geronimo*, 225.

Chapter Six

1. Britton Davis report (Sept. 15, 1885), Crook Collection, No. 349.

2. Gatewood, "Management," 5–6.

3. Davis, "Tribe," 5. Also, see Davis, *Geronimo*, 142.

4. Davis, *Geronimo,* 145.

5. Davis, "Tribe," 6.

6. Ibid., 7.

7. Gatewood, "Management," 6.

8. Britton Davis report (Sept. 15, 1885), op. cit.; Betzinez, *Geronimo,* 129; Davis, "Tribe," 5; Davis, *Geronimo,* 150, 152.

9. Davis quoted in Pierce report (May 17, 1885), Gatewood Collection. Also, see Crook to AG, Division of the Pacific (May 19, 1885), Crook Collection, No. 115.

10. James Parker, *The Old Army, Memories 1872–1918* (Philadelphia: Dorrance & Company, 1929), 153; also, see 152. Crook to Colonel Luther Bradley (May 22, 1885), Crook Collection, No. 148; James Wade report quoted in Robert Walsh to AAG, Department of Arizona, Whipple Barracks (May 18, 1885), Gatewood Collection; Allen Smith to Crook (June 15, 1885), Appendix B in Crook *Annual Report* (Apr. 10, 1886), Crook Collection, 1 (hereafter cited as Crook, *1886 Annual Report*). Smith claims he only had rations for ten days. He did not mention the halt at Black River to await morning before crossing. Also see Davis, *Geronimo,* 151. Davis thought they marched until morning. There may have been as few as eighty soldiers under Smith's command.

11. Crook to CO, Fort Bayard, New Mexico (May 18, 1885), Crook Collection, No. 112.

12. James Wade report quoted in Robert Walsh report (May 18, 1885), Gatewood Collection. Also, see General James Parker, Retired, "Service with Lieutenant Charles B. Gatewood, 6th U.S. Cavalry," Gatewood Collection, 1 (hereafter cited as Parker, "Service"); Davis, "Tribe," 5; and Davis, *Geronimo,* 101.

13. Britton Davis report (Sept. 15, 1885), op. cit.; Parker, "Service," 2.

14. Betzinez, *Geronimo,* 130–31. Betzinez thought Mangus was with Geronimo. Later, however, Crook's information placed Mangus still in New Mexico. See n. 30.

15. Parker, *Memories,* 154; also see 153, 155–156. Crook to Bradley (May 22, 1885), op. cit.; Parker, "Service," 2; Davis, *Geronimo,* 151; Smith to Crook (June 15, 1885), op. cit., 1–2. Smith put the halt at noon and the pack train arrival at 8:00 P.M. He also stated that Davis left for San Carlos the next day (May 19). His mileage estimate for May 19 was twenty-six. Also, see Faulk, *Campaign,* 61, 64. The first day's mileage includes the distance traveled the night of May 17–18. The Lutters have also been identified as George and Chris Luther. The mileage estimates between where the bodies were found varies from one account to another.

16. Crook to Bradley (May 22, 1885), op. cit.; Parker, "Service," 2; Davis, *Geronimo,* 151; Smith to Crook (June 15, 1885), op. cit., 2; Parker, *Memories,* 152, 156. Parker claimed that Gatewood had thirty scouts and that all but five of them—a whopping 83 percent—deserted. I do not believe this is true. Gatewood's scouts were White Mountains. They did not like the Chiricahuas, and would not have joined the outbreak. None of Crook's reports mention this desertion. Davis claims that only three scouts deserted during the entire war, and these

scouts were not with Gatewood. Gatewood, as far as I can find, never made any reference to any of his scouts deserting. Crook's report states Gatewood had ten scouts. Davis thought Gatewood had about twelve scouts with him at this time. Smith claims Gatewood had eleven scouts after Davis left. Eighty-three percent is close to twenty-five men. If twenty-five Indian scouts deserted at one time, surely there would have been loud repercussions. This leads to the conclusion that Parker probably did not realize that when Davis left he took his scouts with him, and mistakenly thought Gatewood's scouts had deserted.

17. Parker, *Memories,* 156. Smith to Crook (June 15, 1885), op. cit., 3. Smith put the mileage at twenty-three on May 21.

18. Crook to Bradley (May 22, 1885), No. 148; and Crook report (June 8, 1885), No. 187, Crook Collection.

19. Parker, "Service," 2; Crook to Bradley (May 24, 1885), op. cit.; Smith to Crook (June 15, 1885), op. cit., 3–4; Parker, *Memories,* 156–60. Parker put the date of the attack as May 21 in "Service," and then May 22 in *Memories.* Smith reported the date as May 22. Crook, quoting Smith, also reported the date of the fight as May 22. Again, Parker could not agree with himself. In "Service," he put the mileage at twenty-five, and in *Memories,* he put the mileage at twelve. Oddly, Thrapp, in *Conquest,* 319, citing Parker, *Memories,* describes the fight differently; Smith is rinsing his bandanna and the command had only stopped for ten minutes when they were hit by the Chiricahuas. I do not know where he came up with this, as Parker does not say this at all. Two partial versions of Smith's June 15, 1885, report of the fight can be found in Parker, *Memories,* 161–162, and in Herbert Welsh, *The Apache Prisoners in Fort Marion, St. Augustine, Florida* (Philadelphia: Office of the Indian Rights Association, 1887), 54 (hereafter cited as Welsh, *Prisoners*). Welsh mistakenly dates the report June 15, 1887. Although he may have already been in Mexico and not at the fight at all, Geronimo has been accused of shooting the White Mountain scout. Supposedly forty Indians attacked. This number seems high.

20. Parker, *Memories,* 159–60; Smith to Crook (June 15, 1885), op. cit., 5. Parker put the mileage at four. He also claimed Smith still had five days' rations left.

21. Crook report (May 26, 1885), Crook Collection, No. 138.

22. Crook report (May 27, 1885), No. 144; Crook report (May 29, 1885), No. 151; and Crook report (June 2, 1885), No. 159, Crook Collection. Thrapp, *Conquest,* 318.

23. Smith to Crook (June 15, 1885), op. cit., 5.

24. Ibid., 5–6.

25. Crook report (May 27, 1885), No. 139; Crook to Emmet Crawford (June 4, 1885), No. 169; and Crook to Crawford (June 5, 1885), No. 171, Crook Collection.

26. Cook, *Years,* 145–46, for all the dialog between Gatewood and Cook. Crook to Major Beaumont (June 3, 1885), Crook Collection, No. 163.

27. Parker, "Service," 3; Crook to CO, Fort Apache (June 6, 1885) Crook Col-

lection, No. 181. Smith was ordered to march back to Apache. Crook to Allen Smith (June 6, 1885), Crook Collection, No. 176.

28. Crook to Crawford (June 5, 1885), No. 171; Crook to Sheridan (June 7, 1885), No. 185; Crook to Bradley (June 7, 1885), No. 186; and Crook to AG, Division of the Pacific (June 11, 1885), Crook Collection.

29. Crook to Sheridan (June 10, 1885), No. 196; Crook to Crawford (June 9, 1885), No. 191; and Crook to Luis E. Torres (June 12, 1885), No. 200, Crook Collection.

30. Crook to Gatewood (June 11, 1885) Crook Collection, No. 198, for this and the next quotation.

31. Crook to Bradley, Commanding the District of New Mexico (June 12, 1885), Crook Collection, No. 202. See Gatewood, "Indians," 42, for the enlistment of this company of scouts. Many of the new enlistees had been serving time for crimes they had committed on the reservation. They gladly signed up to hunt Chiricahuas.

32. Crook to AG, Division of the Pacific (June 13, 1885), Crook Collection, No. 203.

33. Charles B. Gatewood, "Old Black Joe's Devil," edited by Charles B. Gatewood, Jr. Gatewood Collection, 2.

34. Ibid., 3.

35. Ibid., 3–4.

36. Gatewood to Georgia (June 30, 1885), Gatewood Collection, Letter 7, for this quotation and the next three quotations, to Georgia.

37. Crook to AG, Division of the Pacific (June 28, 1885), citing Crawford dispatch of June 25, 1885. Crook Collection, No. 206. Also, see Debo, *Geronimo*, 244.

38. Gatewood, "Old Black Joe's Devil," 4.

Chapter Seven

1. Crook to Bradley, (May 21, 1885), Crook Collection, No. 128.

2. Crook to Roach (July 28, 1885), Crook Collection, No. 218.

3. Crook to AG, Division of the Pacific (June 5, 1885), Crook Collection, No. 175.

4. Georgia to Gatewood, Jr. (Jan. 15, 1928), Gatewood Collection, Letter 176. Other than the fact that Gatewood did not think much of Lockett's performance in the field, it is unknown why Gatewood considered Lockett a fool. However, he must have voiced his opinion to Georgia, as she calls Lockett a fool on more than one occasion.

5. Crook to AG, Division of the Pacific (July 7, 1885). Crook Collection, No. 208. Also, see Crook to Luis E. Torres (June 12, 1885), Crook Collection, No. 200; Crook, *Autobiography*, 255. Some historians, such as Utley, in *Clash*, 60, mistakenly place Gatewood with Wirt Davis at this time.

6. Gatewood to Pierce (Sept. 8, 1885), Appendix O in Crook, *1885 Annual Report,* 38–39.

7. Ibid., 39.

8. Ibid., 40.

9. Gatewood, "Indians," 31. This manuscript convincingly documents his trials and tribulations as a presiding reservation judge.

10. Crook to AG, Division of the Pacific (July 7, 1885), op. cit.

11. Debo, *Geronimo,* 244.

12. Gatewood to AG, Washington, D.C. (Aug. 5, 1885), NA M1395.

13. Crook to AG, Division of the Pacific (Aug. 18, 1885), Crook Collection, No. 225.

14. Debo, *Geronimo,* 244. Also, see Crook to AG, Division of the Pacific (Aug. 17, 1885), Crook Collection, No. 223.

15. Geronimo, *Geronimo,* 136.

16. Ibid., 136.

17. Debo, *Geronimo,* 244–45.

18. Crook to Gatewood (Aug. 9, 1885), Crook Collection, No. 221.

19. Crook endorsements (Aug. 5 and 14, 1885), NA M1395.

20. Davis, *Geronimo,* 187, 192–95; Cruse to Gatewood, Jr. (Jan. 19, 1926), Gatewood Collection, Letter 179; Thrapp, *Conquest,* 332.

21. Gatewood to Pierce (Sept. 8, 1885), op. cit., 38–41.

22. Gatewood, "Arrested," 14. See Gatewood Trial for subpoenas to appear on Sept. 7, 1885, along with the bail bonds filed the next day, Sept. 8. Georgia also made this trip to St. Johns.

23. Gatewood, "Arrested," 15.

24. See Gatewood to Pierce (Sept, 8, 1885), op. cit., 40, for this quotation and the next one as well.

25. Debo, *Geronimo,* 245. Also, see 246.

26. Crook to AG, Division of the Pacific (Sept. 22, 1885), Crook Collection, No. 234; Debo, *Geronimo,* 246.

27. Crook to AG, Division of the Pacific (Sept. 22, 1885), No. 234; also see Crook to AG, Division of the Pacific (Sept. 29, 1885), No. 238, both in Crook Collection; and Thrapp, *Conquest,* 332.

28. Gatewood, "Indians," 52. Also, see 50–51.

29. Ball, *Indeh,* 103; Debo, *Geronimo,* 246–47. Also, see Crook to AG, Division of the Pacific (Sept. 22, 1885), op. cit.

30. Gatewood, "Indians," 55. Also, see 53–54.

31. Ibid., 56–57 for Sanchez's statement and Gatewood's reply. Also, see 58.

32. Crook to AG, Division of the Pacific (Sept. 25, 1885), Crook Collection, No. 235.

33. Gatewood, "Indians," 58. Also, see 59–60 for the rest of the confrontation between Gatewood and the White Mountain Apaches.

34. Crook to Pope (Oct. 2, 1885), NA M1395.

35. Ibid. Crook mistakenly thought that Gatewood's next court appearance would take place on Dec. 7, 1885.

36. AG, Washington, D.C., to Pope (Oct. 3, 1885), NA M1395.

37. Wirt Davis to C. S. Roberts (Mar. 11, 1886), attached to Crook, *1886 Annual Report.* Davis reentered Mexico on Nov. 27, 1885. Also, see Utley, *Clash,* 60; Mazzanovich, *Trailing,* 233. Mazzanovich mistakenly states that Crawford commanded the force that entered Mexico in November. Debo, *Geronimo,* 248, and Thrapp, *Conquest,* 335, state that Crawford reentered Mexico on Nov. 29, 1885. They are also mistaken. See n 44, below.

38. Crook to Crawford (Nov. 14, 1885), No. 245, and Crook to Crawford (Nov. 13, 1885), No. 244, Crook Collection. Crawford's reasoning for Gatewood's quick release is unknown. However, there is a possibility that Gatewood contacted Crawford, who was both his immediate supervisor and a friend, and asked him to make the recommendation. Lockett held the position less than six months.

39. Crook to Sheridan (Nov. 14, 1885), Crook Collection, No. 248. For the past month there had been no Indian depredations in Arizona.

40. Ibid.; Crook to AG, Division of the Pacific (Nov. 24, 1885), No. 249, and (Nov. 25, 1885), No. 251, Crook Collection. There may have been a total of eleven warriors at this time. Thrapp, *Conquest,* 334–35.

41. Utley, *Clash,* 60; Thrapp, *Conquest,* 335.

42. Crook to AG, Division of the Pacific (Sept. 19, 1885), No. 231; Crook to Miles (Sept. 17, 1885), No. 229; Crook to CO, District of New Mexico (Dec. 1, 1885), No. 255. All in Crook Collection.

43. Utley, *Clash,* 60; Thrapp, *Conquest,* 336–39.

44. Marion P. Maus to C. S. Roberts (Apr. 8, 1886), Appendix I in Crook, *1886 Annual Report,* 47. Maus wrote that "on the 6th of December, the command marched south, passing down the Sulphur Spring Valley to the border. It was decided to pursue these renegades to their haunts in southern Sonora, Mexico, and accordingly on the 11th of December, 1885, the Battalion crossed the border and camped twenty miles to the north of Fronteras." Also, see Davis, *Geronimo,* 196. Davis put the reentry into Mexico at about December 15.

45. Gatewood, Jr. (Jan. 26, 1929), Gatewood Collection, Letter 347; Davis, *Geronimo,* 222.

Chapter Eight

1. Headquarters Sixth Cavalry General Orders No. 19 (May 23, 1896), Gatewood Collection, Letter 54.

2. Crook, *1886 Annual Report,* 8.

3. Ball, *Days,* 181.

4. "Probably a Mistake," *Arizona Journal-Miner,* Jan. 8, 1886.

5. Crook, *1886 Annual Report,* 8.

6. Maus to C. S. Roberts (Feb. 23, 1886), Crook Collection, No. 352.

7. Ball, *Days,* 182.

8. Maus to Roberts (Feb. 23, 1886), op. cit. The *Arizona Journal-Miner,* Feb. 8, 1886, printed a Mexican version of Crawford's death: "On the 11th inst[ant] we reached the camp called Teepar or Sierra del Bavis, where we combated a great number of tame and wild Indians, probably over 200, led by foreign (United States) officers . . . ," Santa Ana Perez reported. Continuing, he said, "our safety was due to the treaty with them under the war flag of the United States, to which they pretended to belong, after their captain died. I acceded to their terms for the reason given, though they displayed not a sign of legality."

9. Maus to Roberts, (Apr. 8, 1886), Crook Collection, No. 350. Geronimo's wife was Ih-tedda. See Debo, *Geronimo,* 251, including n. 19. Debo proves without a doubt that Ih-tedda returned to the United States in January 1886. Also, see 304.

10. War Department Statement of Gatewood's Military Service (June 5, 1896), NA M1395.

11. Gatewood to Georgia (June 25, 1886), Gatewood Collection, Letter 12.

12. Betzinez, *Geronimo,* 133.

13. Gatewood, "Arrested," 17; also, see 15–16. See Gatewood Trial for subpoenas to appear on Mar. 22, 24, and 25, 1886; all signed by Judge Shields.

14. See ibid., 18, for this quotation and for Gatewood's reply.

15. Ibid., 20; also, see 21.

16. Ibid., 21–22; also, see 33.

17. See Gatewood Trial for the instructions Shields delivered to the jury.

18. Geronimo, *Geronimo,* 138.

19. Bourke, *Border,* 473; also, see 471. For Bourke's record of the meeting (Mar. 25 and 27, 1886), see Crook Collection, No. 359.

20. Bourke, *Border,* 473–74. A scarp is a line of cliffs formed by the faulting or fracturing of the earth's crust.

21. Ball, *Days,* 184.

22. Crook, *Resumé* (9, 13–14). Also, see Thrapp, *Conquest,* 344. Thrapp cites Crook, *Resumé.* However, his version must be different from mine, as the quotation he cites is not in the version of *Resumé* in my possession.

23. Crook, *1886 Annual Report,* 9.

24. Bourke, *Border,* 474, 476.

25. See Bourke's record of the meeting (Mar. 25 and 27, 1886), op. cit., for this and the rest of the direct quotations made during the two days of meetings. This historic meeting can also be found in Sen. Exec. Doc. No. 88, 51st Cong., 1st sess., 11–17.

26. Geronimo, *Geronimo,* 138.

27. Bourke, *Border,* 476.

28. Crook, *1886 Annual Report,* 9–10.

29. Bourke, *Border,* 476–77.

30. Crook, *1886 Annual Report,* 10.

31. Bourke, *Border,* 478.

32. See ibid., 480, for quotation, and also, see 481; Crook, *1886 Annual Report,* 10; T. J. Clay to Gatewood, Jr. (May 29, 1930), Gatewood Collection, Letter 392; Howard to Drum (Feb. 24, 1887), Sen. Exec. Doc. 117, 49th Cong., 2d sess., 35 (Howard put the total number of Chiricahuas arriving at Bowie at seventy-seven); Davis, *Geronimo,* 217–18. On 213, Davis put the number of Indians who ran at twenty men, thirteen women, three girls, and three boys. Although Robert Tribolet has usually been blamed (see Thrapp, *Biography,* 3:1440–41) for supplying the mescal, it was his brother, Godfrey (known as Charley in Tombstone). George Whitwell Parsons, *The Devil Has Foreclosed: The Private Journal of George Whitwell Parsons,* vol. 2, *The Concluding Arizona Years, 1882–87,* ed. Lynn R. Bailey (Tucson, Ariz.: Westernlore Press, 1997), March 29, 1886, 200–201 (hereafter cited as Parsons, *Devil*). Also, see 204, 207 (*San Francisco Chronicle,* Apr. 1 and 3, 1886). Parsons claimed that on March 29 Geronimo tried to get the others to run with him again, failed, procured some mescal, and got his comrades drunk a second time. When the mescal ran out, he and six or seven warriors rode to a San Bernardino rancho and continued to drink. Here, Geronimo convinced them to run with him. Another version of the final drunk can be found in Leonard B. Radtke, "Sons of Two Famous Indian Scouts Are Now Boy Scouts," *El Paso Times,* Dec. 18, 1927, *Gatewood Scrapbook* (hereafter cited as Radtke, "Scouts"). Radtke claims that when Maus and the Chiricahuas reached a border town, Geronimo went into a tavern to have a drink. Supposedly soldiers, Indians, and scouts celebrated. More and more soldiers entered the building, asking: "Where's Geronimo? Where's Geronimo?" The old warrior, fearing for his life, fled into the night. Bailey wrote (to author, Aug. 22, 1997): "Godfrey was indicted and tried for illegal saleof liquor at Silver Creek in May 1886. He was found not guilty."

33. Sheridan to Crook (Mar. 30, 1886), Crook, *Resumé,* 16. Also, see Sheridan to Crook (Mar. 31, 1886) and Crook to Sheridan (two letters dated Mar. 31, 1886), 16–18; and Parsons, *Devil,* 203.

34. Crook to Sheridan (Apr. 1, 1886), Crook, *Resumé,* 19; also, see 21.

35. Sheridan to Crook (Apr. 5, 1886), Crook, *Resumé,* 21. Crook to Sheridan (Apr. 2, 1886) and Sheridan to Crook (Apr. 3, 1886), 19–20; and Howard to Drum (Feb. 24, 1887), loc. cit.

36. Miles to Mary Miles (Apr. 11, 1886), Brian C. Pohanka, ed., *Nelson A. Miles: A Documentary Biography of His Military Career, 1861–1903* (Glendale, Calif.: The Arthur H. Clark Company, 1985), 149.

37. Nelson A. Miles, *Serving the Republic: Memoirs of the Civil War and Military Life of Nelson A. Miles* (New York and London: Harper & Brothers Publishers, 1911), 225 (hereafter cited as Miles, *Republic*).

38. Howard to Drum (Feb. 24, 1887), loc. cit.

39. William A. Thompson report (Apr. 20, 1886), Sen. Exec. Doc. 117, 49th Cong., 2d sess., 2.

40. Thompson report (Oct. 7, 1886) and Miles report (Sept. 18, 1886), 39, Sen. Exec. Doc. 117, 49th Cong., 2d sess.; Geronimo, *Geronimo*, 140. Also, see Terrell, *Apache Chronicle*, 382. Thrapp, *Conquest*, 351, is in error when he placed Gatewood at Fort Apache during the raid. Gatewood was stationed at Fort Wingate, New Mexico, at this time.

41. Georgia to Gatewood, Jr. (Apr. 4, 1909), Gatewood Collection, Letter 79.

42. Geronimo, *Geronimo*, 140.

43. Notes from Crook's Jan. 2, 1890, visit to Mount Vernon Barracks, Alabama, Sen. Exec. Doc. 35, 51st Cong. 1st sess., 33.

44. Miles report (Sept. 18, 1886), op. cit., 40, and Davis, *Geronimo*, 220, name Kayitah. However, Betzinez, *Geronimo*, 143, documents Massai's desertion. Also, see Debo, *Geronimo*, 270 n. 13. Debo agrees with Betzinez. I am unsure. The locations for the desertions seem to be at odds. I wonder if there were two desertions instead of one.

45. Daly to Gatewood, Jr. (May 28, 1924), Gatewood Collection, Letter 584.

46. James Parker orders to Lawton (May 4, 1886), Sen. Exec. Doc. 117, 49th Cong., 2d sess., 45. Wood, *Chasing*, May 4–5, 1886, 26–27. Wood claimed thirty Indian scouts were enlisted.

47. For the various engagements, see Howard to Drum (Feb. 24, 1887), 35 (for both quotes); and Thompson report (Oct. 7, 1886), 24, op. cit. Davis, *Geronimo*, 219, put the May 3 fight on May 5.

Chapter Nine

1. Gatewood to Georgia (June 12, 1886), Gatewood Collection, Letter 10.

2. Gatewood to Georgia (June 25, 1886), Gatewood Collection, Letter 12.

3. Ibid.

4. Gatewood to Georgia (Mar. 1, 1893), Gatewood Collection, Letter 50.

5. Gatewood to Georgia (June 25, 1886), op. cit.

6. Gatewood to Georgia (July 1, 1886), Gatewood Collection, Letter 14.

7. Gatewood to Georgia (July 2, 1886), Gatewood Collection, Letter 15.

8. Gatewood to Georgia (July 3, 1886), Gatewood Collection, Letter 16.

9. Geronimo, *Geronimo*, 140.

10. Georgia to Gatewood, Jr. (Apr. 4, 1909), Gatewood Collection, Letter 79.

11. Miles report (Sept. 18, 1886), Sen. Exec. Doc. 117, 49th Cong., 2d sess., 40.

12. Samuel E. Kenoi, "A Chiricahua Apache's Account of the Geronimo Campaign of 1886," as recorded by Morris E. Opler, *The Journal of Arizona History* 27, no. 1 (Spring 1986), 73 (hereafter cited as Kenoi, "Account").

13. Ibid., 74. There is some confusion here. Charles Gatewood, Jr., in "Retired Army Officer Here Reveals History of Famous Apache Surrender," *San Diego*

Union, June 8, 1927, claims that Chatto recommended Martine for the assignment at Fort Apache.

14. Radtke, "Scouts." Noche only names Kayitah. Kayitah then chooses Martine to accompany him. Also, see Miles report (Sept. 18, 1886), op. cit., 43; Davis, *Geronimo,* 222.

15. Martine and Kayitah, "The Story of the Final Surrender of Geronimo," as told to O. M. Boggess, Superintendent of the Mescalero Indian Reservation (Sept. 25, 1925), Gatewood Collection, 1 (hereafter cited as Martine/Kayitah, "Surrender"). Also, see Kenoi, "Account," 74. Radtke, "Scouts," claims the meeting between Noche and Miles took place at Fort Bowie. This does not seem possible if both Kayitah and Martine lived near Fort Apache and Noche brought them to Miles the next morning.

16. Safe Conduct Pass, Gatewood Collection, Letter 17.

17. Gatewood, Jr., "Britton Davis, Class of 1881" (unpublished article), Gatewood Collection, Letter 382. Also, see Davis, "Tribe," 5.

18. Charles Gatewood, Jr., to John P. Clum (June 11, 1927), Gatewood Collection, Letter 282.

19. Mazzanovich, *Trailing,* 246.

20. J. A. Dapray, ADC, to Gatewood (July 10, 1886), Gatewood Collection. Cruse mistakenly thought Gatewood was at San Carlos or Fort Grant at this time. Cruse to Gatewood, Jr. (Jan. 19, 1926), Gatewood Collection, Letter 179.

21. Dapray to Colonel Eugene Beaumont (July 9, 1886), Gatewood Collection.

22. Gatewood to Miles (Oct. 15, 1886), Gatewood Collection. There is some confusion regarding the date Gatewood met Miles, received his orders, and headed for Fort Bowie. Dapray to Beaumont (July 9, 1886), op. cit., states Gatewood was en route to Bowie by July 9. But see n. 20; Dapray, on July 10, issued orders for Gatewood to return to Fort Wingate. This mix-up has led me to assume that Dapray's dates have been copied inaccurately. I have chosen to accept Gatewood's dating of July 13.

23. Gatewood, "Surrender," 11–12. This version of Gatewood's account of his mission can be found in print in a number of publications. *The Journal of Arizona History* 27, no. 1 (Spring 1986). This issue of the *Journal* was later published as C. L. Sonnichsen, ed., *Geronimo and the End of the Apache Wars* (Lincoln and London: University of Nebraska Press, 1990). A shortened version of the account was compiled by Charles B. Gatewood, Jr., and presented before the Order of Indian Wars in 1929. This version can be found in *The Papers of the Order of Indian Wars* (Fort Collins, Colo.: The Old Army Press, 1975). Actually, Gatewood wrote two versions of his mission to find Geronimo. The second account is: Charles B. Gatewood, "Gatewood on the Surrender of Geronimo," Gatewood Collection, Box 4, Folder 61 (hereafter cited as Gatewood, "Surrender II").

24. Gatewood to Miles (Oct. 15, 1886), op. cit.

25. Gatewood to Georgia (Aug. 26, 1886), Gatewood Collection.

26. Gatewood, "Surrender," 12. Also, see Mazzanovich, *Trailing,* 246. Miles's written orders to Gatewood have not surfaced. An article, "Son of Heroic Gatewood Tells How Apache Chief Surrendered," *San Diego Union,* Aug. 24, 1933, mistakenly claims Miles gave Gatewood the written authority at Fort Apache (hereafter cited as "Son").

27. Terrell, *Apache Chronicle,* 383.

28. Wratten Interview, 3; Albert E. Wratten, "George Wratten, Friend of the Apaches," *The Journal of Arizona History* 27, no. 1 (Spring 1986), 92, 94, 123 n. 1 (hereafter cited as Wratten, "Friend"); Thompson to Major Mills (July 6, 1886), and Mills to Thomas (July 5, 1886), Gatewood Collection. Wratten apparently left the Indian scouts leaderless when he set out for Bowie with Gatewood. According to Cruse, *Days,* 101, Wratten also spoke Spanish.

29. Gatewood, "Surrender II," 10.

30. Miles to Colonel Royall (July 2, 1886), Gatewood Collection.

31. Lawton report (Sept. 9, 1886), Sen. Exec. Doc. 117, 49th Cong., 2d sess., 47.

32. William C. Endicott, Secretary of War, to the Secretary of the Interior (July 9, 1886), 52; L. Q. C. Lamar, Department of the Interior, to Endicott (July 10, 1886), 53; Sheridan to Miles (July 13, 1886), 53; Sheridan to Secretary of War (July 30, 1886), 52. All in Sen. Exec. Doc. 117, 49th Cong., 2d sess.

33. Miles to AAG, Division of the Pacific (July 7, 1886), Sen. Exec. Doc. 117, 49th Cong., 2d sess., 51.

34. Lamar to Endicott (July 10, 1886), loc. cit.

35. Miles to Sheridan (July 15, 1885), Sen. Exec. Doc. 117, 49th Cong., 2d sess., 55.

36. Miles to AAG, Division of the Pacific (July 7, 1886), 51. Also, see Miles to Sheridan (July 20, 1886), 55. Both in Sen. Exec. Doc. 117, 49th Cong., 2d sess.

37. Davis, as quoted in Hafford, "Chat[t]o," 17.

38. Ball, *Days,* 162, 175.

39. Ball, *Indeh,* 84.

40. Ibid., 47.

41. Dapray to M. Barber, AAG (July 13, 1886), Sen. Exec. Doc. 117, 49th Cong., 2d sess., 53.

42. Wood, *Chasing,* 69–74, 133 nn. 10 and 11; William A. Thompson report (Oct. 7, 1886), 41, and Howard to Dunn (Feb. 24, 1887), 35, both in Sen. Exec. Doc., 49th Cong., 2d sess.; Geronimo, *Geronimo,* 140–41; Davis, *Geronimo,* 220–21. Davis claimed that none of Lawton's white troops took part in the fight. Judging by Wood's words, Brown's scouts hit the camp first, the Indians ran, and then the white troops entered the village. Geronimo claimed that he counterattacked in the afternoon, killed one soldier, and recovered most of the horses. He may have been stretching the truth here. No white accounts mention a counterattack.

43. Davis, *Geronimo*, 221. Also, see 222.

44. Therese O. Deming, *Cosel: With Geronimo on His Last Raid; The Story of an Indian Boy* (Philadelphia: F. A. Davis Company, Publishers, 1938), 79. There are many errors in this manuscript. However, the regret expressed on innumerable occasions for leaving the reservation with Geronimo in 1885 sounds truthful.

45. Wood, *Chasing*, July 14–15, 1886, 73–74.

Chapter Ten

1. Gatewood to Miles (Oct. 15, 1886), Gatewood Collection. Thrapp, *Conquest*, 353, mistakenly claims that Gatewood set out for Mexico on July 13. This could not have happened since he did not arrive at Bowie to outfit until July 15.

2. Gatewood, "Surrender," 13.

3. Wratten Interview, 3.

4. Gatewood, "Surrender," 14.

5. Davis, *Geronimo*, 223; Cruse, *Days*, 227.

6. Gatewood, "Surrender," 54. Also, see Gatewood to Miles (Aug. 7, 1886), Gatewood Collection; and Brigadier General James Parker, "The Geronimo Campaign," *The Papers of the Order of Indian Wars* (Fort Collins, Colo.: The Old Army Press, 1975), 95 (hereafter cited as Parker, "Campaign").

7. Gatewood to the AAAG in the Field, Fort Bowie (July 25, 1886), Gatewood Collection.

8. J. A. Dapray to Eugene Beaumont (July 19, 1886), Gatewood Collection.

9. Gatewood to Miles (Aug. 7, 1886), op. cit. Gatewood to the AAAG in the Field, Fort Bowie (July 25, 1886), op. cit. At this time it was raining just about every night. Wood, *Chasing*, 78, wrote in his journal (July 22, 1886): "It rained all night. Also rained last night and the night before."

10. Parker, "Service," 3. Also, see Gatewood, "Surrender," 15; Richardson to Gatewood, Jr. (Feb. 10, 1926), Gatewood Collection, Letter 201. Richardson called Parker's scouts "Mexicans." He also considered them useless.

11. See Parker, "Campaign," 95, for Parker's suggestion and Miles's reply.

12. Sen. Exec. Doc. 117, 49th Cong., 2d sess.: Miles report (Sept. 18, 1886), 42; also, see Miles report (July 7, 1886), 50–51.

13. Sen. Exec. Doc. 117, 49th Cong., 2d sess.: Miles to Sheridan (Aug. 2, 1886), 56.

14. General James Parker, "The Old Army" (manuscript form), 19, Gatewood Collection (hereafter cited as Parker, "Army").

15. Parker, "Service," 4.

16. See Parker, "Army," 19, for this quotation and Parker's quotation. Thrapp, *Conquest*, 354 n. 14, discounts Parker's account. I am not sure Parker should be dismissed so easily. Gatewood was sick and would get sicker. Also, this would

not be the last time that Gatewood would consider chucking the entire assignment and returning to the United States. Undoubtedly, Parker's willingness to serve as escort influenced Gatewood's decision to continue onward.

17. Davis, *Geronimo*, 193–94.

18. Gatewood to AAAG in the Field, Fort Bowie (July 25, 1886), op. cit.

19. Ibid. George Martine, Martine's son, in Ball, *Indeh*, 109, said: "Miles promised [Kayitah and Martine], 'If you come back alive and Geronimo surrenders I will have the government give you a good home at Turkey Creek and there you will have plenty of good water, grass, and game. Everything you need will be furnished you. And the government will give you seventy thousand dollars if you are successful; you will get the money as soon as Geronimo surrenders and you get back.'" Welsh, *Prisoners*, 10, claimed that Martine and Kayitah told him: "They were offered by General Miles ten ponies apiece if they would find Geronimo, enter his camp and persuade him to surrender."

20. Parker to AAAG, Fort Bowie (July 26, 1886), Gatewood Collection. "Son," *San Diego Union*; Wood, *Chasing*, July 25–26, 1886, 80.

21. Parker, "Campaign," 97–98.

22. Parker to AAAG, Fort Bowie (July 26, 1886), op. cit.

23. Parker, "Army," 20.

24. Lawton to AG, Department of Arizona (Sept. 9, 1886), Sen. Exec. Doc. 117, 49th Cong., 2d sess., 47.

25. Parker, "Army," 20.

26. Parker, "Service," 4.

27. See Parker, "Army," 20, for this quotation and the quotation about the women.

28. Gatewood to Miles (Oct. 15, 1886), op. cit.

29. Ibid.

30. Gatewood to Lawton (July 31, 1886), Gatewood Collection. Bacadéhuachi is also spelled *Bacadenachi* and *Bacadeuachi*.

31. Miles, quoted in C. McKeever, AAG, to AG, Washington, D.C. (July 22, 1886), NA M689, Roll 184.

32. Henry Clay Burke to Cleveland (June 27, 1886), NA M689, Roll 184.

33. Sheridan to Miles (July 31, 1886), NA M689, Roll 184.

34. Henry Daly, "The Capture of Geronimo," *The American Legion Monthly* 8, no. 6 (June 1930), 31 (hereafter cited as Daly, "Capture"); and in the Gatewood Collection, Daly to Gatewood, Jr. (Mar. 2, 1926), Letter 588; (June 18, 1928), Letter 345; (Feb. 6, 1924), Letter 580; (Apr. 25, 1924), Letter 581.

35. William Thompson, AAAG, to Lawton (Aug. 2, 1886), Gatewood Collection.

36. Gatewood to Miles (Aug. 7, 1886). Also, see Parker to AAAG, District of Bowie (Aug. 5, 1886); Parker, "Service," 4; Gatewood to Miles (Oct. 15, 1886); and Lawton to AG, District of Huachuca (Aug. 8, 1886), all in Gatewood

Collection. Gatewood, in "Surrender," 16, stated he found Lawton "perhaps two hundred & fifty miles below the boundary line." If Gatewood traveled some 50 miles into Mexico to meet Parker, and then another 150 (or even 200 miles as Parker claimed) to meet Lawton, there is no way he could have been 250 miles south of the American border. Gatewood did not travel due south for the entire journey, but moved both southwest and southeast in his quest to find either Geronimo or Lawton.

37. Gatewood, "Surrender II," 11–12.

38. Lawton to AG, District of Huachuca (Aug. 8, 1886), op. cit.

39. Gatewood to Miles (Aug. 7, 1886), op. cit.

40. Lawton to AG, District of Huachuca (Aug. 8, 1886); Gatewood to Miles (Aug. 7, 1886), Gatewood Collection.

41. Gatewood to Lawton (Aug. 6, 1886), Gatewood Collection.

42. Parker, "Campaign," 98, for this and the next two Lawton quotations. Parker makes it obvious that he is having the conversation with Lawton. He implies that Gatewood is nowhere close. This is very odd. Gatewood never shied away from his own battles. If he wanted to stay with Lawton, he would not have used Parker to obtain permission.

43. Wood, *Chasing,* Aug. 3, 1886, 88.

44. Gatewood, "Surrender," 15–16.

45. Wood, *Chasing,* Aug. 8, 1886, 93; Lawton to AG, Department of Arizona (Sept. 9, 1886), Sen. Exec. Doc. 117, 49th Cong., 2d sess., 47.

46. Gatewood to Miles (Aug. 7, 1886), op. cit.

47. Richardson to Gatewood, Jr. (Feb. 10, 1926), op. cit.

48. See Wood, *Chasing,* Aug. 7, 1886, 92, for Gatewood and Wood's comments regarding Gatewood's wish to return to the United States.

49. Wood, *Chasing,* 135 n. 7.

50. Lawton to AG, Department of Arizona (Sept. 9, 1886), Sen. Exec. Doc. 117, 49th Cong., 2d sess., 47. Also see Lawton to AG, District of Huachuca (Aug. 8, 1886), op. cit.

51. Lawton to AG, District of Huachuca (Aug. 8, 1886), op. cit. Also see "Geronimo Campaign" as told by Lawrence Vinton, Gatewood Collection; Wood, *Chasing,* Aug. 8, 1886, 93. Gatewood, in "Surrender," 16, wrote: "While there [in Lawton's camp on the Aros River], news came to the effect that the hostiles were several hundred miles to the northwest, & so a movement was made in that direction." It seems strange that Lawton would make no mention of this information.

52. Wood, *Chasing,* journal entry for Aug. 9, 1886, 93. Also, see Aug. 8, 10–11, 1886, 93–94. Lawton to AG, District of Huachuca (Aug. 8, 1886), op. cit.

53. Wood, *Chasing,* Aug. 12, 1886, 95. Also, see 94–95.

54. Ibid., Aug. 15, 1886, 96 (also 95). Also, see Aug. 14, 95.

55. Lawton to Thompson (Aug. 15, 1886), Gatewood Collection.

56. Thomas J. Clay to the Post Adjutant, Fort Huachuca (Aug. 17, 1886), Gatewood Collection.

57. Wood, *Chasing,* Aug. 16–19, 1886, 97–98.

Chapter Eleven

1. O. O. Howard to AG, Washington, D.C. (Aug. 19, 1886), NA M689, Roll 184.

2. Ball, *Indeh,* 106–7, citing Martine and Kayitah's account of Geronimo's surrender. Dahteste is also named as *Mrs. Hugh Coonie.* Martine/Kayitah, "Surrender," 2, listed the women as Mrs. Hugh Coonie and *Dejonah.* Daklugie acted as translator for the version printed in *Indeh.* Ball found the transcript in the Mescalero Reservation records. No interpreter is listed for the Boggess version (in the Gatewood Collection). Also, see Lawton to AG, Department of Arizona (Sept. 9, 1886), Sen. Exec. Doc. 117, 49th Cong., 2d sess., 47; and Jackson, *Madre,* 149. See D. S. Stanley to R. C. Drum (Sept. 30, 1886), Sen. Exec. Doc. 117, 49th Cong., 2d sess., 22, for the peace talks with the Mexicans. Stanley wrote: "In obedience to your instructions, I examined Geronimo and [Naiche] to-day [in San Antonio], separately, and this without raising their suspicions; . . . Both chiefs said they never thought of surrender until Lieutenant Gatewood, Interpreter George Wratt[e]n, and the two scouts came to them and said the Great Father wanted them to surrender."

3. Martine/Kayitah, "Surrender," 1.

4. Gatewood, "Surrender II," 14 1/2.

5. Wood, *Chasing,* Aug. 19, 1886, 98.

6. Gatewood, in "Surrender," 16–17, wrote that he covered seventy miles, but most likely he referred to the entire trek to Fronteras (fifty-five miles plus fifteen miles). Gatewood, in "Surrender II," 15, traveled sixty miles on August 19. When he went into camp that night, he was still some eighteen or twenty miles south of Fronteras. Wood, in *Chasing,* Aug. 19, 1886, 98, claimed that he talked Lawton out of arresting Gatewood: "I urged him not to do this as I believed it would only be the beginning of a long row." He wrote that Gatewood left after midnight with ten soldiers. George A. Forsyth to William A. Thompson (Aug. 21, 1886), Gatewood Collection, spelled Cuchupa, *Cuchuta.* Forsyth does not mention Lawton's troops with Gatewood; instead, he records Gatewood had sixteen Indian scouts. Daly, in "Capture," 31, gave Gatewood six Indians and mistakenly names Tom Horn with him.

7. Bill Hoy, *Spanish Terms of the Sonoran Desert Borderlands* (Calexico, Calif.: Institute for Border Studies, San Diego State University, 1993), 23. A *prefecto* (prefect) was the head of *distritos* (districts), which were major state units of the Mexican government between the years 1837 and 1910. "Before 1861," Hoy writes, "the governor with approval of the State legislature appointed pre-

fects. Between 1861 and 1892, prefects were popularly elected and thereafter were chosen by the governor without legislative approval. Prefect roles included law enforcement, political go-betweens, and approval of political appointments. Sonora divided itself into nine districts based on its geographical regions. Sonora's isolated prefects generally wielded (and often abused) considerable power. The administrative capital of the distrito was the *cabecera*. For example, the Villa de [Arispe] was the cabecera of the Distrito de [Arispe]," which included the pueblo of Fronteras. See L. Arvizu to Governor of Sonora, Mexico (August 31, 1886), Microfilm, Historic Archives of Sonora, Reel 24 (Sonoran State Archives, Roll 24), Arizona Historical Society, Tucson, for the prefect of Arispe's identity. Also, see W. M. Edwa[d]dy to Miles (Aug. 16, 1886); Lawton to CO, District of Huachuca (Aug. 28, 1886); and Thomas J. Clay to Post Adjutant, Fort Huachuca (Aug. 17, 1886), Gatewood Collection. Edwa[d]dy identified the prefect incorrectly.

8. W. E. Wilder to William A. Thompson (August 27, 1886); Forsyth to Thompson (Aug. 21, 1886), Gatewood Collection. Also, see Terrell, *Apache Chronicle*, 383.

9. Forsyth to Thompson (Aug. 21, 1886), op. cit.; Cruse, *Days*, 228; Wood, *Chasing*, Aug. 20, 1886, 99. W. C. Endicott to Drum (Aug. 31, 1886), Sen. Exec. Doc. No. 83, 51st Cong., 1st sess., 25–26; Ball, *Days*, 191; Ball, *Indeh*, 113.

10. Forsyth to Thompson (Aug. 21, 1886), op. cit. Forsyth refers to Jesus Aguirre, the Prefect of Arispe, as *jefe político*—the political leader. Gatewood, in "Surrender," 17, refers to the prefect as the *prefect of the district*.

11. Forsyth to Thompson (Aug. 21, 1886), op. cit.

12. Gatewood, "Surrender," 17–18.

13. Lawton to AG, Department of Arizona (Sept. 9, 1886), Sen. Exec. Doc. 117, 49th Cong., 2d sess., 47.

14. Lawton to CO, District of Huachuca (Aug. 28, 1886), Gatewood Collection; Betzinez, *Geronimo*, 138; Ball, *Days*, 184; Gatewood, "Surrender," 26.

15. Lawton to AG, Department of Arizona (Sept. 9, 1886), loc. cit.

16. Wood, *Chasing*, Aug. 22, 1886, 100. Also, see 99, 136–137 n. 17.

17. R. A. Brown to E. A. Brininstool (Apr. 5, 1921), Gatewood Collection, Letter 89; Davis, *Geronimo*, 224; Cruse, *Days*, 228; Gatewood, Jr. to W. H. Carter (Jan. 20, 1926), Gatewood Collection, Letter 189; Thompson to Miles (Aug. 18, 1886), Gatewood Collection; Mazzanovich, *Trailing*, 241, 251. Cruse claimed Gatewood got Horn from Wilder, but this is not true.

18. Gatewood, "Surrender," 18; Martine/Kayitah, "Surrender," 2; Terrell, *Apache Chronicle*, 383; Wratten Interview, 3; Gatewood, Jr. to Carter (Jan. 20, 1926), op. cit.; "Indian Scout Tells of Geronimo's Surrender; Two Captors Live on New Mexico Reservation," *San Diego Union*, May 24, 1927 (hereafter cited as "Captors"); "Son," *San Diego Union*. There seems to be some confusion as to the exact number of soldiers Gatewood took with him. Gatewood placed the

number at six or eight. Others would estimate as high as ten or twelve and some as low as two or three.

19. Betzinez, *Geronimo,* 138; Ball, *Days,* 184; Gatewood, "Surrender," 26.

20. Gatewood, "Surrender," 19.

21. Wratten Interview, 4. Gatewood, "Surrender II," 19.

22. Wood, *Chasing,* Aug. 24, 1886, 100–101.

23. See Gatewood, "Surrender," 20–21, for this and the next quotation.

24. Martine/Kayitah, "Surrender," 2. Also, see Gatewood, "Surrender," 21; Gatewood, "Surrender II," 20. Gatewood claimed that he located Geronimo's camp before sending out the scouts. Martine and Kayitah claim he sent them out the following morning. To coincide with the correct time frame, I have concluded that both are accurate to a degree—it must have been either late morning or early afternoon when the camp was reached, so close to the noon hour that either Gatewood or Martine and Kayitah mistook the time. Also, I have concluded that the Indians' timeline is off; they could not have waited until the next day to have gone looking for Geronimo.

25. Ball, *Indeh,* 109–10. Also, see Ball, *Days,* 185.

26. Martine/Kayitah, "Surrender," 2. Also, see "Captors," *San Diego Union.*

27. Ball, *Indeh,* 110. In Ball, *Days,* 185, 187, the dialogue is the same with one difference: Yahnosha says to Geronimo, "If there is any more fighting done it will be with you, not them."

28. Gatewood, "Surrender," 21–22.

29. Ibid., 23. Davis, in *Geronimo,* 225, placed Brown's arrival at night. However, Gatewood's wording implies that Brown arrived before Martine returned to camp at sundown.

30. Lawton to Gatewood (Aug. 24, 1886), Gatewood Collection.

31. Martine/Kayitah, "Surrender," 3.

32. Ball, *Days,* 187.

33. Ball, *Indeh,* 110. Also, see Ball, *Days,* 187.

34. See Ball, *Days,* 187, for all the dialogue until Geronimo decides to meet Gatewood. When Kayitah and Martine told Geronimo and Naiche that the Chiricahuas who had surrendered to Crook in March 1886 had been sent to Florida, they did not include in the removal the Chiricahuas who remained at peace on the reservation.

35. Martine/Kayitah, "Surrender," 3.

36. Radtke, "Scouts."

37. Gatewood, "Surrender," 22. Gatewood calls the Teres Mountains the *Torres Mountains.* He has also recorded the date incorrectly, putting it as August 23. Also, see Gatewood to Miles (Oct. 15, 1886), Gatewood Collection. Here, Gatewood records the date correctly.

38. Gatewood to Miles (Oct. 15, 1886), op. cit.

39. Gatewood, "Surrender," 22–23.

40. Martine/Kayitah, "Surrender," 3.
41. Ibid., 3.
42. Wratten Interview, 4.
43. Gatewood, "Surrender," 25.

Chapter Twelve

1. Gatewood, "Surrender," 23–24; Gatewood to Miles (Oct. 15, 1886), Gatewood Collection; Wratten Interview, 4; "Captors," *San Diego Union*; Martine/Kayitah, "Surrender," 3–4; Ball, *Indeh*, 4, 8, 174. Martine and Kayitah claim that Gatewood only took a small portion of the men with him, that most were left at the canebrake. As we shall see, their memories are most-likely faulty here. Geronimo had three half-brothers with him at this time: Perico, Fun, and Eyelash.

2. Brown to E. A. Brininstool (Apr. 5, 1921), Gatewood Collection, Letter 89.

3. Gatewood, "Surrender," 24. Also, see Gatewood to Miles (Oct. 15, 1886), op. cit. In the report, Gatewood states that the messenger delivered the conditions that had to be met before Geronimo and Naiche would meet. This is in agreement with what Brown stated (n. 2, above), but contrary to what Gatewood said in "Surrender." Here, Gatewood claimed the three warriors stated the conditions that had to be met.

4. Gatewood to Miles (Oct. 15, 1886), op. cit.

5. Martine/Kayitah, "Surrender," 4. Again, Martine and Kayitah are slightly confused. They have merged the meeting with the four Chiricahua messengers together with the meeting with Geronimo. It is obvious that here they refer to the actual meeting with Geronimo. See Wratten Interview, 4, for the amount of time before the Chiricahuas appeared; and C. A. Bach to Gatewood, Jr. (Feb. 1, 1926), Gatewood Collection, Letter 193, for the distance from the canebrake. Davis, in *Geronimo,* 225, named the location as a glade. He claimed the distance was only two miles from the canebrake. This does not seem right, as Gatewood would have had to backtrack toward the canebrake to reach the location of the council. Also, see Daly to Gatewood, Jr. (Feb. 5, 1926), Gatewood Collection, Letter 587. Daly erroneously stated that the only white man with Gatewood was Wratten. Wratten Interview, 5, claimed that there were three or four white men in Gatewood's party (Gatewood, Wratten, Horn, and maybe one other). Gatewood, Jr., to Hermann Hagedorn (May 11, 1929), Gatewood Collection, Letter 368, names Koch, a member of the Lawton's Troop B (Fourth U.S. Cavalry), as the soldier with Gatewood. Charles Maurer to Gatewood, Jr. (June 4, 1926), Gatewood Collection, Letter 265, says Koch told him that he (Koch) was with Gatewood when he met Geronimo. I am not sure this is true: Koch is not listed on the Muster Rolls for Troop B for either the months of June or August 1886. See War Department, Adjutant General's Office, Memo, which includes both

Muster Rolls (May 3, 1926); Gatewood Collection, Letter 254. Gatewood, in "Surrender II," 23, describes the movement to the glade slightly differently: "A dozen or so of the bucks joined us, & the usual handshaking & offer of tobacco took place. Then a shot was fired up in their camp, answered by my party. A smoke was sent up, also answered by us. Thus were passed salutations of mutual respect & unity. The white flag that we had been marhing behind was lowered, & the party adjourned some 2 miles to the river."

6. See Wratten Interview, 5 for quotation, and 4. Gatewood to Miles (Oct. 15, 1886), op. cit.

7. Gatewood, "Surrender," 24–25 (25 is the second of two p. 25s in manuscript). Gatewood, "Surrender II," 23–24; Wratten Interview, 5. Wratten's memory is at total odds with Gatewood's regarding the tobacco and food situation. Wratten wrote: "They asked us for tobacco and liquor, but we had but little of the first and none of the second. There wasn't a thing to eat, and I went out with several of the hostiles in search of food. Later, one of Gatewood's soldiers came in with a lot of tobacco and a little food that Gatewood had sent him for." Gatewood, Jr., to Editor, *San Diego Union* (June 7, 1927), Gatewood Collection, Letter 324, claims: "Gatewood carried on his side of the conference [with Geronimo] in their own language [Apache]; the interpreter, Wratten, was along as a witness to the talk, rather than as an interpreter." Charles Gatewood, Jr., in "Retired Army Officer Here Reveals History of Famous Apache Surrender," *San Diego Union*, June 8, 1927, again claims that Gatewood did all the talking, that Wratten merely listened (hereafter cited as Gatewood, Jr., "Retired"). Gatewood, Jr.'s conclusions are strange. Why have three interpreters if you are not going to use them? However, going along with Gatewood, Jr.'s conclusion, I have seen no mention of Horn or Yestes's roles in the meeting, other than named as being present. In Gatewood to Miles (Oct. 15, 1886), op. cit., Gatewood records what Geronimo said to him on August 26, followed by: "This is the substance of what he said as near as could be interpreted." As the meeting with Geronimo on the twenty-sixth was as important as the all-day powwow on the twenty-fifth, and as Gatewood obviously depended on an interpreter's translation on the twenty-sixth, I see no reason to believe he would have relied totally upon his mastery of Apache and/or pidgin English-Spanish-Apache on the twenty-fifth. He knew the importance of the meeting. Although it is uncertain just how much Gatewood used his interpreters, I cannot help but believe that he did use them. And finally, in "Surrender II," 25, Gatewood wrote: "I want to say that in this talk I used interpreters because of the importance of the occasion . . ."

8. Gatewood, "Surrender II," 24. *Anzhoo* translates to "How are you? Am glad to see you."

9. Gatewood, "Surrender," 25 (second of two p. 25s in manuscript).

10. Gatewood, "Surrender II," 16. Also, see 17.

11. Ibid., 24.

12. Gatewood, "Surrender," 25 (second of two p. 25s in manuscript). In Gatewood to Miles (Oct. 15, 1886), op. cit., Gatewood placed the warrior count at twenty-one.

13. Ball, *Indeh,* 110–11; Ball, *Days,* 184.

14. There has been a lot of confusion concerning the date of Gatewood's meeting with Geronimo. Much of the confusion stems from documents written a month and even years after the meeting took place. Lawton, in his report to the AG, Department of Arizona (Sept. 9, 1886), Sen. Exec. Doc. 117, 49th Cong., 2d sess., 47, put the date of the meeting on August 24; as does Gatewood, "Surrender," 24, when he lists the day before the meeting as August 23; and Cruse, *Days,* 229. Both Thrapp, *Conquest,* 360, who states that Gatewood, Geronimo, and Lawton started for the United States on August 25; and Debo, *Geronimo,* 285, accepted this date. However, it is off by a day. The meeting took place on August 25. On August 24, 1886, Lawton wrote Gatewood that he had just arrived in Brown's old camp and could not reach him that day; Gatewood Collection. On August 25, Wood recorded: "It seems that about half an hour after leaving Lawton he struck the Indian trail and wanted us to follow it with as little delay as practicable, in order that his whole command might be concentrated. That is to say, the whole outfit join[ed] Brown and the Scouts, who are on ahead with Gatewood and his Indians." Wood, *Chasing,* 101. Gatewood to Miles (Oct. 15, 1886), op. cit., states that Kayitah and Martine entered Geronimo's camp on August 24, and that he met with him the next day. Finally, Gatewood to Georgia (Aug. 26, 1886), Gatewood Collection, states: "Well, I've had a talk with Geronimo in person. It took all day yesterday [August 25] and made me very tired."

15. See "Inevitable," *Mississippi Republican,* for this quotation and the next two quotations.

16. Gatewood to Georgia (Aug. 26, 1886), op. cit.

17. Gatewood, "Surrender," 26.

18. "Son," *San Diego Union.*

19. See Gatewood, "Surrender," 26–27, for Gatewood's quotation and Geronimo's comments regarding drinking.

20. "Inevitable," *Mississippi Republican.*

21. See Gatewood to Georgia (Aug. 26, 1886), op. cit., for this and the next quotation.

22. "Geronimo's Surrender," *Prescott Courier,* Oct. 22, 1886.

23. Gatewood, "Surrender," 27–28.

24. Ibid., 28.

25. "Inevitable," *Mississippi Republican.*

26. Gatewood to Georgia (Aug. 26, 1886), op. cit. Also, see Gatewood, "Surrender," 28–29; Gatewood to Miles, (Oct. 15, 1886), op. cit.

27. Stanley to Dunn (Sept. 30, 1886), Sen. Exec. Doc. 117, 49th Cong., 2d sess., 22.

28. Wood, *Chasing,* Aug. 25, 1886, 101.

29. Gatewood to Miles, (Oct. 15, 1886), op. cit. Also, see Gatewood, "Surrender," 29. In the report, Gatewood put the time at 11:00 A.M.; in the article, he logged the time as 12:00 noon.

30. See Gatewood, "Surrender," 29–31, for this quotation through Gatewood's gamble. Although the reservation Chiricahuas had been rounded up, they had not been shipped east yet.

31. Gatewood, "Surrender II," 28. Also, see 29.

32. Gatewood, "Surrender," 31; and Gatewood, "Surrender II," 31–32.

33. Gatewood, "Surrender," 32.

34. Ibid., 33.

35. Lawton to AG, Department of Arizona (Sept. 9, 1886), Sen. Exec. Doc. 117, 49th Cong., 2d sess., 47; Wood, *Chasing,* Aug. 25, 1886, 101.

36. Gatewood, "Surrender II," 32–33. Also, see Gatewood, "Surrender," 33.

37. Gatewood, "Surrender," 33–34.

38. Ibid., 34.

39. Gatewood, "Surrender II," 36. Also, see 35.

40. Gatewood to Miles, (Oct. 15, 1886), op. cit.

41. Gatewood to Georgia (Aug. 26, 1886), op. cit. Also, see Gatewood, "Surrender," 35.

42. Gatewood to Georgia (Aug. 26, 1886), op. cit.

43. Gatewood, "Surrender," 34.

44. Gatewood to Georgia (Aug. 26, 1886), op. cit. Also, see Gatewood, "Surrender," 35.

45. Gatewood, "Surrender," 35.

46. Ball, *Indeh,* 54.

47. Gatewood, "Surrender," 36. Geronimo later told Gatewood that he was pleased that Bay-chen-daysen cared enough about his son's welfare to send him back against Chappo's wishes.

48. Lawton to AG, Department of Arizona (Sept. 9, 1886), loc. cit. Lawton claimed he had to talk Gatewood out of riding to Miles. This seems farfetched, as Gatewood had already told Geronimo he would not make the trip to Miles. Also, Gatewood knew that the Chiricahuas would be delivering their answer in the morning. See Gatewood to Georgia (Aug. 26, 1886), op. cit., for his condition at the end of the day.

49. J. A. Cole to Mazzanovich (Apr. 14, 1928), Gatewood Collection, Letter 344. Kaywaykla, in Ball, *Days,* 189, called the wife with Geronimo his "Mescalero wife," meaning Ih-tedda. However, Debo, in *Geronimo,* 254, 304, proves Kaywaykla's memory to be wrong. She shows that Zi-yeh, captured in 1885, and Ih-tedda, who returned to Arizona with Maus in January, were both in Florida at this time.

50. Ball, *Days,* 181. Kaywaykla claims Nana was one of the warriors who wanted to remain free. This is an error. Nana returned to the United States in January with Maus.

51. Ball, *Indeh,* 104.

52. Gatewood to Miles, (Oct. 15, 1886), op. cit. Gatewood, in "Surrender," 36–37, does not name the interpreters who accompanied him. I am assuming he used the same three men as the day before. Also, see Gatewood, "Surrender II," 38–39; Gatewood, Jr., "Retired."

53. Gatewood, "Surrender," 37–38. In Gatewood, "Surrender II," 39, the text is slightly different, but the meaning is the same.

54. Gatewood to Miles, (Oct. 15, 1886), op. cit.

55. Lawton to AG, Department of Arizona (Sept. 9, 1886), loc. cit. Also, see Gatewood, "Surrender," 38. Gatewood, in "Surrender II," 39–40, describes the smoking incident during the meeting with Lawton. Here, however, he does not mention the starvation camp.

56. Gatewood to Georgia (Aug. 26, 1886), op. cit. Gatewood did eventually begin work on a book of his experiences with the Apaches. Unfortunately, he died before completing the project.

57. Wood, *Chasing,* Aug. 26, 1886, 102.

58. Miles, *Republic,* 226.

Chapter Thirteen

1. Gatewood to Miles (Oct. 15, 1886), Gatewood Collection.

2. Cook, *Years,* 158.

3. Charles Riepert to Gatewood, Jr. (Jan. 15, 1927), Gatewood Collection, Letter 304.

4. Forsyth to Thompson (Aug. 29, 1886), Gatewood Collection.

5. Lawton to Mame Lawton (Aug. 27, 1886), as quoted in Wood, *Chasing,* 103.

6. Donald F. MacCarthy to Owen P. White (Apr. 1, 1933), Gatewood Collection, Letter 420; Wood, *Chasing,* Aug. 27, 1886, 103–4, 137 n. 2).

7. Wood, *Chasing,* Aug. 27, 1886, 104.

8. Ibid., 104.

9. Wratten Interview, 3–4.

10. Wood, *Chasing,* Aug. 28, 1886, 104. Gatewood, in "Surrender," 39, continues to be off with his dating. Here, he states that the advance northward began on August 24. In "Surrender II," 41, Gatewood is again off on his dating. Here, however, he states that the northbound journey began on August 25. Others who wrote later also have used erroneous dates. Both Cruse, *Days,* 231, and Thrapp, *Conquest,* 360, put the date as August 25.

11. Gatewood, "Surrender II," 41; Wood, *Chasing,* Aug. 28, 1886, 105; Martine/Kayitah, "Surrender," 4; R. D. Walsh to Gatewood, Jr. (May 3, 1926), Gatewood Collection, Letter 256. Gatewood estimated the number of Mexicans at two hundred, as did Walsh. Martine and Kayitah put the Mexican force at six hundred soldiers. Gatewood placed this incident on the second day of the jour-

ney. Most likely, he meant the second day after Geronimo agreed to return to the United States.

12. Martine/Kayitah, "Surrender," 4.

13. Gatewood, "Surrender II," 41. Also, see 42.

14. Gatewood, "Surrender," 39.

15. Lawton to CO, District of Huachuca (Aug. 28, 1886), Gatewood Collection; Wood, *Chasing*, Aug. 28, 1886, 105–6.

16. Gatewood, "Surrender," 40; Walsh to Gatewood, Jr. (May 3, 1926), op. cit.; Lawton to CO, District of Huachuca (Aug. 28, 1886), op. cit.; Wood, *Chasing*, Aug. 28, 1886, 106. The distance does not jive with the gait at which Gatewood said they traveled for an hour. However, this seems a more reasonable distance.

17. Gatewood, "Surrender II," 43. Also, see 42.

18. Walsh to Gatewood, Jr. (May 3, 1926), op. cit.; Gatewood, "Surrender," 40–41; Wood, *Chasing*, Aug. 28, 1886, 106; "Inevitable," *Mississippi Republican*. Walsh claimed that the Mexicans and Apaches remained mounted during the entire meeting, but that the American officers were dismounted. He also stated that the prefect and Geronimo were each accompanied only by two others. Naiche was one of the seconds with Geronimo. The *Republican* also had both groups mounted, including Gatewood. Gatewood, in "Surrender II," 43, has the prefect sitting under a cottonwood tree when he and Geronimo appear.

19. "Inevitable," *Mississippi Republican*.

20. Walsh to Gatewood, Jr. (May 3, 1926), op. cit.

21. "Inevitable," *Mississippi Republican*. Also, see Gatewood, "Surrender II," 44.

22. Gatewood, "Surrender," 41.

23. "Inevitable," *Mississippi Republican*.

24. Wood, *Chasing*, Aug. 28, 1886, 107; Walsh to Gatewood, Jr. (May 3, 1926), op. cit. Wood claimed that he, Clay, and Lawton jumped between the two sides to prevent shooting. Neither Gatewood, Walsh, nor Lawton confirm this. Both Wood and Walsh stated that the American officers feared that Geronimo and his followers would kill the Mexicans if a shoot-out commenced.

25. Gatewood, "Surrender II," 45.

26. Gatewood, "Surrender," 41.

27. "Inevitable," *Mississippi Republican*. Gatewood, in "Surrender," 42, cited Geronimo as saying "I am, because I can trust them," in reply to the prefect's question.

28. See Gatewood, "Surrender," 42, for this quotation and the rest of the quotations in the section.

29. Walsh to Gatewood, Jr. (May 3, 1926), op. cit.

30. Wood, *Chasing*, Aug. 28, 1886, 107.

31. Martine/Kayitah, "Surrender," 4. Also, see Mazzanovich, *Trailing*, 252.

32. Lawton to the CO, District of Huachuca (Aug. 28, 1886), op. cit.

33. Wratten Interview, 5.

34. Wood, *Chasing*, Aug. 29, 1886, 107; Gatewood, "Surrender," 42. Gatewood states that they traveled for "a day or two, . . . having marched about a day's journey (15 to 20 miles), we halted & waited for the command." This is a strange statement, contradicting itself. I believe that at the time he wrote this he had forgotten exactly how much time had passed before Geronimo's group traveled the fifteen to twenty miles. As Apaches could easily travel this distance— even in rugged country—in a day, I am certain that Gatewood refers to only one day: August 29. Wood confirms the date and puts the total mileage for the day at twenty (with eight of the twenty miles still to come after the halt).

35. Gatewood, "Surrender," 43. Also, see Wood, *Chasing*, Aug. 30, 1886, 108.

36. Gatewood, "Surrender," 43–44. Gatewood spelled Perico, *Periquo*. He also called the warrior Geronimo's brother-in-law, rather than his half-brother. Gatewood, in "Surrender II," 46–47, told the story of the meal slightly differently.

37. Wood, *Chasing*, Aug. 29, 1886, 107.

38. Gatewood, "Surrender," 44.

39. Lawton to AG, Department of Arizona (Sept. 9, 1886), Sen. Exec. Doc. 117, 49th Cong., 2d sess., 48; Martine/Kayitah, "Surrender," 5. The timing of when these messengers were sent out is uncertain. However, their departure must have been shortly after Gatewood ate with Perico.

40. Thomas J. Clay, "Some Unwritten Incidents of the Geronimo Campaign," in *The Papers of the Order of Indian Wars* (Fort Collins, Colo.: The Old Army Press, 1975), 115 (hereafter cited as Clay, "Incidents").

41. Wood, *Chasing*, Aug. 30, 1886, 107–8.

42. Lawton to CO, District of Huachuca (Aug. 28, 1886), op. cit.

43. Frank C. Lockwood, *The Apache Indians* (1938; repr., Lincoln and London; University of Nebraska Press, 1966), 306. Lockwood thought this statement was made at the San Bernardino Ranch. If it had been made, it must have been said on the trail before Lawton left for the ranch.

44. Wood, *Chasing*, Aug. 30, 1886, 108, 137 n. 3.

45. Lawton to Miles (Aug. 30, 1886), Gatewood Collection, Letter 403. Gatewood and Geronimo were closer to Lawton at this time than he realized.

46. Clay to Mazzanovich (May 25, 1930), Gatewood Collection, Letter 391.

47. Wratten Interview, 5.

48. MacCarthy to White (Apr. 1, 1933), op. cit.

49. Wood, *Chasing*, Aug. 30–31, 1886, 108.

50. Miles to Lawton (Aug. 31, 1886), Gatewood Collection, Letter 403.

51. Miles to Lawton (Aug. 31, 1886), Gatewood Collection, Letter 403. This dispatch, although dated the same (and held in the same grouping in the Gatewood Collection) as the dispatch in n. 50, is a separate communiqué.

52. Gatewood, "Surrender," 45.

53. Hermann Hagedorn to Gatewood, Jr. (Apr. 18, 1929), Gatewood Collection, Letter 349.

54. Gatewood, "Surrender," 45.

55. Gatewood, Jr. to Hagedorn (May 11, 1929), Gatewood Collection, Letter 368.

56. Gatewood, "Surrender," 46, for this quotation and the next two quotations.

57. Gatewood, Jr. to Hagedorn (May 11, 1929), op. cit. Also, see Gatewood, Jr. to Hagedorn (Apr. 2, 1929), Gatewood Collection, Letter 362. Gatewood, Jr., wrote: "Two days later, the same officers [Smith and Wood] and men who had advocated this attack on the Indian party hatched a scheme to invite Geronimo and [Naiche] to a conference to talk and feast, and then kill them." It is obvious that Gatewood, Jr., is of the opinion that there were two separate instances of conflict with the United States troops: one at Guadalupe Canyon and another a day or two later. Most likely, he bases this theory on Gatewood, "Surrender," 47, where Gatewood, obviously making a nod to his unsure memory, stated: "It was in this camp or the next one, that several young officers proposed to kill Geronimo during one of their talks." Wood, who kept a good running account of daily occurrences only made one reference to this trouble. See Chasing, Aug. 31, 1886, 108. I disagree with Gatewood, Jr. As Lawton returned to the camp in Guadalupe Canyon on August 31, this next attempt would have taken place on September 2 at Skeleton Canyon. Finding nothing that indicates any murder attempt was planned or activated at Skeleton Canyon, I am certain that the attempt must have taken place just prior to Lawton's return to his command. There was only one confrontation and it was about to happen. Hagedorn to Gatewood, Jr. (Apr. 18, 1929), Gatewood Collection, Letter 349, defended Wood of the damning charge: "I question the story concerning the proposed [murder of Geronimo] . . . because Wood, with all his faults, was not that sort of man." Lane, ed., in Wood, Chasing, 138 n. 7, dismissed all intended wrongdoing by the Americans. He wrote: "The Smith incident was of only minor importance. The Indians were excited by Miles's reluctance to meet with them, which prolonged the final surrender and made them vulnerable to an attack by the Mexicans." I do not agree wih Lane's conclusion. Gatewood, Lawton, and Geronimo had not yet reached Skeleton Canyon, the proposed location for the surrender. And although Lawton and Gatewood were aware that Miles might not appear, they would have downplayed this information with Geronimo. Besides, the Indians, now on American soil, had much more to fear from U.S. troops than they did from Mexicans, who did not have much of a track record of crossing the border to attack.

58. Gatewood, Jr., to Hagedorn (May 11, 1929), op. cit. Regarding the confrontation, as cited by Wratten, Gatewood, Jr. wrote: "Col. M. W. Day, who served throughout the Geronimo campaign, under Crook as well as under Miles, told me that he had the story direct from Gatewood confidentially. (Day and

Gatewood were classmates and especially close friends). He repeated exactly what Wratten had told me in 1906 [in Washington D.C.]. So far as I know, Gatewood himself never told anyone else of this incident. In 1926, I asked Frank Huston (packer with Gatewood) if these facts were true. He asked in return, 'Where the Hell did you get that? You're not far wrong.' Charles Maurer, a sergeant, 4th Cavalry, overheard part of the argument between Gatewood and A. L. Smith concerning the proposed attack on the Indians." Also, see Gatewood, "Surrender," 47; Wood, *Chasing,* Aug. 31, 1886, 108; and Hagedorn to Gatewood, Jr. (Apr. 18, 1929), op. cit.

Chapter Fourteen

1. See T. J. Clay to Mazzanovich (May 25, 1930), Letter 391, Donald P. MacCarthy to Owen P. White (Apr. 1, 1933), Letter 420, Gatewood Collection; and Clay, "Incidents," 115, for Gatewood's ability to soothe the Indians and keep them from running.

2. Wood, *Chasing,* Aug. 31, 1886, 108–9.

3. See Gatewood, "Surrender," 48–49, for this and the next quotation. Also, see Gatewood, Jr., to Hagedorn (May 11, 1929), Letter 368, and (Apr. 2, 1929), Letter 362, Gatewood Collection. Obviously, murder hovered in everyone's minds. Gatewood wanted out because he felt the entire mission collapsing around him, not because Lawton turned his back on the so-called attempted murder incident. If this happened, Gatewood, who was fairly frank in his accounts, would have hinted that this terrible breach of military conduct was the reason he wanted to leave. It also follows that he would have tendered his request to leave on August 31 and not on September 2, when he was at Skeleton Canyon and the end was near.

4. Wood, *Chasing,* Sept. 1, 1886, 109.

5. Lawton to Miles (Sept. 2, 1886), Gatewood Collection.

6. Wratten Interview, 5; Lawton to Miles (Sept. 2, 1886), op. cit.; Wood, *Chasing,* Sept. 2, 1886, 109. Wratten put the arrival on the fifth or sixth day of travel (September 2), which agrees with Wood and Lawton. There have been a number of articles and books that have completely missed the correct arrival date. For example, Daly, "Capture," claimed the arrival took place on August 31; and Mazzanovich, *Trailing,* 253, stated the arrival date was several days before Miles made his appearance, which was on September 3.

7. Lawton to Miles (Sept. 2, 1886), op. cit.

8. R. A. Brown to E. A. Brininstool (Apr. 5, 1921), Gatewood Collection, Letter 89; Wratten Interview, 6; Wood, *Chasing,* Sept. 2, 1886, 109. Brown put the camp at two or three miles distant, while Wood claimed it was only one and a half miles from the soldiers. Also, see Gatewood, Jr., to Brininstool (June 4, 1925), Gatewood Collection, Letter 99.

9. Howard to Drum (Sept. 2, 1886), Sen. Exec. Doc. 117, 49th Cong., 2d sess., 6.

10. Miles to Drum (Aug. 28, 1886), Sen. Exec. Doc. 117, 49th Cong., 2d sess., 6.

11. Miles to Lawton (Aug. 31, 1886), Gatewood Collection.

12. Miles to Lawton (Aug. 31, 1886), Gatewood Collection. Note that the message cited in n. 11, along with the messages cited in nn. 50 and 51 in chap. 13, are separate dispatches that Miles sent to Lawton, all on the same date.

13. Lawton to Miles (Sept. 2, 1886), op. cit.

14. Wood, *Chasing*, 109.

15. Thompson to Miles (Sept. 3, 1886), Gatewood Collection.

16. Wood, *Chasing*, Sept. 3, 1886, 109; Thompson to Miles (Sept. 3, 1886), op. cit.

17. Geronimo, *Geronimo*, 142.

18. Gatewood, "Surrender II," 48.

19. Miles to AG, Division of the Pacific (Sept. 24, 1886), 19, and D. S. Stanley to Headquarters, Department of Texas (Oct. 27, 1886), 29, Sen. Exec. Doc. 117, 49th Cong., 2d sess.; Gatewood, "Surrender," 49.

20. Stanley to Headquarters, Department of Texas (Oct. 27, 1886), loc. cit.

21. Geronimo, *Geronimo*, 142.

22. Miles to AG, Division of the Pacific (Sept. 24, 1886), loc. cit., for quotation and Miles's comment.

23. Geronimo, *Geronimo*, 142.

24. Miles to AG, Division of the Pacific (Sept. 24, 1886), loc. cit.

25. Geronimo, *Geronimo*, 143.

26. Stanley to Drum (Sept. 30, 1886), Sen. Exec. Doc. 117, 49th Cong., 2d sess., 22.

27. See Geronimo, *Geronimo*, 143, for this quotation through Miles's quotation about Geronimo not being arrested. In an interesting aside, Geronimo said in his book that he had been arrested twice since the surrender for drinking whiskey.

28. Stanley to Headquarters, Department of Texas (Oct. 27, 1886), loc. cit.

29. Miles to AG, Division of the Pacific (Sept. 24, 1886), loc. cit.

30. See Gatewood, "Surrender," 49–50, for this quotation and Geronimo's comment.

31. Geronimo, *Geronimo*, 143.

32. Gatewood, "Surrender," 50.

33. Ibid., 50–51.

34. Miles to AG, Division of the Pacific (Sept. 24, 1886), loc. cit. Also, see 20.

35. Clay, "Incidents," 115. Also, see Gatewood, "Surrender," 51.

36. See Gatewood, "Surrender," 51, for this quotation and Naiche's reply. I do not know who this missing brother was. Naiche became the last chieftain of the Chokonen (central Chiricahuas) when Taza, his older and perhaps only brother, died in 1876. I have seen no references to any other named sons by Cochise or of named half-brothers. This, however, does not mean that Naiche did not have another brother or half-brother. Wood, *Chasing*, Sept. 3 and 8,

1886, 109, 111, refers to the missing brother, whom he called "a fairly well grown boy."

37. See Clay, "Incidents," 115, for Gatewood's quotation and Naiche's reply.

38. Gatewood, "Surrender," 52.

39. Miles, *Republic,* 227.

Chapter Fifteen

1. Howard to AG, U.S. Army, Washington, D.C. (Sept. 7, 1886), Sen. Exec. Doc. No. 117, 49th Cong., 2d sess., 7; Charles Farson to Gatewood, Jr. (Jan. 16, 1926), Letter 177, Miles to L. Q. C. Lamar, Jr. (Sept. 6, 1886), Gatewood Collection. There is some confusion as to exactly how many Apaches rode to Bowie with Miles. Howard put the number at six. Both Farson and Miles put the number at five.

2. Endicott to Drum (Aug. 31, 1886), Sen. Exec. Doc. No. 83, 51st Cong., 1st sess., 25–26; Ball, *Indeh,* 114.

3. Clay, "Incidents," 115.

4. See Utley, *Clash,* 79, for Geronimo's quotation and Miles's reply.

5. Gatewood, "Surrender," 52; and Howard to AG, U.S. Army, Washington, D.C. (Sept. 7, 1886), loc. cit. Also, see Clay, "Incidents," 115, who put the mileage at seventy.

6. Wratten Interview, 6. Miles to Lamar, Jr. (Sept. 6, 1886), loc. cit.

7. Utley, *Clash,* 79.

8. Wratten Interview, 6.

9. Stanley to Drum (Oct. 1, 1886), Sen. Exec. Doc. 117, 49th Cong., 2d sess., 22.

10. Howard to AG, U.S. Army, Washington, D.C. (Sept. 7, 1886), loc. cit. Howard concluded this report with the question: "What shall be done with Geronimo and the hostiles now prisoners of war?" Apparently Howard's order to Miles did not survive.

11. Field Orders No. 89 (Sept. 6, 1886), Sen. Exec. Doc. 117, 49th Cong., 2d sess., 7. The orders carry an asterisk and a footnote in the executive document: "There is no record in the Department of a telegram of September 4, 1886, or any other date, from the Acting Secretary of War to General Miles, directing him to send Geronimo and band to Fort Marion, Fl[orida]. No such order was given." Italics in document.

12. Miles, *Republic,* 228.

13. Wood, *Chasing,* Sept. 7, 1886, 111; Miles to Lamar, Jr. (Sept. 6, 1886), op. cit; Martine/Kayitah, "Surrender," 5.

14. Cleveland to Drum (Sept. 7, 1886), Sen. Exec. Doc. No. 117, 49th Cong., 2d sess., 8.

15. Gatewood to Georgia (Aug. 26, 1886). Charles B. Gatewood, Jr., "Lieu-

tenant Charles B. Gatewood, 6th U.S. Cavalry and the Surrender of Geronimo," 2–3. Gatewood Collection.

16. Miles to Sheridan (Sept. 7, 1886), Sen. Exec. Doc. No. 117, 49th Cong., 2d sess., 9. Italics in document. Also, see Howard to Drum (Sept. 2, 1886), NA M689, Roll 184.

17. Sheridan to Miles (Sept. 7, 1886), Sen. Exec. Doc. 117, 49th Cong., 2d sess., 9–10. Italics in document.

18. Miles to Sheridan (Sept. 7, 1886), Sen. Exec. Doc. 117, 49th Cong., 2d sess., 10.

19. Wood, *Chasing,* Sept. 8, 1886, 111, 138, n. 9; Howard to Drum (Feb. 24, 1887), Sen. Exec. Doc. No. 117, 49th Cong., 2d sess., 36; Davis, *Geronimo,* 231–32.

20. Wood, *Chasing,* Sept. 8, 1886, 112 for quotation, and 111. Also, see Miles, *Republic,* 228; Hermann Hagedorn, *Leonard Wood, A Biography,* 2 vols. (New York and London: Harper & Brothers Publishers, 1931), 1:102–3 (here-after cited as Hagedorn, *Wood1*); and Lockwood, *Apache Indians,* 309.

21. Sheridan to Terry (Oct. 29, 1886), Sen. Exec. Doc. No. 117, 49th Cong., 2d sess., 27.

22. Ball, *Indeh,* 131.

23. Drum to Stanley (Sept. 10, 1886), Sen. Exec. Doc. No. 117, 49th Cong., 2d sess., 13.

24. See Ball, *Indeh,* 131, for Geronimo's quotation, Wratten's reply, and Kanseah's quotation.

25. Hagedorn, *Wood1,* 105. Also, see 104, 106.

26. The supposition that Wood had it in for Gatewood cannot be taken lightly. Thirteen years after Gatewood's death, Georgia wrote Gatewood, Jr. (Apr. 4, 1909), Gatewood Collection, Letter 79, regarding writing about his father: "When the papers first began to announce [Geronimo's] death and to follow up with articles mentioning Lawton, Miles & that Wood man, or thing, I was stopped everywhere and I must say these people, all, said they knew it was your father did it all, alone, but none of the articles said so, except an editorial in a Cumberland paper, and I grew so enraged and sore and felt so helpless, . . . I real-ized your position in regard to Wood and I tell you, cautious as you may be, you will incur his enmity if you say a word without mentioning him, for he don't want the subject uncovered at all, & I seem to stand alone in my opinion of his unscrupulous vanity, & as he perjured himself for Miles,—for his own advance-ment, so will Miles perjure himself now to uphold them both, & others will keep quiet." Also, see Howard to AG, Washington, D.C. (Sept. 14, 1886), Sen. Exec. Doc. No. 83, 51st Cong., 1st sess., 28. The train carrying the Chiricahuas passed through Albuquerque at 2:30 A.M. on September 14.

27. Drum to Terry (Sept. 12, 1886), Sen. Exec. Doc. No. 83, 51st Cong., 1st sess., 27.

28. "Crook's Protégés," *San Francisco Chronicle* (the date presumed to be the latter half of 1889), Gatewood Scrapbook. Also, see Welsh, *Prisoners*, 8.

29. Undated and untitled news clipping in Gatewood Scrapbook.

30. Charles Riepert to Gatewood, Jr. (Jan. 15, 1927), Gatewood Collection, Letter 304.

31. Charles Maurer to Gatewood, Jr. (June 4, 1926), Gatewood Collection, Letter 265.

32. Lawton to AG, Department of Arizona (Sept. 9, 1886), Sen. Exec. Doc. No. 117, 49th Cong., 2d sess., 48.

33. Miles, *Recollections*, 512.

34. "A Deserving Officer," *Arizona Citizen*. The debate continued into the twentieth century with well-defined sides. Although many officers remained in the Miles/Wood camp, Britton Davis never wavered in his support of Gatewood's accomplishment. For example, when James Parker, a retired general in 1929, gave little credit to Gatewood when he spoke at an Order of Indian Wars meeting, Davis attacked his speech. Davis to General S. W. Fountain (July 18, 1929), *The Papers of the Order of Indian Wars*, 123: "I claim that [Geronimo] actually surrendered the morning of his second talk with Gatewood, when he accepted the terms of surrender."

35. Thompson to Miles (Sept. 10, 1886), Gatewood Collection, Box 1, Folder 5.

36. NA M1395. The same document is in Department of Arizona, U.S. Army Department of Arizona General Orders and Circulars, 1870–1886, Microfilm Roll 5 (1883–1886), Arizona Historical Society. However, here it is listed as General Orders No. 24.

37. See Gatewood to Miles (Sept. 18, 26, 27, 29, and 30, 1886), Gatewood Collection.

38. Sen. Exec. Doc. No. 117, 49th Cong., 2d sess., Sheridan note returned to Drum, the (Acting) Secretary of War (Sept. 25, 1886), 18.

39. Ibid., Miles to Cleveland (Sept. 25, 1886), 20.

40. Ibid., Drum to Miles (Sept. 26, 1886), 20.

41. Ibid., Miles to Drum, the Acting Secretary of War (Sept. 29, 1886), 21.

42. "Thrice-told," *St. Louis Republican*.

43. Howard to AG, Washington, D.C. (Oct. 20, 1886), Sen. Exec. Doc. No. 117, 49th Cong., 2d sess., 75.

44. Ball, *Indeh*, 115.

45. Davis, *Geronimo*, 231.

46. Ball, *Indeh*, 118. Italics in text.

47. Sheridan to Terry (Oct. 29, 1886), loc. cit.

48. J. M. Schofield to AG of the Army, Washington, D.C. (Oct. 25, 1886), Sen. Exec. Doc. No. 117, 49th Cong., 2d sess., 29.

49. Geronimo, *Geronimo*, 145.

50. Ball, *Indeh*, 134.

51. "Sunburned Warriors," *San Francisco Chronicle*, Oct. 20, 1886; *Kalama-*

zoo Telegraph, Oct. 27, 1886.

52. General Orders No. 37 (11/15/86), Department of Arizona, U.S. Army Department of Arizona General Orders and Circulars, 1870–1886, Microfilm Roll 5 (1883–1886), Arizona Historical Society.

53. Daly to Gatewood, Jr. (May 28, 1924), Letter 584; Daly to Gatewood, Jr. (June 18, 1928), Letter 345; Daly to Gatewood, Jr. (Apr. 25, 1924), Letter 581, Gatewood Collection, for the Daly/Gatewood meeting. Daly surmised that someone overheard their conversation and reported Gatewood to Miles.

54. For File with "Efficiency Reports" Summary of Reports by Commanding Officers, NA M1395.

55. Miles recommendation (Dec. 28, 1886), Gatewood Collection; and Papers and Recommendations filed in Connection with the Application of Charles Gatewood, NA M1395. The endorsements included letters from New Mexico Governor Edmund G. Ross, among others.

56. AG to Thomas McColloh, Dec. 4, 1886, NA M1395.

Epilogue

1. Ball, *Indeh,* 133.

2. Ibid., 122.

3. Gatewood to AG, USA, Washington, D.C. (Feb. 7, 1887); Special Orders, No. 88 (Feb. 15, 1887), NA M1395.

4. Betzinez, *Geronimo,* 149–59; Ball, *Indeh,* 140–51. Both Betzinez and Daklugie, after realizing that their lives had changed forever, made the most of their schooling. However, the schooling affected them differently. Whereas Betzinez grew to appreciate the opportunity presented him, Daklugie's hatred grew, never allowing him to forget or forgive the attempt to destroy his heritage.

5. Ball, *Indeh,* 153 n. 5, 154. Chappo contracted the coughing sickness, tuberculosis. He was sent home to Geronimo to die.

6. Ibid., 152; also, n. 1. Also, see Debo, *Geronimo,* 326, 334.

7. Geronimo, *Geronimo,* 145.

8. John D. Weaver, *El Pueblo Grande: A Non-Fiction Book about Los Angeles* (Los Angeles: Ward Ritchie Press, 1973), 37.

9. Hagedorn, *Wood1,* 109.

10. Miles to AG of the Army, Washington, D.C. (May 31, 1887), NA M1395.

11. This is supposition on my part. Gatewood to Georgia (Mar. 1, 1893), Gatewood Collection, Letter 50. Writing from Arizona Territory, Gatewood mentions the sale of two lots. These lots may very well have been in Arizona.

12. Wood, *Chasing,* 117; Thrapp, *Biography,* 3:1590. Wood was honored in 1898.

13. Georgia to Gatewood, Jr. (May 5, 1909), Gatewood Collection, Letter 82. Also, see Georgia to Gatewood, Jr. (date unknown/letter incomplete), Gatewood Collection, Letter 58.

14. Hagedorn, *Wood 1*, 111.

15. Miles, *Recollections*, 532.

16. Hagedorn, *Wood 1*, 111.

17. Georgia to Gatewood, Jr. (date unknown/letter incomplete), quoting a San Francisco newspaper, op. cit.

18. Daly to Gatewood, Jr. (May 15, 1925), Gatewood Collection, Letter 583.

19. Georgia to Gatewood, Jr. (date unknown/letter incomplete), op. cit. Again, if we can believe Georgia, one of Miles's practices that he did not want scrutinized was his backing of Amos Kimball. Miles allowed Kimball to make a lot of money by granting him a contract to sell stoves to the army.

20. Georgia to Gatewood, Jr. (May 5, 1909), op. cit.

21. Wratten interview, 6; Wratten, "Friend," 106; Ball, *Indeh*, 175.

22. Sen. Exec. Doc. No. 83, 51st Cong., 1st sess., Notes of an interview between Crook and Chiricahua Apaches (Jan. 2, 1890), 35.

23. Ibid., Howard to AG, U.S. Army, Washington, D.C. (Dec. 23, 1889), 37.

24. NA M1395, Gatewood to AAG, Division of the Pacific (June 2, 1890).

25. Ibid., Headquarters, Division of the Pacific, Special Orders, No. 41 (June 2, 1890).

26. Note received, AG's Office (Aug. 26, 1890)/S.o. 215 Par. 8 (Sept. 13, 1890); Headquarters of the Army, Washington, D.C., Special Orders, No. 215 (Sept. 13, 1890); Acting AG, Headquarters of the Army, to Gatewood (Sept. 15, 1890); and Gatewood to AG, USA (Sept. 18, 1890); all in NA M1395.

27. Lawton died in 1899 (rank, major general of volunteers). Parker retired in 1918 (rank, major general). Smith retired in 1918 (rank, brigadier general). Wood became a brigadier general during the Spanish American War and eventually rose to chief of staff of the U.S. Army. Many others also attained high rank.

28. See Utley, *History*, 335, for this quotation and Wovoka's quotation, and 334, 338. Also, see Thrapp, *Biography*, 1:348, 350. Crook, who became a major general on April 6, 1888, commanded the Division of the Missouri until his death by heart attack on March 21, 1890.

29. Statement of the Military Service of Charles B. Gatewood, 38373 A.G.O., AG's Office (June 5, 1896), NA M1395.

30. Utley, *History*, 338, 340–41.

31. Gatewood to Post Adjutant (Feb. 16, 1891); Medical Certificate—both in NA M1395.

32. Gatewood's Efficiency Report (1895); NA M1395.

33. Lieutenant-Colonel W. H. Carter, *From Yorktown to Santiago with the Sixth U.S. Cavalry* (Baltimore: The Lord Baltimore Press, 1900), 265.

34. Ibid., 268–69.

35. Certificate in the case of C. B. Gatewood, 6th Cavalry. Appendix A, NA M1395.

36. Examination for Promotion, Case No. 481481 (Oct. 3, 1892), NA M1395.

37. Headquarters of the Army Special Orders, No. 258 (Nov. 3, 1892), NA M1395.

38. Gatewood to the AG, U.S.A. (Nov. 22, 1892), NA M1395.

39. M. F. Bowers, Sheriff, El Paso County, Colorado, request for Gatewood's services (June 4, 1894); AG's Office, Washington, D.C., 1st Endorsement, to H. M. Teller, U.S. Senator (June 13, 1894)—both in NA M1395.

40. Gatewood to AG, U.S. Army (Oct. 10, 1894). Also, see C. W. Hine to AG, U.S. Army, Washington, D.C. (Sept. 10, 1894); Gatewood to AG, U.S.A., Washington, D.C. (Sept. 28, 1894); AAG, Headquarters of the Army, to Charles W. Hine (Oct. 28, 1894); Lobban & Hine General Merchandise statement (Dec. 18, 1894). All in NA M1395.

41. Captain A. P. Blocksom to Regimental Adjutant, Sixth Cavalry (May 2, 1895); 1st Endorsement by Colonel D. B. Gordon (May 3, 1895); 2d Endorsement by Miles (May 29, 1895); Joseph B. Doe, Acting Secretary of War, 6th (and final) Endorsement (June 24, 1895); Medal of Honor, Case of Lieutenant Charles B. Gatewood (20635 A.G.O.). All in NA M1395.

42. Surgeon Edward B. Mosley to Miles (May 21, 1896); Surgeon Mosley to AG, U.S. Army (May 21, 1896); AG's Office statement (May 21, 1896); Gilmore, AAG, to CO, Fort Myer (May 22, 1896); Record of Death and Interment. All in NA M1395. For Gatewood's seniority, see Constance Wynn Altshuler, *Cavalry Yellow and Infantry Blue: Army Officers in Arizona Between 1851 and 1886* (Tucson: The Arizona Historical Society, 1991, 139.

43. Ball, *Indeh,* 175. Also, see 159, 173–74.

44. Ibid., 176. Also see Wratten, "Friend," 118–19.

45. Ball, *Indeh,* 179, 181; Betzinez, *Geronimo,* 198. Betzinez claimed Geronimo fell in a ditch after getting drunk.

46. C. L. Sonnichsen, "From Savage to Saint: A New Image for Geronimo." *The Journal of Arizona History* 27, no. 1 (Spring 1986), 30.

47. Ibid., 31.

48. Ball, *Indeh,* 112.

Bibliography

Archival Sources

Arizona Historical Society, Tucson.
> Microfilm, Historic Archives of Sonora, Reel 24 (Sonoran State Archives, Roll 24).
> U.S. Army Department of Arizona General Orders and Circulars 1870–1886. Microfilm; four rolls (3 through 6). Roll No. 5 deals with the years 1883–1886.

Arizona State Archives, Department of Library, Archives, and Public Records, Archives Division, Phoenix, Arizona. The holdings include RG1, Office of the Governor, SG8, Bisbee-Naco Water Company: Indictment for False Imprisonment of Thomas M. Zuck by Charles B. Gatewood (No. 49), Indictment for False Imprisonment of Thomas F. Jones by Charles B. Gatewood (No. 50), Indictment for False Imprisonment of Joseph C. Kay by Charles B. Gatewood (No. 51); all were filed in District Court of the United States for the Territory of Arizona, Third Judicial District, Feb. 10, 1885.

National Archives—Pacific Southwest Region, Laguna Niguel, Calif.
> Record Group 21: Records of the District Court of the United States for the Territory of Arizona, Third Judicial District, 1869–1910, Criminal Cases A83–5 to A-85–19, Box No. 4, No. 52 (T. M. Zuck, T. F. Jones, and J. C. Kay Trial).
> National Archives Record Group 75: Microcopy 348; rolls 45, 46. 47. Report Books of the Office of Indian Affairs.

National Archives, Washington, D.C.
> Letters Received by the Commissioner of Indian Affairs (1882—1886): letters 23038 and 4140.
> Microfiche Publication M1395 (five fiche), Letters Received by the Appointment, Commission, and Personal Branch of the Adjutant General's Office, 1871–1894.
> Microfilm 689—Letters Received, 1881–1889
> 1066 AGO 1883; rolls 173, 174, 175, 180, 184. Papers relating to the war between the United States government and Apache Indians, 1883–1886.
> 1749 AGO 1882; roll 96: deals with events that occurred in 1882.

Rutherford B. Hayes Memorial Library, Fremont, Ohio
    The George Crook Collection (annual reports, official correspondence, and
        other papers concerning Crook's Arizona service). Letter Books I (with
        numbered reports and letters), and Letter Books II (with unnumbered
        reports and letters).

Manuscript Sources

Davis, Britton. "A Short Account of the Chiricahua Tribe of Apache Indians and
    the Causes Leading to the Outbreak of May, 1885." Arizona Historical
    Society, Tucson, Gatewood Collection.
Gatewood, Charles B. "Gatewood on Experiences among the Apaches." Arizona
    Historical Society, Tucson, Gatewood Collection. Two manuscripts with
    the same title.
———. "Gatewood on the Apache Indians, Government Relations, Reserva-
    tions, Courts, and Scouts." Arizona Historical Society, Tucson, Gatewood
    Collection.
———. "Gatewood on the Control and Management of the Indians (including
    the Outbreak of May 1885)." Arizona Historical Society, Tucson, Gate-
    wood Collection.
———. "Gatewood on the Surrender of Geronimo." Arizona Historical Society,
    Tucson, Gatewood Collection.
———. "How the Judge was Arrested and Tried." Arizona Historical Society,
    Tucson, Gatewood Collection.
———. "Old Black Joe's Devil," ed. Charles B. Gatewood, Jr. Arizona Histori-
    cal Society, Tucson, Gatewood Collection.
———. "The Judge's Trial." Arizona Historical Society, Tucson, Gatewood Col-
    lection.
———. "The Surrender of Geronimo." Arizona Historical Society, Tucson,
    Gatewood Collection, 1895.
———. "The Trial Chapt[er]." Arizona Historical Society, Tucson, Gatewood
    Collection.
———. "Lieutenant Charles B. Gatewood, 6th U.S. Cavalry and the Surrender
    of Geronimo." Arizona Historical Society, Tucson, Gatewood Collection.
    Undated typewritten manuscript, which includes a biographical sketch of
    Gatewood.
Huddleson, S. M. "An Interview with Geronimo and His Guardian, Mr. G. M.
    Wratten." Arizona Historical Society, Tucson, Gatewood Collection.
Martine and Kayitah, "The Story of the Final Surrender of Geronimo," as told
    to O. M. Boggess, Superintendent of the Mescalero Indian Reservation,
    Sept. 25, 1925. Gatewood Collection.
Parker, General James, Retired, "Service with Lieutenant Charles B. Gatewood,
    6th U.S. Cavalry." Arizona Historical Society, Tucson, Gatewood Collection.
———. "The Old Army." Arizona Historical Society, Gatewood Collection.

Government Documents

Senate Executive Document No. 117, 49th Congress, 2d sess.
Senate Executive Document No. 83, 51st Congress, 1st sess.
Senate Executive Document No. 88, 51st Congress, 1st sess.

Books

Adams, Alexander B. *Geronimo.* New York: G. P. Putnam's Sons, 1971.
Altshuler, Constance Wynn. *Cavalry Yellow and Infantry Blue: Army Officers in Arizona Between 1851 and 1886.* Tucson: The Arizona Historical Society, 1991.
Ball, Eve, with Nora Henn and Lynda Sanchez. *Indeh: An Apache Odyssey.* Provo, Utah: Brigham Young University Press, 1980.
Ball, Eve, and James Kaywaykla. *In the Days of Victorio: Recollections of a Warm Springs Apache.* Tucson: University of Arizona Press, 1970.
Betzinez, Jason, with Wilbur Sturtevant Nye. *I Fought With Geronimo.* 1959. Reprint: Lincoln and London: University of Nebraska Press, 1987.
Bourke, John G. *An Apache Campaign in the Sierra Madre.* 1886. Reprint, with foreword by Joseph C. Porter, Lincoln and London: University of Nebraska Press, 1987.
———. *On the Border with Crook.* 1891. Reprint, Lincoln: University of Nebraska Press, 1971.
Carroll, John M., introduction, and preface by Colonel George S. Pappas. *The Papers of the Order of Indian Wars.* Fort Collins, Colo.: The Old Army Press, 1975.
Carter, Lieutenant-Colonel W. H. *From Yorktown to Santiago with the Sixth U.S. Cavalry.* Baltimore, Md.: The Lord Baltimore Press, 1900.
Cook, James H. *Fifty Years on the Old Frontier as Cowboy, Hunter, Guide, Scout, and Ranchman.* 1923. Reprint, with foreword by J. Frank Dobie, introduction by Charles King, and foreword to the paperback edition by Joseph C. Porter, Norman and London: University of Oklahoma Press, 1980.
Crook, George. *General George Crook: His Autobiography.* Edited and annotated by Martin F. Schmitt. Norman: University of Oklahoma Press, 1946.
Crook, Brigadier Gen'l. George. *Resumé of Operations against Apache Indians, 1882 to 1886.* 1886. Reprint, with notes and introduction by Barry C. Johnson, London: The Johnson-Taunton Military Press, 1971.
Cruse, Thomas. *Apache Days and After.* 1941. Reprint, Lincoln and London: University of Nebraska Press, 1987.
Davis, Britton. *The Truth about Geronimo.* Edited by M. M. Quaife. 1929. Reprint, with foreword by Robert M. Utley, New Haven and London: Yale University Press, 1963.
Debo, Angie. *Geronimo.* Norman: University of Oklahoma Press, 1976.

Deming, Therese O. *Cosel: With Geronimo on His Last Raid; The Story of an Indian Boy.* Philadelphia: F. A. Davis Company, Publishers, 1938.

Dunlay, Thomas W. *Wolves for the Blue Soldiers: Indian Scouts and Auxiliaries with the United States Army, 1860–90.* Lincoln and London: University of Nebraska Press, 1982.

Faulk, Odie B. *The Geronimo Campaign.* New York: Oxford University Press, 1969.

Forsyth, General George A. *Thrilling Days in Army Life.* 1900. Reprint, with introduction by David Dixon, Lincoln and London: University of Nebraska Press, 1994.

Geronimo. *Geronimo: His Own Story.* Edited by S. M. Barrett; newly edited with introduction and notes by Frederick W. Turner III. New York: E. P. Dutton & Co., 1970.

———. *Geronimo's Story of His Life.* Taken down and edited by S. M. Barrett. New York: Garrett Press, 1969.

Gardner, Mark. *Fort Bowie National Historic Site.* Tucson: Southwest Parks and Monuments Association, 1994.

Hagedorn, Hermann. *Leonard Wood, A Biography.* 2 vols. New York and London: Harper & Brothers Publishers, 1931.

Hatfield, Shelley Bowen. *Chasing Shadows.* Albuquerque: University of New Mexico Press, 1998.

Hill, Edward E., comp. *Guide to Records in the National Archives of the United States Relating to American Indians.* Washington, D.C.: National Archives and Records Service, 1981.

Hoy, Bill. *Spanish Terms of the Sonoran Desert Borderlands.* Calexico, Calif.: Institute for Border Studies, San Diego State University, 1993.

Hutton, Paul Andrew, *Phil Sheridan and His Army.* Lincoln and London: University of Nebraska Press, 1985.

Jackson, Donald Dale, and Peter Wood. *The Sierra Madre.* Alexandria, Va.: Time-Life Books, 1975.

Lockwood, Frank C. *The Apache Indians.* 1938. Reprint, Lincoln and London: University of Nebraska Press, 1987.

Lummis, Charles F. *General Crook and the Apache Wars* Edited by Turbesé Lummis Fiske. Flagstaff, Ariz.: Northland Press, 1966.

Mails, Thomas E. *The People Called Apache.* 1974. Reprint, New York: BDD Illustrated Books, 1993.

Malone, Dumas, ed. *Dictionary of American Biography.* 10 vols. and supplement. 1935. Reprint, New York: Charles Scribner's Sons, 1936.

Mazzanovich, Anton. *Trailing Geronimo.* Edited and arranged by E. A. Brininstool. Los Angeles, Calif.: Gem Publishing Company, 1926.

Miles, Nelson A. *Personal Recollections and Observations of General Nelson A. Miles.* Chicago & New York: The Werner Company, 1896.

———. *Serving the Republic: Memoirs of the Civil War and Military Life of*

Nelson A. Miles. New York and London: Harper & Brothers Publishers, 1911.

Nevin, David. *The Soldiers.* Alexandria, Va.: Time-Life Books, 1974.

Opler, Morris Edward, *An Apache Life-way: The Economic, Social, and Religious Institutions of the Chiricahua Indians.* 1941. Reprint, New York: Cooper Square Publishers, 1965.

Ortiz, Alfonso, ed. *Handbook of North American Indians: Southwest,* vol. 10. Washington, D.C.: Smithsonian Institution, 1983.

Parker, James. *The Old Army: Memories, 1872–1918.* Philadelphia, Pa.: Dorrance & Company, 1929.

Parsons, George Whitwell. *The Concluding Arizona Years, 1882–87.* Vol. 2, *The Devil Has Foreclosed: The Private Journal of George Whitwell Parsons.* Transcribed, edited, annotated, indexed, and with foreword by Lynn R. Bailey. Tucson, Ariz.: Westernlore Press, 1997.

Pohanka, Brian C., ed. *Nelson A. Miles: A Documentary Biography of His Military Career, 1861–1903.* Glendale, Calif.: The Arthur H. Clark Company, 1985.

Reedstrom, E. Lisle. *Apache Wars: An Illustrated Battle History.* 1990. Reprint, New York: Barnes and Noble Books, 1995.

Sonnichsen, C. L., ed. *Geronimo and the End of the Apache Wars.* 1986. Reprint, Lincoln and London: University of Nebraska Press, 1990.

Terrell, John Upton. *Apache Chronicle.* New York: World Publishing, 1972.

Thrapp, Dan L. *The Conquest of Apacheria.* Norman: University of Oklahoma Press, 1967.

———. *Encyclopedia of Frontier Biography.* 3 vols. Glendale, Calif.: The Arthur H. Clark Company, 1988.

———. *Encyclopedia of Frontier Biography.* Vol. 4. Spokane, Wash.: The Arthur H. Clark Company, 1994.

———. *General Crook and the Sierra Madre Adventure.* Norman: University of Oklahoma Press, 1972.

Thrapp, Dan L., ed. *Dateline Fort Bowie: Charles Fletcher Lummis Reports on an Apache War.* Norman: University of Oklahoma Press, 1979.

Utley, Robert M. *A Clash of Cultures: Fort Bowie and the Chiricahua Apaches.* Washington, D.C.: National Park Service, 1977.

———. *The Indian Frontier of the American West, 1846–1890.* Albuquerque: University of New Mexico Press, 1984.

Utley, Robert M., ed. *Life in Custer's Cavalry: Diaries and Letters of Albert and Jennie Barnitz, 1867–1868.* New Haven and London: Yale University Press, 1977.

Utley, Robert M. and Wilcomb E. Washburn. *The American Heritage History of the Indian Wars.* New York: American Heritage Publishing Co., 1977.

Weaver, John D. *El Pueblo Grande: A Non-Fiction Book about Los Angeles.* Los Angeles: The Ward Ritchie Press, 1973.

Welsh, Herbert. *The Apache Prisoners in Fort Marion, St. Augustine, Florida.* Philadelphia: Office of the Indian Rights Association, 1887.

Wharfield, Colonel H. B. *Apache Indian Scouts.* El Cajon, Calif.: privately printed, 1964.

Wood, Leonard. *Chasing Geronimo: The Journal of Leonard Wood; May-September, 1886.* Edited, with introduction and epilogue by Jack C. Lane. Albuquerque: University of New Mexico Press, 1970.

Articles

Clay, Lieutenant Thomas J. "Some Unwritten Incidents of the Geronimo Campaign." In *The Papers of the Order of Indian Wars,* introduction by John M. Carroll and preface by Colonel George S. Pappas, 114–15. Fort Collins, Colo.: The Old Army Press, 1975.

Daly, Henry W. "The Capture of Geronimo." *The American Legion Monthly* 8, no. 6 (June 1930): 30–31.

Davisson, Lori. "Fort Apache, Arizona Territory: 1870–1922." *The Smoke Signal* 33 (Spring 1977): 62–80.

Fiebeger, Colonel G. J. "General Crook's Campaign in Old Mexico in 1883: Events Leading up to it and Personal Experiences in the Campaign." In *The Papers of the Order of Indian Wars,* introduction by John M. Carroll and preface by Colonel George S. Pappas, 193–20. Fort Collins, Colo.: The Old Army Press, 1975.

Gatewood, Charles, Jr. "Retired Army Officer Here Reveals History of Famous Apache Surrender." *San Diego Union,* June 8, 1927.

Hafford, William. "Chat[t]o the Betrayed." *Arizona Highways* 69, no. 2 (February 1993): 14–18.

Kenoi, Samuel E. "A Chiricahua Apache's Account of the Geronimo Campaign of 1886," as recorded by Morris E. Opler. *The Journal of Arizona History* 27, no. 1 (Spring 1986): 71–90.

Kraft, Louis. "Assignment: Geronimo." *Wild West* 12, No. 3 (October 1999): 36–41.

———. "Lieutenant Charles Gatewood's Civil Difficulties in Arizona Territory Began with Judge Thomas Zuck." *Wild West* 12, No. 3 (October 1999): 20, 22, 74.

Mazzanovich, Anton. "Facts about a Great Hero, Lieut. Charles B. Gatewood." *Progressive Arizona and the Great Southwest* 7, no. 3 (September 1928): 29, 32–33.

Simmons, Marc. "The McComas Massacre." *New Mexico* 74, no. 1 (January 1996): 60–65.

Sonnichsen, C. L. "From Savage to Saint: A New Image for Geronimo." *The Journal of Arizona History* 27, no. 1 (Spring 1986): 5–31.

Wratten, Albert E. "George Wratten, Friend of the Apaches." *The Journal of Arizona History* 27, no. 1 (Spring 1986): 91–124.

Newspapers

Arizona Citizen
Arizona Journal-Miner
El Paso Times
Kalamazoo Telegraph
Mississippi Republican
Prescott Courier
San Diego Union
San Francisco Chronicle
St. Louis Republican

Index